Working with Microsoft® Visual Studio® 2005 Team System

Richard Hundhausen

PUBLISHED BY
Microsoft Press
A Division of Microsoft Corporation
One Microsoft Way
Redmond, Washington 98052-6399

Library of Congress Control Number 2005933120

Printed and bound in the United States of America.

2 3 4 5 6 7 8 9   QWT   9 8 7 6 5

Distributed in Canada by H.B. Fenn and Company Ltd.

A CIP catalogue record for this book is available from the British Library.

Microsoft Press books are available through booksellers and distributors worldwide. For further information about international editions, contact your local Microsoft Corporation office or contact Microsoft Press International directly at fax (425) 936-7329. Visit our Web site at www.microsoft.com/learning/. Send comments to *mspinput@microsoft.com*.

Microsoft, Active Directory, BizTalk, Developer Studio, Excel, InfoPath, IntelliSense, Microsoft Press, MSDN, MSN, Outlook, SharePoint, Visio, Visual Basic, Visual C#, Visual C++, Visual J#, Visual SourceSafe, Visual Studio, Windows, and Windows Server are either registered trademarks or trademarks of Microsoft Corporation in the United States and/or other countries.

The example companies, organizations, products, domain names, e-mail addresses, logos, people, places, and events depicted herein are fictitious. No association with any real company, organization, product, domain name, e-mail address, logo, person, place, or event is intended or should be inferred.

This book expresses the author's views and opinions. The information contained in this book is provided without any express, statutory, or implied warranties. Neither the authors, Microsoft Corporation, nor its resellers, or distributors will be held liable for any damages caused or alleged to be caused either directly or indirectly by this book.

Acquisitions Editor: Ben Ryan
Project Editor: Valerie Woolley
Copy Editor: Nancy Sixsmith
Indexer: Richard Shrout

Body Part No. X11-50126

Table of Contents

Foreword xi

Acknowledgments xiii

Introduction xv

Part I Introducing Team System

1 Overview of Team System 3

Life Without Visual Studio 2005 Team System 3

Global Communication 4

Too Many Tools 5

Solving Your Problems 6

Goals of Visual Studio 2005 Team System 6

The Need for a Methodology 8

Microsoft Solutions Framework 8

How Team System Supports These Methodologies 11

Customizing Methodologies 13

Visual Studio 2005 Team System 13

Visual Studio 2005 Team Edition for Software Architects 14

Visual Studio 2005 Team Edition for Software Developers 14

Visual Studio 2005 Team Edition for Software Testers 14

Visual Studio 2005 Team Foundation Server 15

Visual Studio 2005 Team Suite 15

Roles Within Team System 15

Visual Studio 2005 Editions 16

Visual Studio 2005 Express Editions 17

Visual Studio 2005 Standard Edition 17

Visual Studio 2005 Professional Edition 17

Integration with Other Microsoft Products 17

Summary 18

2 Team Foundation Server 19

Team Foundation Server Components 19

Team Foundation Server Architecture 20
    Data Tier 20
    Application Tier 22
    Client Tier 23
Software Configuration Management (SCM) 24
    Work Item Tracking (WIT) 25
    Version Control 27
    Build and Release Management 35
Summary 36

3   Team System Client Applications 37
Tools for Project Managers 38
    Visual Studio 2005 Team Explorer 38
    Microsoft Excel 39
    Microsoft Project 43
Tools for Architects 44
    Dynamic Systems Initiative (DSI) 45
    System Definition Model (SDM) 46
    Domain-Specific Languages 48
    DSL Tools in Team System 50
Tools for Developers 62
    Source Control Explorer 62
    Class Designer 63
    Pending Checkins 64
Tools for Testers 65
Internet Explorer for All Team Members 66
Command-Line Utilities 66
Tools by Roles 67
Summary 68

Part II   Team System for the Entire Team

4   Project Managers 71
Organizing the Team 71
Starting a New Project 72
    Selecting a Methodology 72
    Configuring the Project Portal 73

Configuring Version Control Settings..74

Managing the Ongoing Project...75

Configuring Security 76

Creating Classifications...78

Creating Iterations 78

Setting Check-In Policies 79

Uploading Documents and Other Assets...81

Adding and Managing Work Items 82

Summary 91

5   Architects 93

The Architect Role..94

Infrastructure Architect 94

Application Architect 95

DSI, SDM, and DSL Revisited..96

The Distributed System Designers 96

Security 97

Interoperability..97

Unified Modeling Language (UML) 98

Custom Assemblies...99

Other Languages 99

Existing Code Libraries 99

Web Services, J2EE, BizTalk Server, and SQL Server 99

The Logical Datacenter Designer 100

Creating Logical Datacenter Diagrams...100

The Application Designer..107

Creating Application Diagrams...108

Connecting Endpoints...110

Reusing Custom Application Prototypes...111

Implementing the Classes 112

Settings and Constraints...115

The System Designer 117

The Deployment Designer..119

Validating the Deployment...120

Generating a Deployment Report..121

What's Next?...123

Summary 124

6   Developers..**125**

Viewing Work Items...125

Implementing the Web Application or Service...............................127

Using the Class Designer...128

Version Control..130

Associating Check-Ins with Work Items....................................131

Version Control Explorer...133

Pending Check-Ins...133

Shelving and Unshelving...134

Version Control Check-In Policies...136

Integrated Testing...136

Test-Driven Development..137

Unit Testing...138

Code Coverage...141

Static Analysis...142

Profiling...144

Team Foundation Build..145

Build Type...147

Executing a Build..150

Viewing the Build Results...151

Reports...151

Impact on Code Development..153

Summary..154

7   Testers **155**

Viewing Work Items...156

Managing Tests..157

Test Manager...157

Test View...158

Test Projects...158

Testing in Visual Studio 2005..159

Authoring Tests...159

Manual Tests..160

Generic Tests...162

Web Tests...164

Load Tests..167

Ordered Tests...169

Test Results and Tracking Bugs 170
    Test Run Configuration..171
Summary 172

Part III   Methodologies and Extensibility

8   Microsoft Solutions Framework **175**
    MSF and Team System..176
    Choosing a Process Template 177
What's New in MSF 4.0 177
    MSF 4.0 Key Concepts 180
    MSF 4.0 Structure..181
    The MSF 4.0 Team Model..183
    MSF 4.0 Cycles and Iterations..184
    MSF 4.0 Governance 185
MSF for Agile Software Development..186
    Roles...186
    Work Streams...188
    Disciplines 191
    Qualities of Service 191
    Governance and Tracks...192
MSF for CMMI Process Improvement..193
    Principles 195
    Mindsets 196
    Roles...199
    Work Item Types..206
    Disciplines and Qualities of Service 207
    Governance 207
Implementing MSF 4.0 with Team System..208
    Customization and Extensibility..210
Summary 210

9   Customizing and Extending Team System **211**
Customizing Versus Extending...211
    Customizing Team System 212
    Extending Team System 224
    Visual Studio 2005 Tool Integration 238

Extensibility Toolkit 239

Partners 239

    Borland 239

    SourceGear 240

    AutomatedQA 241

    Identify 241

    Compuware 242

    AVIcode 243

    Mercury Interactive Corporation 243

    Serena 244

    Conchango 244

    Osellus 244

Summary 246

10   Wrapping It Up: The Endgame and Deployment **247**

Team Build 247

Deploying the Application 248

Closing Down the Current Iteration 248

    Continuing to Track Bugs and Defects 248

    Reporting 249

    Project Integration 257

Summary 258

Part IV   Appendixes

A   A Day in the Life of Team System **261**

The Adventure Works Scenario 261

The Adventure Works Team 262

    Stakeholder 262

    Business Sponsor 262

    Business Analyst 262

    Project Manager 263

    Architect 263

    Lead Developer 263

    Developers 263

    Testers 264

Operations Manager 264

Using MSF for Agile Software Development 264

Project Timeline 266

Iteration 0: Project Setup and Planning (3 weeks) 266

Iteration 1: Release Candidate 1 (3 weeks) 268

Iteration 2: Release Candidate 2 (3 weeks) 270

Iteration 3: Stabilize and Deploy (3 weeks) 272

B   Distributed System Designer Reference **275**

Logical Datacenter Designer 275

Windows Client 276

IIS Web Server 276

Database Server 277

Generic Server 278

Zone 279

Application Designer 279

Windows Application 280

ASP.NET Web Service 280

ASP.NET Web Application 281

Office Application 282

External Web Service 282

External Database 283

BizTalk Web Service 283

Generic Application 284

Class Designer 284

Class 285

Enum 285

Interface 285

Abstract Class 286

Struct 286

Delegate 286

C   Codenames **287**

Index 289

Foreword

Software development will never be the same again. How can I say that? Let's look at today's reality. Teams work in isolation, not just geographically, but within our own offices. It's sometimes difficult to pass information among project managers, architects, developers, and testers—and it's even harder to pass that information to IT. We spend our time in meetings, on the phone, and exchanging e-mail, and many of our projects are delayed, over budget, or don't meet our original requirements.

Microsoft looked at how we could change this—how we could use the most productive developer tool, Microsoft® Visual Studio®, and expand it to include further roles, providing stronger support for your software development life cycle. Visual Studio 2005 Team System is the result of this vision, hard work, and invaluable customer and partner feedback.

Software development life cycle tools have been available for some time, but they have been costly, difficult to use, and hard to support. You also might have had to bend and change your internal processes—the very things that make your development successful—so that you could use them. In the first vision of Visual Studio 2005 Team System, you would be able to use your strengths—such as your design, development, and testing procedures—with Team System from the start. Microsoft has built two process guidance frameworks: the Microsoft Solutions Framework for Agile Software Development methodology, and the Microsoft Solutions Framework for CMMI Level 3 methodology. These two process frameworks can be used as they are or can be customized, and Microsoft also supplies tools for building your own process guidance framework.

As important as the first vision was, roles in your development life cycle needed to be integrated so that they could share information easily and re-use components. For example, project managers work best with project management tools such as Microsoft Office Project or even Microsoft Office Excel®. However, developers want to use their Visual Studio integrated development environment (IDE). One of Microsoft's goals for Visual Studio 2005 Team System was to enable people to use the tools they're comfortable with and to enable those tools to share information seamlessly.

As a member of the development team for Visual Studio 2005, I can attest that before we even thought about modeling environments, integrated testing, or developer enhancements, we ensured that this new release would increase your team's productivity and enable you to reuse or choose your development methodologies. We then looked deeply at the specific development roles—architects, developers, testers, and project managers—and at the tools that these team members needed to support each role.

In doing this, we focused on the premier priorities of current and future applications. For architects, being able to visually model service-oriented applications and validate them against their IT environments not only provided vast improvements to developer productivity, but it also enabled the identification of problems between development and deployment early in the cycle. For developers, being able to check the actual grammar of their code, look for security issues, and profile code will provide higher quality earlier in development. For testers, being able to integrate and share the same environment will mean more effective testing, better quality, and better real-life results. Finally, for project managers, knowing the status of a project at any time and running reports about real business metrics, instead of only about bugs and code, will provide greater analytical depth and range than ever before.

If you're an expert developer, new to developing software, or even if you're not involved in the development process, this book is for you. Richard Hundhausen has provided an insightful look into the value of software development life cycle tools and how Visual Studio 2005 Team System can be practically used. Richard focuses on each role in the development process, how it integrates with other roles, and how, together, they make the process stronger. For those involved directly in developing solutions, this book will highlight how to dramatically increase your predictability of success and quality. For those of you not directly involved in application development or in supporting IT solutions, this book will provide a view of how you can be productively involved earlier in the design and delivery of end-user solutions.

Michael Leworthy

Lead Product Manager, Visual Studio

Microsoft Corporation

Acknowledgments

What you are holding in your hands would simply not exist without the help of some key people. Writing a book on pre-release software requires several "friends at the factory" and many more people on the outside to act as sounding boards and counselors. Needless to say, I had much help with this effort.

Thanks especially to Steven Borg, Martin Danner, Kris Horrocks, John Alexander, Dave Bost, Martin Nagel, and Dennis Minium for supplying great content for this book. It was a sprint to the finish to get the book published in time for Tech-Ed 2005 and, with the help of this crew, we were able to do it. I'd like to thank them again for helping me fine-tune it for the release of Team System.

My friends at the factory include Michael Leworthy, Eric Lee, Ajay Sudan, Rob Caron, Randy Miller, David Anderson, Erik Gunvaldson, David Chesnut, Rick Rainey, and Tom Arnold. Thank you, gentlemen, for giving me direct access to whatever I needed. I also appreciate the time that Dmitriy Nikonov, Keith Short, and Bill Gibson spent with me at various events over the last couple of years, especially at Tech-Ed 2004 in San Diego, where they let me ask question after question about Whitehorse. My friends at Microsoft Press, Valerie Woolley and Ben Ryan, were also essential in helping me get this done.

I'd also like to acknowledge the input of Donis Marshall, Cory Isakson, Bill Sempf, Scott Cate, Darrel Carver, Brian Randell, and Chris Kinsman. These are all influential people in my life and regular guests on my MSN Messenger. Readers like Peter Nowak, Jason Camp, and my compadres at Solid Quality Learning have also provided valuable feedback.

Last, but not least, I'd like to thank my loving wife Kristen for allowing me the time to write this book in my already hectic life, and for putting up with many more instances of "I'll just be another minute" than anyone should rightfully have to.

Introduction

Welcome to *Working with Microsoft® Visual Studio® 2005 Team System*. I am very excited about how the new Team System role-based editions of Visual Studio 2005 can integrate the entire team.

Who Is This Book For?

This book will be of interest to most members of software development teams. These include, but are not limited to, project managers, architects, developers, and testers. Team members in these roles interact directly with Team System. On the periphery of a project, IT operations professionals can benefit from using Team System to negotiate a successful software deployment, thus making their jobs easier. Beyond this core team, any project stakeholder or other developer can use this book to learn the capabilities of Team System and what to expect of a team that uses it properly.

Organization of This Book

Working with Microsoft Visual Studio 2005 Team System is divided into parts and chapters. Because there's so much information to cover, I've sliced the book into four parts, each containing a list of chapters and an opening paragraph or two about those chapters. Naturally, I recommend reading the book from cover to cover, but I realize that we're all busy professionals. A more strategic approach might be to read the first three chapters in Part 1 to get an idea of what Team System is and what front-end and back-end software and services make it work. Then read the chapters in Part 2 that apply directly to you. Parts 3 and 4 provide deeper coverage and discussion of real-world use of Team System. Time permitting, you can then read any chapters that you might have skipped.

Here is a brief summary of what each part of the book contains:

- Part 1, "Introducing Team System," provides an overview of the software—including the back-end Team Foundation Server and the various client applications—that you and your team will use to interact with Team System.

- Part 2, "Team System for the Entire Team," provides a detailed look at Team System, covering the relevant tools and tasks for each team member by their role.

- Part 3, "Methodologies and Extensibility," includes a detailed look at Microsoft Solutions Framework 4.0 and how it integrates with Team System, an overview of the extensibility found within Team System, and guidelines for wrapping up a software development cycle or iteration.

■ Part 4, "Appendixes," includes a reference section, for both infrastructure and application architects, on Microsoft Distributed System Designers. You'll also find a fun storyboard-like scenario where a fictitious software development team uses Team System throughout a project iteration.

Prerelease Software

This book was reviewed and tested against the July 2005 Community Technical Preview (CTP) of Visual Studio 2005 Team System. This book is expected to be fully compatible with the final release of Visual Studio 2005 Team System. If there are any changes or corrections to the content that appears in this book, they will be collected and added to a Microsoft Knowledge Base article. See the "Support for This Book" section in this Introduction for more information.

Online Companion Content

The online companion content page has content and links related to this book, including a link to the Microsoft Press Technology Updates Web page. (As technologies related to this book are updated, links to additional information will be added to the Web page. Visit the page periodically for updates on Visual Studio 2005 Team System and other technologies.) The online companion content page for this book can be found at

http://www.microsoft.com/mspress/companion/0-7356-2185-3.

Support for This Book

Every effort has been made to ensure the accuracy of this book and the companion content. As corrections or changes are collected, they will be added to a Microsoft Knowledge Base article. To view the list of known corrections for this book, visit the following article:

http://support.microsoft.com/kb/905038/

Microsoft Press provides support for books and companion content at the following Web site:

http://www.microsoft.com/learning/support/books/

Questions and Comments

If you have comments, questions, or ideas regarding the book or the companion content, or questions that are not answered by visiting the sites above, please send them in e-mail to Microsoft Press at:

mspinput@microsoft.com

Or via postal mail at:

Microsoft Press
Attn: *Developer Series Editor*
One Microsoft Way
Redmond, WA 98052-6399

Please note that Microsoft product support is not offered through the above addresses.

Part I
Introducing Team System

In this part:

Chapter 1: Overview of Team System...3
Chapter 2: Team Foundation Server...19
Chapter 3: Team System Client Applications.........................37

In this section, I'll provide an overview of Team System and discuss why you need it. Software projects, regardless of size and team, typically suffer from common problems: lack of communication; too many tools to install, learn, and use; and difficulties arising because some team members are working remotely. Team System solves these problems by providing both state-of-the-art tools and designers in new editions of Visual Studio 2005, as well as high-performance, secure, scalable back-end services and databases to enable the team to work more effectively, both as individuals and as a team.

Chapter 1
Overview of Team System

In this chapter:

Life Without Visual Studio 2005 Team System 3
The Need for a Methodology 8
Visual Studio 2005 Team System. 13
Roles Within Team System 15
Visual Studio 2005 Editions 16
Visual Studio 2005 Express Editions 17
Visual Studio 2005 Standard Edition 17
Visual Studio 2005 Professional Edition. 17
Integration with Other Microsoft Products. 17
Summary. 18

This chapter reminds us of just how complicated our jobs and responsibilities can be. It seems that the faster and more capable computer hardware and software become, the more complicated it is to build intelligent systems that sit on top. Is it that we now have a broader range of software design options that makes things more complicated? Or is it that we are suffering from the same old problems that we always have? To quote any good consultant: "It depends."

Life Without Visual Studio 2005 Team System

We've all been there. The rollout deadline is upon us, the developers are at odds with the architects about something, the testers are sitting around doing nothing, and programmers are busy adding features that don't map to requirements. To make matters worse, the customer is calling. Does this sound familiar?

Building software these days is very difficult. Enterprise developers can no longer generate a single Microsoft® Visual Basic® executable and deploy it with a Microsoft Office Access database on a floppy disk. No, today's enterprise-scale applications have many layers and services. These projects require more development effort and are held to a higher standard than similar projects from a few years ago. You must consider also that more and more customers, Chief Information Officers (CIOs), and other stakeholders are reading magazines and Weblogs. Although they might not be as technical as the developers, they know what they want, and, more importantly, they probably know what they don't want: a simple .exe and .mdb combination.

Enterprise-scale software has significantly more moving pieces than it did 10 or 15 years ago. Web-based applications, XML, and Web services might make systems easier and better, but this is from the architect's, stakeholder's, or user's point of view. The reach, interoperability, and extensibility benefits cannot be matched. The downside is that these systems are not easy to build. All of these services, stacks, versions, and application programming interfaces (APIs) known as "XML Web services" make it challenging for any sized team to plug the various elements together and make them work efficiently.

Global Communication

Geographically separated teams are a roadblock to successfully building and implementing enterprise-scale applications. In a modern-day environment that includes telecommuting and outsourcing, the chances are good that you have at least one team member who is performing project management, design, development, or testing from a remote workstation. Not everyone on the team can access the LAN or enjoy virtual private network (VPN) access. It can be advantageous to have team members who work remotely. A physical separation between the development team and the daily business noise is a key benefit in most development methodologies. When a project has team members working remotely, however, it's important for all communication, including code, to flow smoothly through any firewalls. Using LAN-based tools such as Microsoft Visual SourceSafe® 6.0 to work remotely has historically not been practical. Anyone who has attempted this will know what I am talking about. It was doable, but only after you established a VPN connection to your SourceSafe database. Visual SourceSafe was never intended to be used as a thin-client application over port 80 and through firewalls.

 Note   That said, one of the new features with Visual SourceSafe 2005 is the ability to use it remotely through port 80, via an HTTP Web Service interface.

Whether the team is distributed across the globe, country, city, or cubical farm, communication is never easy. Team members tend to live in their own silos, seeing the project through their own personal portal. Hopefully, e-mail, telephone, or instant messaging (IM) is being used for communication—especially IM. I can't tell you how easy it is to collaborate remotely using this tool. Copying and pasting code, transferring files, and just getting a quick question answered from a teammate are all tasks that IM handles with ease. When I was first learning Microsoft .NET, I regularly pinged my online buddies to ask quick and simple questions such as, "In which namespace would I find the *StringBuilder* class?" If it's not abused, instant messaging can greatly increase the efficiency of communication among like-minded professionals on a project. Online live meetings and conference calls can be productive as well, and e-mail serves as a great archive for questions asked in the past and resources provided by other teammates.

One drawback to all these various forms of communication is that they force developers to use a tool outside of Visual Studio. Visual Studio is supposed to be our primary development environment. Many developers will spend eight or more hours per day inside this interface. Leaving Visual Studio and launching a separate tool such as Microsoft Office Outlook®, or some other custom task or bug-tracking utility, isn't an efficient use of your time. It's a fact that managers and other developers will send tasks in lots of different ways: e-mail, instant message, voice mail, or even a sticky note on the door. It requires a lot of effort to properly aggregate and organize these work items.

Rather than requiring you to embed Outlook or another collaboration tool inside Visual Studio, Microsoft has developed Team System, which integrates the sending and receiving of tasks, bugs, and accomplishments right inside the integrated development environment (IDE). As you'll see later, you don't have to leave Visual Studio to communicate with other team members about a project. If everyone on the team uses it, everyone wins.

Too Many Tools

If you study any sized software development team, you'll find an array of products in use. Project managers use Microsoft Office Project and Microsoft Office Excel® to track requirements, iterations, phases, milestones, and deliverables. Architects use Microsoft Office Visio® or third-party tools to diagram their datacenters, networks, application services, and classes. The developers have it easy. They have and will continue to use Visual Studio to implement these services and classes. Developers and testers who want to test their software will also need tools to perform unit tests, code coverage, static analysis, load and Web testing. If the testers are lucky, these testing utilities will plug into Visual Studio or at least run in managed code. The end result of using so many tools is a hard drive full of software from various manufacturers. Newly hired team members will need weeks of training to gain experience on all these niche applications. Welcome to life without Team System.

Another potential weakness to a project is a lack of guidance. This is not to say that the project managers or team leads are weak individuals. Quite the contrary. Consider what I said earlier about how complex today's systems can be. Guidance can be the best way to assemble all those services and frameworks. Guidance can also be the methodology to follow to successfully create the software, specifying the team members, phases, and deliverable items.

I have met some extremely sharp developers and architects, both inside and outside Microsoft. The Microsoft Regional Director and MVP programs are full of such folks. However, no single person can know it all. With a good search engine, an appetite for reading, and plenty of spare time, a person *can* come close. Unless such a rare person joins your project, you'll need process guidance and best practices, preferably compiled by scores of domain experts. With this safety harness, you can go forward and write code, confident that you are proceeding according to published and agreed-upon best practices. Even then, any guidance implemented in the development process needs to be customizable. This requirement is important because it enables your team's patterns and practices to trump those compiled by Microsoft.

> **Note**   Documenting and publishing best practices is exactly the job of the Microsoft
> Patterns and Practices team. This team is internally known as Prescriptive Architecture and
> Guidance (PAG). Their documentation gives best practice advice in every area imaginable:
> data, security, configuration, and deployment, just to name a few. You can find and download
> these Patterns and Practices online for free at *http://www.microsoft.com/patterns*.

Another problem with using multiple tools relates back to communication. Not between
team members, but with the project. The project itself needs to communicate with the
project manager and other stakeholders. These individuals need to have their fingers on
the pulse of the project at all times. Today's managers have to rely on Project or Excel to
provide them with such a detailed and accurate view. The status of the project presented
by these tools, however, is only as accurate as the data recently typed into Project or Excel
documents. This is a dependency that can cause problems when ad hoc reports are needed
and the data is missing. Ideally, the project metrics should be relayed to the project manager
in real time, without additional aggregation. Such metrics might include outstanding tasks,
satisfied tasks, code churn, team efficiency, and bugs. These metrics should be available
remotely and accessed in an easy-to-use way, such as from a Web browser.

Solving Your Problems

Some software development problems will never be solved. In many problematic situations,
the customer, team, project, budget, and/or time frame difficulties are beyond the help
of any tool or methodology. Straightening out such problematic situations is beyond the
scope of this book and Team System. I suggest improving communication among all the
people involved—and not just from a technical viewpoint, but also from a psychological or
philosophical one.

What about the specific problems that I spent the last few pages enumerating? You know,
the poor team communication, problems with working remotely, tools that don't integrate,
lack of guidance, and lack of insight into the project's status. Your best chance for success
comes from the following list of principles: adequate planning, good designs, following best
practices, testing, and effective communication. Given that, wouldn't it be great if there were
a tool that was available to guide you in achieving these goals? Wouldn't it be great if this tool
plugged right into your familiar development environment that you already use for 8 to 18
hours a day? This tool now exists and it's called Microsoft Visual Studio® 2005 Team System.

Goals of Visual Studio 2005 Team System

Microsoft did something unique with Visual Studio 2005 Team System: It took a step
back and studied the ways that software shops and teams successfully, and sometimes
unsuccessfully, developed software. Then it tactically built a product that will increase
the predictability of a successful project. From start to finish, Team System provides the
guidance and collaboration to achieve this level of predictability. With Team System,

Microsoft will also change the way we think about Visual Studio. No longer is Visual Studio just a slick IDE for development. Team System transforms it into a powerful tool that integrates the entire team with the entire solution across the entire life cycle.

At its core, Team System is based on the same suite of tools that Microsoft uses internally to successfully plan, build, and deploy its software to customers like you and me. Even though your company may not be a multibillion dollar software development firm, Microsoft knows that other software development teams face the same challenges it does. It made sense for Microsoft to polish up this suite of tools for resale and thereby share its internal best practices with the rest of us.

Visual Studio 2005 Team System is designed to achieve these primary goals:

- Increase the project's predictability of success
- Increase the team's productivity by reducing the complexity of delivering modern service-oriented solutions
- Increase the team's collaboration by integrating all the tools
- Increase the team's capability by allowing remote users to work in a robust, secure, and scalable environment
- Be extensible by allowing its tools and services to be customized and extended

The last goal means that third parties must be able to introduce Team System add-ins. If your team happens to use an alternate methodology, designer, source-code control, or testing infrastructure, then those tools can be integrated with Team System. This goal also reflects Microsoft's ongoing commitment to its partners and developer communities, such as those in independent software vendor (ISV) and Visual Studio Integrator Program (VSIP) programs today.

> **More Info**   Be sure to read Chapter 9 for many ways to customize and extend Team System, including how to customize the guidance documentation and templates.

Providing Process Guidance and Methodology

Is having a tool that dictates a methodology a good thing? Some developers and architects I've talked with would caution Microsoft to stay out of the "how-to-build-software" business and stick to just providing the tools for building it. For the most part, I agree. People don't like having a methodology or process forced upon them. That's exactly the position that Microsoft took when building Team System. Going back to extensibility, Team System is customizable and extensible at every angle. If the guidance or methodology questions being asked by the tool aren't satisfactory or don't fit your team, you can change them. If your version control check-in policies are too restrictive or not restrictive enough, you can change them. If the number or types of tasks your team is receiving is causing strife, you can change them.

I've been teaching architecture, development, and best practices to software teams for many years. These people are the most demanding and fussy group of professionals out there. They know exactly what they want. More importantly, they know exactly what they *don't* want. They don't want tools, training, or advice that gets in the way of their work. They don't want a new methodology. They've seen too many come and go. They just want something lightweight that demonstrates best practice and a productivity increase. If this thing also happens to generate code, then that's a bonus for them. Microsoft, being made up of such personality types, knew from the beginning that Team System would only be successful if it was extensible.

The Need for a Methodology

Let's back up for a moment. I believe, and most would agree, that having a methodology is important, no matter what kind of methodology it is. If your methodology is to write down all the tasks you're going to do for the day onto sticky notes, prioritize them, stick them to your wall, and then remove them when you've completed them, you have a methodology. Even the term "methodology" is not very concrete. It simply means that you have a concise and consistent approach to accomplishing something. There are well-known methodologies as well as obscure ones. This area has fascinated me for many years because it represents an intersection of soft organizational skills with hard technical ones.

Note   Team System itself is not a methodology. It is simply a tool that provides guidance and communicates which items need to be worked on. It does so according to whatever methodology you happen to be using. That said, I love the irony in Team System: Some teams need a tool to get them to use a methodology to guide them to use the tool.

The next few pages will highlight some of the more popular methodologies, including the two Microsoft Solutions Framework (MSF) methodologies that will be included with Team System.

More Info   Be sure to read Chapter 8 for a deeper look at the MSF methodologies.

Microsoft Solutions Framework

Microsoft Solutions Framework (MSF) is a set of software development processes, principles, and proven practices that enable developers to achieve success in the software development life cycle (SDLC). MSF is rooted in well-known industry best practices. First introduced in 1994, MSF has aggregated 25 years of guidance from both internal and external sources.

Over the years, MSF has morphed to meet the changing needs of developers. MSF version 4.0, which ships with Team System, breaks down into two versions, which are essentially two philosophies on how to develop software: *MSF for Agile Software Development* and *MSF for CMMI Process Improvement*. MSF for Agile Software Development will appeal to the "agilists" out there—that is, teams accustomed to more rapid, ready-for-change environments that are tightly coupled with the customer. MSF for CMMI Process Improvement will appeal to larger shops or larger projects that feature many reporting levels. These are typically projects in which long-range planning and communication are more important than constant deliverables and feedback.

MSF for Agile Software Development

The MSF for Agile Software Development process is brand new. It is intended for smaller shops, with 5 to 20 members on the development team. Was MSF for Agile Software Development created specifically for Team System? Probably. Was Team System created to complement MSF for Agile Software Development? Probably. The integration of the process and the tool is very natural.

Officially, the agile process model was created by a council known as the Agile Alliance. Here are some tenets that the Agile Alliance agrees on:

- Individuals and interactions are more important than processes and tools.
- Customer collaboration is more important than contracts.
- Working software is more important than comprehensive documentation.
- Responding to change is more important than following a plan.

Delivering consistent and quality software defines an agile process. Gone are the days of formal specification phases. With MSF for Agile Software Development, Microsoft demonstrates its recognition that throwing hard-and-fast specifications and requirements over the wall to the developers often results in failed projects.

MSF for Agile Software Development is the default methodology in Team System. You can really feel that tight coupling when you use it. The default artifacts, which include tasks and bugs, are intuitive to developers who have used Visual Studio.

MSF for CMMI Process Improvement

CMMI stands for Capability Maturity Model Integration. Its purpose is to provide a model for continuous process improvement. This results in reduced software development–cycle times, improved ability to meet cost and schedule targets, and improved quality. It is a formal methodology managed by the Software Engineering Institute of Carnegie Mellon University.

One of the major advantages of using CMMI is that it is an evaluated standard by which you can compare your ability to develop software against other firms. Specifically, the U.S. Department of Defense and other large software consumers often look at the CMMI rating achieved by their vendors in order to determine who should receive a development contract.

Team System implements CMMI for Process Improvement that is specific to software engineering. This is an excellent process to use on your project if your company is attempting to achieve a measured baseline competency in software development. Far more status documents and reports must be completed in this model than in MSF Agile, but this more formal development process reduces risk on large software projects and provides a baseline that can be used to achieve certifications in the various CMMI levels or ISO 9000/9001.

eXtreme Programming (XP)

eXtreme Programming is another agile SDLC methodology that enables the team (developers, customer(s), and project lead) to handle changes throughout the development of a project. As you know, requirements can change frequently during a project. For that matter, in XP, just about everything can change—including the members of the customer and development team, along with the business environment. Waterfall and other fixed SDLCs cannot easily handle changes, especially later in their respective cycles. XP is an SDLC that not only handles changes but also deals with them elegantly. Instead of trying to control a change, the XP practices enable team members to adjust to that change easily.

> **Tip**   "Everything in software changes. The requirements change. The design changes. The business changes. The technology changes. The team changes. The team members change. The problem isn't change, per se, because change is going to happen; the problem, rather, is the inability to cope with change when it comes."
>
> —Kent Beck, *eXtreme Programming Explained*

There are many advantages to XP:

- Customers get the first product on which they can start working within one customer iteration. (The first actual iteration might be for the development team to set up its environments.)
- Developers are working on the most important features, as prioritized by the customers.
- The most important functionality and features of the system get the most testing.
- The product delivered meets the needs of the customer.

> **Note**   This is just an overview of XP. Full descriptions of these values and practices are available in many excellent books currently available.

Scrum

Scrum is another agile development methodology that focuses on incremental delivery using small development teams, short development cycles, and a facilitator who keeps the team focused and productive.

A Scrum project is broken up into one or more *sprints*, a well-defined development cycle that is typically four to six weeks in duration. After the initial project planning is complete, the deliverables for the first sprint are determined jointly by the customers and the development team. Then the team begins the sprint, focusing on it to the exclusion of all other tasks. The short duration of the sprint creates a sense of immediacy that keeps the team motivated. Sprints help the team keep the end in sight because the end is, at most, a few short weeks away. Each sprint finishes with a retrospective, where the team reviews how the sprint went and explores ideas for improving the next sprint. The end of one sprint signals the beginning of the next sprint. This cycle continues until the project is complete.

At the center of the team is the *scrum master*, a facilitator whose primary and often *only* responsibility is to guide the team through a successful sprint. The scrum master conducts a daily *scrum*, which is a short meeting of the entire development team. The agenda for the daily scrum consists of three simple questions for each team member:

- What have you accomplished since the last scrum?
- What do you plan to accomplish by the next scrum?
- What is impeding your progress?

Any other discussions that come up during the scrum are deferred to follow-up meetings with the appropriate people. This keeps the scrum meeting short and productive for all who attend.

The scrum master is responsible for removing the impediments identified in the scrum meetings. This function, which is often missing in development teams, is a key component of the scrum process. Impediments ranging from equipment issues to pending decisions to missing upstream deliverables can have a major impact on a development team. Giving one person responsibility for these distractions clears the way for the developers to focus on the task at hand.

By applying these simple techniques, a software development team can achieve significant improvements in productivity and morale.

 Note This methodology gets its name from the sport of rugby. *Scrum* is short for *scrummage*, which evolved into the term *scrimmage* used in American football.

How Team System Supports These Methodologies

No matter how lofty and theoretical your methodology is, you still need to bring it down to earth, implement it, and get your work done. This is where Team System comes in. Team System takes a work-stream approach, which means that it defines a process by offering a collection of activities and subactivities. This model fits well with most methodologies.

For example, Team System knows about the MSF for Agile Software Development elements: roles, work items, activities, and work streams. *Roles* are identified as business analyst, project manager, architect, developer, tester, and release manager. *Work items* are the various scenarios, quality of service requirements, risks, tasks, or bugs. These work items might link to artifacts, such as documents, spreadsheets, project plans, source code, and other tangible output from activities. Work items are created when certain activities are completed. They can also be prerequisites to perform an activity. *Activities* are a pattern of work performed together for a single purpose. An activity can use or produce work products and can be tracked by a work item. Activities are grouped together into work streams. *Work streams* are activities composed of other activities. They are the simple building blocks of the process and can be assigned to single or multiple roles.

Scenario

A *scenario* is a type of work item, recording a single path of user interaction through the system. As the person attempts to reach a goal, the scenario records the specific steps that he or she will take. Some scenarios will record a successful path; others will record an unsuccessful one. When writing scenarios, be specific. Because there are an infinite number of possible scenarios for all but the most trivial systems, it is important to be discerning in deciding which scenarios to write.

> **Note**   A scenario is often compared to use case in Unified Modeling Language (UML).

Quality of Service Requirement

Quality of Service (QoS) Requirements document characteristics of the system, such as performance, load, availability, stress, accessibility, serviceability, and maintainability. These requirements usually take the form of constraints on how the system should operate.

> **Note**   Quality of Service Requirements are not the same as functional requirements.

Task

A *task* work item communicates the need to do some work. Each role has its own requirements for a task. For example, a developer uses development tasks to assign to component owners work that has been derived from scenarios or quality of service requirements. The tester uses test tasks to assign the job of writing and running test cases. A task can also be used to signal regressions or to suggest that exploratory testing be performed. Finally, a task can be used generically to assign work within the project. On the work item form, certain fields are used only in cases when a task relates to a particular role.

Risk

An essential aspect of project management is to identify and manage the inherent risks of a project. A *risk* is any probable event or condition that can have a potentially negative outcome on the project in the future. A risk work item documents and tracks the technical or organizational risks of a project. When concrete action is required, these risks can translate into tasks to be performed to mitigate the risk. For example, a technical risk can set off an architectural prototyping effort. The team should always regard risk identification in a positive way to ensure contribution of as much information as possible about the risks it faces. The environment should be such that individuals identifying risks can do so without fear of retribution for honest expression of tentative or controversial views. Teams creating a positive risk management environment will be more successful at identifying and addressing risks earlier than teams operating in a negative risk environment.

Bug

A *bug* is a work item that communicates that a potential problem exists or has existed in the system. The goal of opening a bug is to accurately report bugs in a way that allows the reader to understand the full impact of the problem. The descriptions in the bug report should make it easy to trace through the steps used when the bug was encountered, thus allowing it to be easily reproduced. The test results should clearly show the problem. The clarity and understandability of this description often affects the probability that the bug will be fixed.

Customizing Methodologies

As I've said previously, Team System is not a complete methodology tool. For example, it only supports the core development team. It won't schedule meetings, prepare budgets, send e-mail, or facilitate communication with the customer or other stakeholders directly. In an enterprise where the customer is on-site, possibly in another division or department, this functionality might be missed. For an ISV selling software online, this functionality would not be missed.

Team System does a great job of organizing all your project work items, expectations, and collaboration tasks. Real people and real meetings, however, will still be required to implement a methodology, and this is outside the scope of Team System.

Visual Studio 2005 Team System

Team System is more than an edition of Visual Studio. It is actually a series of role-based editions. Team System is not really intended for solo professionals or consultants. Its value is realized for teams that include project manager, architect, developer, and tester roles. If, as an individual, you wear all these hats, then you might want to get your hands on it as well.

> **Note**   Team System is optimized for teams of 5 scaling to 500 active members.

Visual Studio 2005 Team Edition for Software Architects

This edition is specifically designed for both the infrastructure and application architect roles. It includes visual designers, referred to as the *distributed application designers* or *service-oriented architecture (SOA) designers*. The architect can create diagrams to represent the logical datacenter, the application, application systems, and the deployment of the application. These designers follow a simple drag, drop, and connect heuristic that has long been popular with Visual Studio. More than just pretty shapes, the diagrams have intelligence and metadata that can be validated against well-known and custom-defined constraints, and then turned into code with a quick click. Behind the scenes of these elegant diagrams, Microsoft is persisting the information in System Definition Model (SDM) files, which are implementations of Dynamic Systems Initiative (DSI).

> **More Info**   You'll learn more about Team Edition for Architects in Chapter 5.

Visual Studio 2005 Team Edition for Software Developers

This is the edition for the developers or programmers on the team. This will probably be the most common of the Team System role-based editions. In addition to all of the base Visual Studio 2005 professional features, developers will get the static code analyzer (akin to FxCop), unit testing (akin to NUnit), code coverage, and code profiler. Some of these features are shared with the Visual Studio 2005 Team Edition for Software Testers. Microsoft knows that it is hard to determine which role (developer or tester) should be in charge of writing and running these source code tests, so it provided them in both editions.

> **More Info**   You'll learn more about Team Edition for Developers in Chapter 6.

Visual Studio 2005 Team Edition for Software Testers

Whether a team member is a developer or exclusively a tester, this edition will provide access to all the coverage, quality, and load-testing facilities needed to thoroughly test a project, ensuring that it works from all angles. The Team Edition for Testers includes load Web testing (akin to the Application Center Test), Unit Testing, Code Coverage, as well as test-case management tools for managing all the tests and running and monitoring them from a centralized area. The ability to plug in whatever manual tests you might have is also supported in Team Edition for Testers. Some of these tests are shared with Team Edition for Developers.

> **More Info**   You'll learn more about Team Edition for Testers in Chapter 7.

Visual Studio 2005 Team Foundation Server

This edition of Visual Studio will provide many back-end databases and Web services to enable the team to collaborate, by sharing work items, source code, builds, and other artifacts. If you intend to run Team System for a team, as it is advertised, you'll need this product to connect all your team members together. Team Foundation Server is more than just an "edition" of Visual Studio 2005 Team System. It's the engine behind your software development life cycle.

Team Foundation Server includes a standalone client called Team Explorer. This client is essentially a lightweight edition of Visual Studio 2005 that offers an alternate way—besides using one of the other Visual Studio editions, Excel, or Project—of creating and managing work items. It's intended for the "casual stakeholder": the person on your team who has to check in documentation, manage images for a Web project, and so on.

> **More Info**   You'll learn more about Team Foundation Server in Chapter 2, and you'll learn more about the various clients in Chapter 3.

Visual Studio 2005 Team Suite

For the team member who plays more than one role, or for the consultant who plays all the roles, there's the Team Suite. Microsoft has wrapped up all three role-based editions (architect, developer, and tester) into a single edition for simplicity.

> **Note**   When Visual Studio 2005 launches, MSDN® Universal and MSDN Enterprise will no longer be available for purchase. At that time, active MSDN Universal subscribers will be offered an upgrade to MSDN Premium Subscription and their choice of Visual Studio 2005 Team Edition for Software Architects, Visual Studio 2005 Team Edition for Software Developers, or Visual Studio 2005 Team Edition for Software Testers at no additional cost. For those that want each of the Visual Studio Team System role-based editions, special pricing will enable MSDN Universal subscribers to upgrade to Visual Studio 2005 Team Suite. Check the Team System Web site on MSDN for the latest information and updates.

Roles Within Team System

Remember that a role doesn't necessarily mean a person. In fact, it's doubtful that any team will exactly fit the Team System model, with every role covered perfectly and no overlap. As you read through this section, remember what I've been saying about the flexibility of Team System.

Here are the four Team System roles:

- Project Manager
- Architect
- Developer
- Tester

If you get creative, you can come up with a few more roles. For example, you can break the architect role into two subroles:

- Application Architect—designs software and services
- Infrastructure Architect—designs deployment environments, including network and infrastructure

Another role that is affected by Team System includes the IT professional (IT Pro) staff that will be asked to deploy the finished product into the environment. With that in mind, you can come up with some other pseudo and combination Team System roles:

- IT Professional—software deployment
- Tester/IT Professional—software testing and deployment
- Developer/Tester—software development and testing
- Application Architect/Developer—software design and development

Visual Studio 2005 Editions

Team System is not part of all editions of Visual Studio. For novices, hobbyists, students, and professional developers, there are express, standard, and professional editions of Visual Studio.

- Visual Studio 2005 Express Editions
- Visual Studio 2005 Standard Edition
- Visual Studio 2005 Professional Edition
- Visual Studio 2005 Team Edition for Software Architects
- Visual Studio 2005 Team Edition for Software Developers
- Visual Studio 2005 Team Edition for Software Testers
- Visual Studio 2005 Team Foundation Server
- Visual Studio 2005 Team Suite

Note   All Team System editions are based on the professional edition.

Visual Studio 2005 Express Editions

The Visual Studio 2005 Express Editions are great for children, hobbyists, students, novices, and enthusiasts in general. You can select from Microsoft Visual C#® Express, Visual Basic Express, Visual C++®, Visual J#®, and Web Developer Express. Express editions are made available to almost anyone who wants them so that developers will start using Visual Studio 2005.

Visual Studio 2005 Standard Edition

Similar to standard editions of the previous versions of Visual Studio, this is the entry level for anyone who is serious about developing applications. The intended audience includes Web professionals, Visual Basic 6.0 developers, and part-time developers who want to build standalone applications in Visual Basic .NET or C#.

Visual Studio 2005 Professional Edition

Similar to the professional editions of the previous versions of Visual Studio, this is the edition for serious development in Visual Studio. This edition is for consultants, solo professionals, and those who work in small teams for which Team System may be more than they need. The professional edition also differs from the standard edition in that it has all the features required to build distributed applications.

Integration with Other Microsoft Products

Team System is composed of many pieces and parts. In the client-only editions, Team System is simply Visual Studio 2005 Professional Edition with the appropriate add-ins. Team Foundation Server, which you will learn more about in Chapter 2, is an entire architecture of services.

Here are some other Microsoft products and how they integrate:

- **Microsoft SQL Server™ 2005**   Repository for all work items, source code, and build data, including all team artifacts. Analysis Services (OLAP cubes) and Reporting Services support the portal and various team reports.

- **Microsoft Windows® SharePoint® Portal Services (but not SharePoint Portal Server)**   The software behind the team project portal.

- **Visual Studio 2005**   Primary environment for all roles.

- **Microsoft Project 2003 (but not Project Server)**   An alternate tool for project managers.

- **Microsoft Excel 2003**   An alternate tool for project managers.

- **Microsoft Internet Explorer**   Used to interact with the team project portal and view reports.

> **Note**   Microsoft is planning to release a Microsoft Source Code Control Interface (MSSCCI) plug-in as a download sometime after Visual Studio 2005 launches. This will enable basic source control integration between Team Foundation Version Control and previous versions of Visual Studio. Until then, and for all other software packages or platforms, you can use the various command-line utilities or APIs as a way to extend or integrate with other development environments.

In addition to these tools, Microsoft and its partners have announced many Team System integrated tools and services. Microsoft is planning to include migration utilities for Microsoft Visual SourceSafe, and other partners have promised additional modeling tool support, requirements gathering support, and testing tools.

Summary

Team System was created by Microsoft, a company who knows a thing or two about designing, developing, and shipping large-scale software products. When you use Team System to develop your service-oriented solutions, you will be increasing your project's predictability of success by improving the communication and productivity of your team through the use of integrated tools, regardless of whether your team is working on a LAN or in a distributed, worldwide environment. Methodology and guidance are provided out of the box, as well as the ability to customize and extend Team System in many, many ways.

Chapter 2
Team Foundation Server

In this chapter:

Team Foundation Server Components. 19

Team Foundation Server Architecture 20

Software Configuration Management (SCM) 24

Summary. 36

I thought it important to start with the heart of Microsoft® Visual Studio® 2005 Team System, which is its back-end infrastructure. Microsoft Visual Studio 2005 Team Foundation Server isn't required to run the various Visual Studio 2005 Team System role-based editions, but without it your team won't collaborate as well as it could. You might say that Team Foundation Server is to Visual Studio Team System what Microsoft Exchange Server 2003 is to Microsoft Office Outlook®. You can run Outlook by itself, but without Exchange Server, you'll be missing many features.

Team Foundation Server Components

Team Foundation Server is a partnering product to Visual Studio 2005, but in many cases it will be purchased as a separate solution. It is used in environments where teams need communication tightly integrated inside Visual Studio, scalable version-control software, and an integrated Web portal for the project. I guess it sounds like most teams will need Team Foundation Server.

Tip Topics related to installing, configuring, and troubleshooting Team Foundation Server are beyond the scope of this book. For more information, please refer to the appropriate installation guides or visit the main Team System site at *http://msdn.microsoft.com/teamsystem*.

Here are the features that you get with Team Foundation Server:

- Project management—Create and manage team projects

- Work item tracking—Create and manage requirements, tasks, and bugs

- Change management—Version control to manage changes to the project

- Build server—Automated and extensible project-build tool

- Project site—Microsoft Windows® SharePoint® Services (WSS) portal provides a collaborative work area

- Reporting—Management and status reports are available to the entire team

These are important features to teams of every size. These features serve to unify the entire team in various ways. Without Team Foundation Server, each team member would be architecting, developing, or testing within his or her own silo. This is a problem we want to avoid.

> **Tip**   Microsoft recommends using Visual Studio 2005 Team System with Active Directory® directory service. However, this is not a requirement. If you want to install Team Foundation Server on a single server, it can belong to a workgroup. Dual-server installations will require Active Directory.

Team Foundation Server Architecture

Team Foundation Server is a multitiered architecture, composed of an application tier and a data tier. It is similar to what many enterprises are building in-house for their own business applications. Team Foundation Server was constructed by using best-of-breed software, such as ASP.NET 2.0, WSS, and Microsoft SQL Server™ 2005.

Data Tier

Team Foundation Server's data tier is hosted on SQL Server 2005. Ideally, this should be a dedicated server that does nothing but support your team. Team Foundation Server needs to run on the default instance of SQL Server 2005, thus freeing up other instances. Team Foundation Server will use both the database engine and analysis services features of SQL Server 2005. You should follow the Team Foundation Server setup guide explicitly when preparing a SQL Server 2005 for Team System.

The following databases are installed in the data tier:

- **TFSIntegration**   Team Foundation Server core services (project metadata, notifications, security groups, and so on)

- **TFSWarehouse**   Team Foundation Data Warehouse

- **TFSWorkItemTracking**   Team Foundation Server work item tracking database

- **TFSWorkItemTrackingAttachments**   Team Foundation Server work item attachment database

- **TFSVersionControl**   Team Foundation Server version control database

- **TFSActivityLogging**   Team Foundation Server version control event log

- **TFSBuild**   Team Build data (results, code coverage, test results, and so on)

An advantage of Team Foundation Server being hosted on SQL Server 2005 is that it becomes a central place to maintain and back up the assets of your development projects: work items, report data, and most important—code! Just create a couple of simple maintenance plans to run periodically, and you're covered! You also can take advantage of any other availability features of SQL Server 2005, such as database mirroring and clustering. Look for Microsoft to issue guidance down the road to keep your development team's assets protected.

Reporting Services

Another benefit of hosting Team Foundation Server on SQL Server 2005 is that Team Foundation Server has built-in reporting capability. As you might know, Microsoft started shipping a server-based reporting solution, known as Reporting Services, with SQL Server 2000. It's available out of the box with SQL Server 2005 and is the cornerstone to Team System's informative, real-time reporting.

Microsoft will offer many prebuilt reports within Team System. These will include beneficial reports that pull from the data warehouse, such as project health, code churn (changes in code between check-ins), test pass, test effectiveness, active bugs, and efficiency reports. Reporting Services will also provide advanced BI and trending analysis tools for your Team Foundation Server data, enabling you to build and execute "what if" reports. Examples might include "When is our project expected to end based on current trending?" or "If I drop certain scenarios how does that effect timelines?"

> **More info**   For a list of reports and some screen shots, read Chapter 10.

With just a little knowledge of the database or data warehouse structure and some experience with authoring Reporting Services reports, you'll be able to create any other custom reports you might need. In turn, these reports can be displayed through the project portal by using a Microsoft WSS reporting Web part.

> **More info**   For information on customizing and extending the reporting capabilities of Team System, read Chapter 9.

With SQL Server 2005, Microsoft will provide us with Report Builder, a new component that allows business users to create their own reports using a user-friendly model of their data. Report Builder leverages the Reporting Services platform to bring ad hoc reporting to end users. Users create and edit reports with the Report Builder client, a ClickOnce application deployed via the browser. They start by selecting report layout templates containing predefined data sections such as tables, matrices, and charts. Users can then drag and drop report items from the model to the design surface and set constraints to filter the report data. The model contains all of the necessary information for the Report Builder to automatically generate the source query and retrieve the requested data.

Application Tier

The application tier is composed of ASP.NET (ASMX) Web services, which are called from the various client applications as well as WSS, which supports the team portal.

> **Note**   Because both WSS and the Team Foundation Server Web services reside on the same Internet Information Services (IIS) 6.0 installation, they need to have different port numbers. The Beta 1 port numbers are as follows: the IIS 6.0 Default Web Site (port 80), WSS (port 16083), and the Team Foundation Server Web services (port 8080).

The following ASP.NET Web services are installed in the application tier:

- **<install path>\WebServices\Services**   Application Programming Interface (API) for the Team Foundation Server core services

- **<install path>\WebServices\VersionControl and <install path>\WebServices\ VersionControlProxy**   API for the Team Foundation Server version control

- **<install path>\WebServices\Build**   API for Team Build

- **<install path>\WebServices\Warehouse**   API for Team Foundation Data Warehouse

- **<install path>\WebServices\WorkItemTracking**   API for Work Item Tracking (as shown in Figure 2-1)

> **Tip**   Those of you who want to interact directly with Team System should use the Team Foundation client object model. The Web services are not intended for direct interaction. The software development kit (SDK) has documentation for doing this. That said, it's definitely possible to add a Web reference to the appropriate Web service and interact directly. You should be careful, however, because these Web service APIs are complex. Sticking with the client object model is probably your best bet.

Windows SharePoint Services (WSS)

WSS provides a clean and quick way to create a collaborative portal environment for teams of any size. If you haven't had any experience with WSS before, it's a great framework for building nice sites. It's not exclusively a Team System feature, but it integrates very well with the experience. Great features of WSS portals are that they look clean and all the upload, download, security, menus, check-in, check-out, and versioning capabilities are built in. You don't have to write any code. WSS is a natural fit for Visual Studio 2005 Team System. Figure 2-2 shows you a sample team portal.

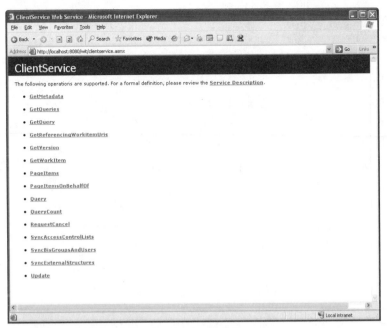

Figure 2-1   A Web service that tracks work items

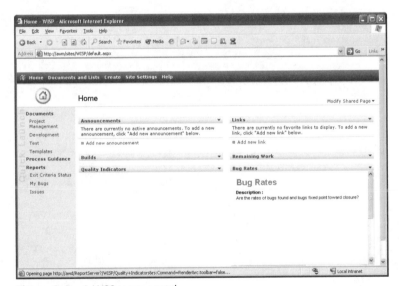

Figure 2-2   A WSS team portal

Client Tier

The client tier of Team Foundation Server includes whatever client application you're running. These client applications will communicate with Team Foundation Server by means of the aforementioned Web services. Microsoft will supply several clients, and third parties will undoubtedly supply more. More importantly, you can create your own, interacting with the Microsoft client object model or accessing the Web services directly.

In the next chapter, we'll look closely at the various Team System client applications, which are listed here:

- Visual Studio 2005–Popular development environment, which your development team probably already uses

- Microsoft Office Excel®–Popular spreadsheet software

- Microsoft Office Project–Powerful project management software

- Microsoft Internet Explorer–A browser that allows all team members access to the team portal

- Team Explorer–A Visual Studio add-in or standalone tool for creating and managing Team System projects

Software Configuration Management (SCM)

Proper Software Configuration Management (SCM) can be a lot of work. Companies and teams that lack insight into how to integrate their projects are headed for failure. Using an effective software development tool with built-in SCM can enable a team and company to manage the unmanageable.

Team System improves your team's SCM in the following ways:

- Enables you to develop and manage multiple versions of a product at the same time

- Enables multiple developers to work on the same files simultaneously

- Relates bugs and bug fixes back to their origin

- Merges changes from one release to another

- Manages software builds

- Manages releases

As I mentioned in the initial chapter, improving team communication is a great start for solving problems related to design and development. It's also the basis for improving SCM. Team-based software development is like an orchestra during a symphony, where all the members need to be in sync, watching their manager, and working in unison to bring the deliverable to fruition on time. Managers regularly need to know what state the project is in, how much code churn is in the nightly builds, when the project has reached zero new bugs, and so on. Requiring team members to pull out of their task at hand so that they can answer these questions is quite distracting.

Depending on the methodology you choose, your approach to software development might be quite different from project to project or from team to team, but your need to intelligently store information will be the same as any other. Your team must constantly manage repositories of work items and artifacts, including tasks, risk items, requirements, source code, bugs, and reports. Scattering each of these item types to different tools fractures the already brittle communication pathways of teams and software.

Team System's core concepts of proper software configuration management are as follows:

- Work item tracking
- Version control
- Build and release management
- Team communication
- Reporting

I will explain work item tracking, version control, and build and release management in this chapter. You'll see them further explained throughout the chapters in Part 2, which show you Team System in a role-based approach, focusing on the team members and their activities. Team communication will also become evident as you read through those chapters. Although reporting will be used throughout your project's life cycle, I won't cover it until Chapter 10.

Work Item Tracking (WIT)

The term *work item* abstracts or generalizes the various concepts of software development. A work item can define any actionable unit of information that is part of the software development life cycle. Examples of work items include requirements, tasks, and bugs. Work items have properties, such as title, date, status, and name of the team member they are assigned to. If you allow them to be, these items become the foundation of your software process. As you pass through the various phases and iterations of your project, the work items move with you.

The actual type and format of work items is dictated by the methodology you choose for your project. Microsoft Solutions Framework (MSF) for Agile Software Development defines different work items that ask different questions than other methodologies. Figure 2-3 shows what information MSF Agile specifies for a task.

Note   If you choose the MSF for Agile Software Development methodology for your Team System project, the five work item types you'll have available are risks, bugs, tasks, scenarios, and Quality of Service (QoS) requirements. You will learn more about the various MSF 4.0 methodologies in Chapter 8.

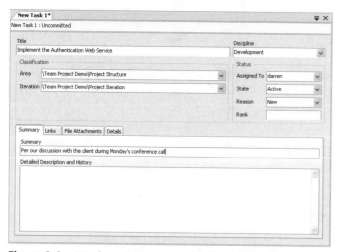

Figure 2-3   A task work item as defined by MSF Agile

A powerful feature of work items is the ability to link them to other artifacts, which is key to an effective SCM strategy. Linking a work item to a set of code checked into version control allows the developer or the project manager to track which changes are related to which requirements or bugs. Tough questions such as, "Why was the change made?" and "Who authorized the change?" can now be easily answered. All these linkages can be queried and reported. You also need to know which builds contained which work items. This information is displayed clearly on the Links tab of a work item.

> **Note**   Ask yourself this: How many times have you or a developer you know become side-tracked in writing a "cool feature" or adding some functionality that's not called for explicitly by a functional requirement or bug fix? These excursions can cost a project time or money.

If, as a project manager, you're already tracking bugs and requirements in Excel or Project, you should keep doing so. By using the integrated Team System toolbar, you can synchronize work items, allowing you to work in an environment you're comfortable with—even when you're disconnected from the network—if you choose.

Once committed to the Team Foundation Server database, all of these work items are just records in tables in SQL Server 2005. The familiar interfaces and lightweight operational maintenance of SQL Server result in a very short learning curve and back-end extensibility if necessary. You also know that your valuable intellectual property enjoys transactional integrity and robust security.

Customizing Work Item Tracking

Microsoft realizes that the work items it developed for its MSF methodologies won't satisfy everyone's needs. For example, you might want to assign an hourly rate, dollars, security classification, or budget information to a task. Currently, the MSF 4.0 methodologies don't support those definitions.

Team System, however, allows you to add, edit, or delete the actual work item fields, including how they appear in the user interface and any rules and workflow associated with them. These new or altered work items will surface in the various tools and reports throughout your development process based on the methodology templates, just like those work items Microsoft provides by default.

More info   Be sure to check out Chapter 9 for a useful section on how to customize and extend Team System.

Pluggable Methodology vs. Built-In Processes

So how can you have a completely flexible and pluggable methodology? You can't, but let me explain. For example, I can't alter Work Item Tracking so that after 50 new bugs are entered team members need to physically attend a team meeting. I also can't change the infrastructure and workflow of Team Foundation Server.

For example, a typical methodology describes the following items:

- Role
- Work stream
- Activity
- Types of work items

A methodology, however, can't alter these built-in rules of the underlying meta-model:

- Users belong to security groups.
- Users own work items.
- Roles perform work streams.
- Work streams are sequences of activities.
- Work items track activities.
- Activities produce and consume work products.
- Iterations group and schedule work items.

Why am I mentioning this? While you are learning about all the ways in which you can customize and extend Team System, keep in mind that there are basic, intrinsic rules when you use Team System.

Version Control

Team Foundation Version Control (TFVC) was built new, from the ground up. Microsoft did not just update Microsoft Visual SourceSafe® and change the name. The new version control is a multitiered architecture and, as such, offers the same benefits as those enjoyed by the work item tracking architecture. Unlike Visual SourceSafe, TFVC supports large distributed development teams and projects.

TFVC introduces a new concept called a *changeset*. With other version control products, the individual files you work on have no linkage or context. They are just separate files checked in at the same time. Hopefully, your comments are enough to glue them together, giving them context and fidelity. In TFVC, changesets describe a group of associated file modifications. This allows for better accounting and workflow, as well as simplified administration. Internally, each changeset is given a unique identifier for tracking and reporting.

As a developer works on the files under version control, the changes are made to a local workspace. Later, he or she can check them in, specifying any required documentation and associating the changeset with one or more work items, such as a task or bug.

> **Note**   The internal team at Microsoft responsible for building Team Foundation Server is located in North Carolina. Microsoft has a rather substantial campus there and has been "dogfooding" (using) this same version control throughout the development of Team System. They have been synchronizing builds with the team members on the Redmond, Washington campus.

If you have both Visual SourceSafe and TFVC installed, you can switch back and forth by selecting a different plug-in. This way, you can continue to support any Visual SourceSafe projects, as well as any new development efforts under the Team System Version Control (see Figure 2-4). Remember also that Microsoft includes a migration tool to move your Visual SourceSafe artifacts over to TFVC. Microsoft, or other partners, may release similar migration tools down the road.

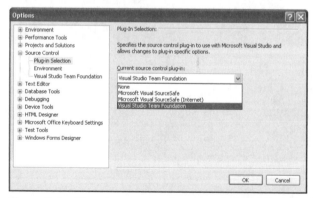

Figure 2-4   Choosing your version control plug-in inside Visual Studio

You'll learn more about the version control integration in Chapter 6, which covers the Visual Studio 2005 Team Edition for Software Developers.

Tip   There is also a command-line utility (*tf.exe*) for interaction with TFVC. This utility allows you to interact from any environment, not just Visual Studio 2005.

How does version control work in environments involving many development shops or teams in different sites? What if they are working over slow connections? In the past, this would be a nightmare of virtual private network (VPN) connections. With TFVC, the solution is to have all the sites connect to the same application tier. Remember that the application tier is just an XML Web service. The integrated tools inside Visual Studio 2005 will natively interact with these Web services.

I'll provide an overview of the TFVC capabilities for branching, merging, and shelving, which are really its unique features.

Branching

Branching in TFVC is similar to *copying* items from one project to another; however, it is done intelligently. The origin, context, and history of the copied items are maintained so that future changes can be merged back into the original path. This capability is important to software configuration management because it allows multiple builds and releases to be maintained efficiently. These branches are easy to visualize and navigate in the Visual Studio Source Control Explorer. This tool enables a developer to work simultaneously on many branches of the same code, as is sometimes necessary.

Branching can be performed by date, label, or version. You can branch from an existing project in the Source Control Explorer (as shown in Figure 2-5) or when you begin a new team project (as shown in Figure 2-6). All changes that you make to the newly branched code are done locally, in your local workspace, until you check in the changes to the TFSC. The advantage of this process is that you can make any necessary changes, build the code, and test it to make sure it works properly before checking it back in as a new branch.

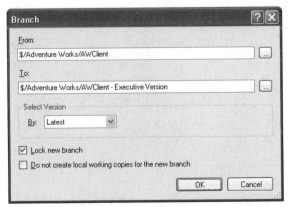

Figure 2-5   Creating a new branch from Source Control Explorer

> **Note**   The Source Control Explorer allows you to move and rename items from one team project to another. This explorer will be available only in Visual Studio 2005. Microsoft is planning to release a Microsoft Source Code Control Interface (MSSCCI) plug-in as a download sometime after Visual Studio 2005 launches. This will enable basic version control integration between TFVC and previous versions of Visual Studio.

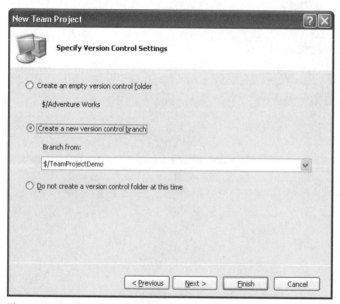

Figure 2-6   Creating a new version control branch at project creation

Another benefit of branching is that of storage space efficiency. TFVC minimizes the required storage by only maintaining one copy of content, regardless of how many source files contain it. This is similar to how Exchange Server keeps only one large attachment even though it's being sent to many people. For example, in TFVC, only one copy of a 3 MB file will be saved, even when there are 10 copies of the file in various projects and branches. For this reason, new branches consume very little space. As the developers start making changes to particular files, the additional storage will be used for those changes. TFVC stores only the differences, or deltas from the original files, which is very efficient.

Security can be configured on these branches just as you would set permissions on any directory folder in Microsoft Windows. Remember that branches are essentially paths, so you can use the same access control list (ACL) security model that you are used to. Just right-click on a branched folder, choose Properties, and set permissions.

Merging

Merging is at the core of TFVC's high level of efficiency. This intelligent process reconciles all the changes you've made in your branched code ("the source") with its original code ("the target"). This is why TFVC remembers the origin and relationships when branching. Merging is more than just blending text. It's almost transactional in nature, because it will merge additions, deletions, un-deletions, and renames from the source to the target environment.

Team System projects can be configured for *multiple checkout*. This feature allows more than one user to edit the same file simultaneously. The same engine that merges changes between branched projects can also merge changes from two or more checked-out projects back to the source. This feature is not enabled by default.

> **Note** In the case that both the source and target code were changed during a session, the merge will result in a conflict. TFVC will communicate this message to the developer, providing guidance and options on how to resolve the conflict. For straightforward conflicts, you can simply choose whether the source or target should take precedence. For more complex conflict resolution, you can use the included graphical three-way merge tool. This tool is the same as the one you may have used in the past with Visual SourceSafe.

You can choose which changes you want to merge. For example, you can merge the code that fixed a single bug without merging anything else that you were working on. After merging, TFVC updates the merge history for the items. This information is tracked automatically and can be viewed from inside Visual Studio or accessed from the command-line utility.

From the developer's point of view, it's a simple process. Microsoft includes a Merge Wizard in Visual Studio 2005, which leads the user through the process, allowing him or her to choose what changes to merge. The possible answers in the wizard are constrained to keep mistakes to a minimum. For example, if you've branched a particular project twice, only those other two projects would be listed as possible targets for the merge.

Shelving

Shelving is another new, key concept to TFVC. Shelving allows a developer to store pending changes to the server without checking them in. TFVC introduces the concept of a *shelveset*, which is similar to a changeset except that it's used to store *shelved* files in a personal space on the server. You can upload pending changes, comments, and associated work items to this personal space for whatever reason. This is not to suggest that developers should start keeping their source code and project files in their own personal area away from other team members. That goes against why we are using version control in the first place. Figure 2-7 shows the shelving feature from inside Visual Studio.

There are many reasons that you might want to shelve your code, including the following ones:

- You need to switch to a different project to perform work with higher priority.
- Your code fails a check-in policy, and you can't fix it immediately.
- Your code is not complete enough to share with others.
- You need to leave suddenly, and you want to upload your work to the server for safekeeping.

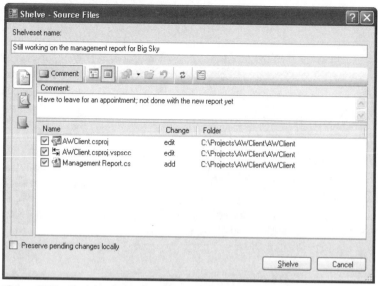

Figure 2-7   Shelving code from Visual Studio

Each user can have as many shelvesets as desired. Other users are able to see what shelvesets are available, but they can't access them unless permission is explicitly granted.

> **Note**   Shelving is a great feature, but it can be abused. It's intended for unforeseen inter-ruptions during a development session. As a best practice, however, all contributors to a project should check in their files and documentation normally to the shared folders only after all check-in policies are satisfied.

Work Item Integration

From a management standpoint, one of the coolest features is the ability to associate a work item with your check-in. This capability will enable others to see *why* code was changed. Ideally, they'll always see a code change linked back to a requirement or bug. This type of managerial oversight is important in any project in which developers shouldn't be able to add features or make unnecessary changes.

Check-In Policies

Even though a project manager or team lead might tell his or her developers, "You can't check in your code until you perform a clean build" or "Don't even think of uploading code that fails its unit tests," these are just words, and words can be ignored. With Team System, policies can be created and enabled inside Visual Studio 2005 that will enforce the two example conditions I just cited, as well as others. Figure 2-8 shows the various check-in policy types.

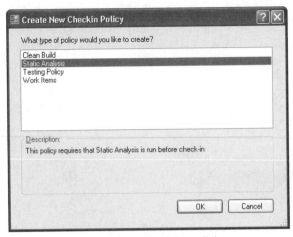

Figure 2-8   Team System check-in policies

- **Clean Build**   The project must compile without errors before check-in.
- **Static Analysis**   A static analysis test must be run before checkin.
- **Testing Policy**   Check-in tests, such as unit tests, must be run before checkin.
- **Work Items**   One or more work items must be associated with the checkin.

Team System projects can also be configured to track additional notes at check-in. Figure 2-9 shows some standard notes associated with the MSF Agile methodology as well as how easy it is to create a new required note. The project administrator can create new notes and set any note to be required. This becomes another type of check-in policy.

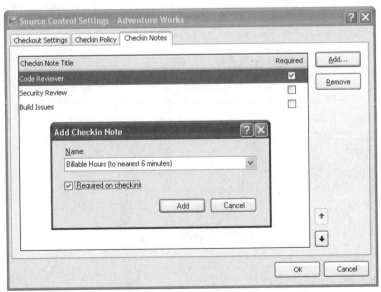

Figure 2-9   Creating a new check-in note

If a developer needs to override a policy, he or she could shelve the changes instead, or override the policy. Figure 2-10 shows the flexibility in Team System to allow for a policy override. This might be required in an emergency situation where a fix is required at 2 A.M., for example, and there may be need to check in code that hasn't been fully reviewed.

> **Note**   The fact that a check-in policy has been overridden is made known to the adminis-trator, so a developer can't simply ignore checkin policies with impunity.

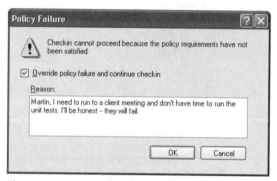

Figure 2-10   Overriding a check-in policy

TFVC and Sarbanes-Oxley Requirements

If your shop needs to comply with the Sarbanes-Oxley (SOX) Requirements, then you'll need to have tight controls over your source code and related configuration management. Security permissions are a good start, but they are not enough. You also need to have tight auditing in place—that is, you'll need to track which developers are assembling which parts of the application and when. Implementing these types of controls is different from how most shops perform their normal day-to-day routine, but we are developing software under different circumstances now than we did ten years ago.

One of Team Foundation Server's answers to SOX is to manage *promotion* levels by using branches. Successive levels of promotion are handled in different branches of a project's source code. Developers will typically do their work in the branch that corresponds with the lowest promotion level. Changes then get merged to higher levels of promotion when they are ready. Remember that TFVC branches by using a path-space method, so it can use standard file system ACLs to manage access rights. This ability allows a manager or lead developer to lock down each branch so that only authorized users are allowed to check in code.

To help your project achieve SOX compliance, Microsoft suggests creating at least two promotion levels:

- A *developer* branch for the day-to-day work
- An *approved* branch where approved changes are merged

The manager or lead developer would lock down the approved branch so that only authorized users could perform check-ins. TFVC provides native audit trail support of who changed what, which allows you to prove that only authorized people have been making changes in that branch.

What Happened to Visual SourceSafe?

I've been asked and answered that question many times recently. Most developers are aware of the limitations of Visual SourceSafe. Many of you have probably hit the same walls I have when using it: scalability limitations, remote operation limitations, and (occasionally) corruption of data. But love it or hate it, we have to agree that it's the easiest version control tool out there.

Rest assured, Visual SourceSafe is alive and well. Although it's not being built by the same group as Team System, Microsoft continues to research and develop Visual SourceSafe. There's a new release of Visual SourceSafe to accompany certain Visual Studio 2005 editions. It contains a big feature that is shared with Team Foundation Version Control: HTTP access through Web service interfaces.

Some other features we'll see in Visual SourceSafe 2005 include the following:

- A copy-modify-merge model, to reduce lock contention
- A local area network (LAN) performance booster, to use remote procedure calls (RPC) to increase performance
- Asynchronous file opening, so that you can start working before loading is completed
- Better support for projects with developers in multiple time zones
- Better support for multiple languages and Unicode

Remember that Visual SourceSafe 2005 is intended for use by smaller teams, with perhaps no more than five users, and it's intended to be used for version control only. It doesn't have deep SCM support. For any medium-to-large teams (from 5 to 500 users), Team Foundation's version control is optimized for the job.

Build and Release Management

The term *build* refers to the compilation of all the files, libraries, or components into a new set of executables, libraries, or components. Team System's build management provides an easy, end-to-end solution to produce daily builds, with complete testing and automation. It will pull all the related project files out of Team Foundation Version Control.

Pressing F5 or using the Build menu option inside Visual Studio 2005 works great for smaller applications, where you have local access to all the source-code files and don't have any additional requirements. Larger projects tend to have many other tasks bundled with the actual compile process. Build automation allows for the following additional pre-build and post-build requirements:

- Check out version controlled files for the build
- Run static analysis, unit tests, or both
- Compile sources
- Save code churn, test, code coverage, and other build information
- Drop the binaries into a predefined location
- Generate reports

The Visual Studio Team System build Automation Tool provides an out-of-the-box solution to meet these requirements. Its wizard helps you create automated build scripts so that you can easily automate these tasks. Reports can then be studied to determine the general health of the project and the *velocity* of the development effort.

Team Build

The Team Build product uses MSBuild internally, which means that it has the flexibility to accommodate many scenarios. By creating and plugging in MSBuild tasks, you can customize your process and accomplish a number of custom tasks.

> **Note**   You will learn more about Team Build in Chapter 6 and more about extending it in Chapter 9.

Summary

I hope you see now that Team Foundation Server is the beating heart of Team System. Without it, your team is designing, developing, and testing in isolation. The integration between their Visual Studio 2005 environments simply won't be. Sure, Visual SourceSafe is still available and does include some great improvements, but the enterprise-scale version control available in Team Foundation Server, with its ability to link work items, is a must.

Chapter 3
Team System Client Applications

In this chapter:

Tools for Project Managers 38
Tools for Architects 44
Tools for Developers 62
Tools for Testers 65
Internet Explorer for All Team Members 66
Command-Line Utilities 66
Tools by Roles 67
Summary 68

Now that you have an understanding of and appreciation for the back end of Team System, I want to spend some time with the front-end products, tools, and designers that you'll be using. Some of these client applications work directly with Team Foundation Server and some can be used as standalone components. From a product perspective, the various Team System clients are the following:

- Microsoft® Visual Studio® 2005–The newest edition of Visual Studio, which your development team already uses

- Microsoft Office Excel® 2003–Popular spreadsheet software, which is part of Microsoft Office

- Microsoft Office Project Professional 2003–Powerful project management software

- Internet Explorer–A browser that allows all team members access to the team portal

- Command-line tools–Various tools that enable scheduled, batch interaction with Team System

I'll cover each of the tools and designers from a role-based point of view, both in this chapter as well as in the rest of the book. At the end of this chapter, you'll see–listed by edition of Visual Studio and Team System–which tools and designers will be available. Checking that list will enable you to focus on the tools and designers that are available within the edition you're using.

Tools for Project Managers

I'll start with project managers because most projects start with project managers. The Team System duties that a project manager performs include definition of work items such as the scenarios, quality of service requirements, and tasks for the other team members. Before a project manager can start performing these duties, he or she must set up the project infrastructure by defining the project, selecting a methodology, determining version control settings, and creating a team project portal to view any reports.

Project managers create the project from inside Visual Studio. This could be any of the various Team System editions, Team Suite, or the standalone Team Explorer that accompanies the Team Foundation Server edition. Once the project is created, work items can be managed from Microsoft Excel or Microsoft Project, providing several unique client applications to satisfy most skill sets.

Visual Studio 2005 Team Explorer

Team Explorer accompanies all Visual Studio 2005 Team Editions. It can be used by all roles provided that the security permissions have been set up appropriately. For project managers, the Team Explorer will be the most popular of the tools. Project managers can use Team Explorer to create new team projects, configure settings and security, and create new work items. It's a familiar, hierarchical tree view with lots of context menus and functionality.

Here are some of the tasks you can perform from Team Explorer:

- Connect to a specific Team Foundation Server
- Configure Team Foundation Server settings, such as groups, security, process templates (as shown in Figure 3-1), and file types under version control
- Create new team projects
- Configure project settings, such as groups, security, classifications, and check-in policies
- Add and manage work items, document libraries, and documents within a project
- Create, execute, and save queries to return an exact list of work items
- Create and execute Team Builds

Not all of these preceding tasks will be performed by all roles. For example, it's highly unlikely that a tester would be creating new team projects or that a project manager would be configuring and executing Team Builds. Visual Studio Team System, however, can be configured so that anybody on the team can have permission to execute any of these tasks.

Some Team Explorer tasks that you perform, such as creating document libraries and uploading documents, are simply acting directly on the Microsoft Windows® SharePoint® Services (WSS) Project Portal site. Changes that you make in Team Explorer are visible from the portal, and vice versa. For example, if you create a document library named *UML Diagrams* from Team Explorer and then upload some Microsoft Visio® diagrams, these changes will be seen immediately by anyone visiting your Project Portal from a browser. If the portal user creates an additional document library named *Specifications* and then uploads some Excel spreadsheets, those changes will be seen from within Team Explorer as soon as you click the Refresh button.

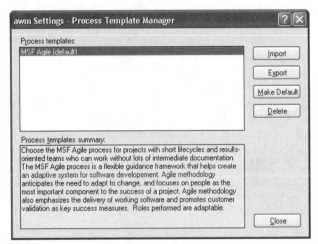

Figure 3-1   Managing methodology templates from Team Explorer

Note   Microsoft Excel and Project documents can be created and launched from inside Team Explorer. Each of these tools, as you will see, has advantages over using Team Explorer directly.

Note   To access Team Foundation Server, you must first install Team Explorer. Team Explorer is both a standalone application with Team Foundation functionality only, and an addition to Visual Studio that provides integrated Team Foundation functionality. If your team members don't need the full capabilities of Visual Studio 2005, you can just install Team Explorer as a standalone application on their computers. The installation binaries are found on the Team Foundation Server media.

Microsoft Excel

Excel is the most popular project management tool in use. All managers and team leads that I've met keep at least some of their schedule, tasks, requirements, milestones, or deliverables in an .xls spreadsheet somewhere. For this reason, the Visual Studio product team made it a priority to integrate Excel with Team System. This integration is handled by a managed Excel add-in, which gives access to the Team Foundation Server via a Work Item toolbar and menu.

Another advantage to using Excel is that it's a great offline Team System client. A project manager can connect to a Team Foundation server, create a new work item list, select the available properties (columns), and then detach and work on the list while he or she is at home or traveling.

The first step is to connect to a particular Team Project on a Team Foundation server. One way of doing this is to launch Excel from within the Visual Studio 2005 Team Explorer. If you do this, you'll already be connected to a server and a project. If you launch Excel by itself, however, you'll need to specify a connection to a server and select a project, before creating or editing lists of work items. Figure 3-2 shows Microsoft Excel connecting to a Team Foundation server. You can also see the new toolbar and menu.

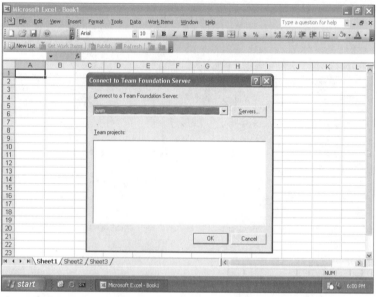

Figure 3-2   Connecting to a Team Foundation server from Excel

Once you're connected to the Team Foundation server, you can create a new list of work items or query Team Foundation Server for a list of existing work items that you might want to update. When creating a new list, you're presented with the entire list of properties (columns) that you can track for a given work item type. This comprehensive list, which can be quite long, is specific to the product's chosen methodology. Items in boldface type are required by Team System. You can use the Add Required button to select them in a batch, as shown in Figure 3-3.

> **Note**   Excel and Project reflect any customizations you make to the default work item types. For example, if you add another field to the Task work item type to track the Security Clearance level required to accomplish that task, it shows as a selectable column. See Chapter 9 for more information on customizing and extending Team System.

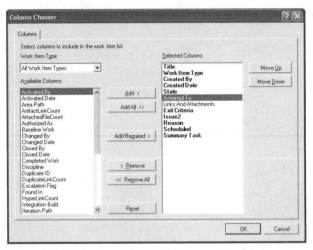

Figure 3-3   Selecting columns for a new list of tasks

After adding the work items to your spreadsheet, you need to publish them back to Team Foundation Server. This can be done by selecting Publish Changes from the toolbar or the Work Items menu. (See Figure 3-4.) If there are no errors and all required fields have been specified, the work items will be uploaded to the server. If any errors are encountered, the add-in will present you with a message box and then with a screen listing all the work item publishing errors so that you can see what's wrong with the batch. (See Figure 3-5.)

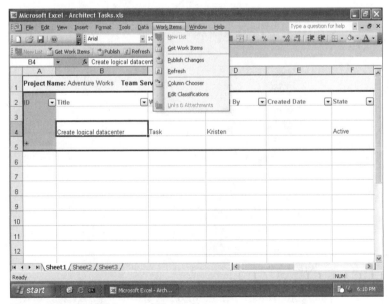

Figure 3-4   Publishing work item changes

> **Tip**   When you create new work items, you must leave the work item ID blank. Team Foundation Server will assign it the next available number when it is published.

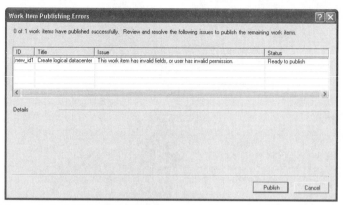

Figure 3-5   Work item publishing errors

Once published, the work items are visible to all other Team System users who have the appropriate permission. Later, a project manager can come back to Excel and pull down a list of work items, making changes to items in that list. Instead of selecting New List, he or she can run a Get Work Items query and retrieve one or more work items to edit. (See Figure 3-6.)

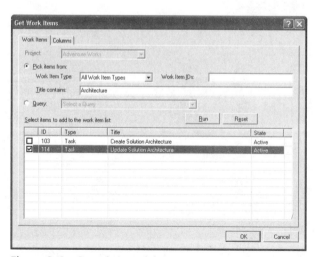

Figure 3-6   Querying work items

Work items can also be related to other work items, artifacts, hyperlinks, and other attachments. As I mentioned in the last chapter, this is a very powerful feature that's used to properly support Software Configuration Management. You must remember that you get out of Team System only what you put into it. The more context and relevance you add to your work items, the better the whole experience will be for everyone involved. Figure 3-7 shows the deep support available for this inside Excel.

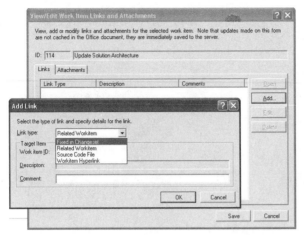

Figure 3-7   Associating linked artifacts and other attachments to work items

When you're finished, you should save your Excel spreadsheet. Technically, Team System doesn't require this. You are allowed to use Book1.xls as a throwaway shell to create or query work items and then publish them back to Team Foundation Server. I recommend, however, giving each worksheet a unique name and saving it to the hard drive or team portal. This way, the metadata regarding your list and queries is saved, as well as any additional items on other spreadsheets contained in that workbook. It'll save you time when you have to work on that same list again. Another benefit is that you can send it as an attachment to new Team System users.

Microsoft Project

Microsoft Project support for Team System is identical to that in Excel. Rather than adding work items into or retrieving them from a spreadsheet, you're doing so within a project plan. Microsoft provided this alternative to Excel simply as an option to project managers who prefer the Microsoft Project environment to Excel or Visual Studio. Project managers are also welcome to use any of the built-in features of Microsoft Office Project, such as milestones, project/subproject rollups, and reports.

> **Note**   Team System requires Microsoft Project 2003 Professional Edition.

The work item add-in also defines field mappings between work item types and Microsoft Project. Unlike Excel, Microsoft Project uses a limited set of columns, including predefined columns such as Task Name, and custom fields. When a user publishes or refreshes work item data from a Microsoft Project file, a special field map is used to determine which fields in the work item database match the columns in Microsoft Project. The field map is located in an XML file named MsProjProp.xml. After a team project is created, these mappings cannot be changed for that team project.

You can customize the mappings—for example, to support a new field that you created or to map fields to predefined columns instead of custom columns.

> **Tip**   If you choose to install Microsoft Project Professional 2003 using a different type of installation, such as *custom install*, you must be certain to install the .NET Programmability Support feature for Microsoft Office Project for Windows. This feature installs the Primary Interop Assemblies that allow programmability with the .NET Framework and is required for integration with Team Foundation.

Tools for Architects

The design and development of distributed systems is more complex now than ever. Architects need new ways of reducing this complexity to increase the predictability of deployment. To do this, they must find new techniques for diagramming these systems by using rich metadata about both the design and the deployment's operational requirements.

Ask yourself this: how many times has the IT operations team locked down the servers or implemented restrictive group policies that lessened your application's chance of deployment? What usually ends up happening? The result is compromise during crunch time—which isn't good. On the other end of the spectrum, the IT group could inundate the developers with paperwork or meetings, outlining every service pack, version, and configuration of their datacenter. This, too, is counterproductive. What the developers want to know is whether Microsoft SQL Server™ will work and whether their ASP.NET Web services will be able to access it!

The best solution is to have *application* architects communicate their designs effectively to the IT operations team and to have *infrastructure* architects and operations communicate information about their hosting environments back to the developers.

> **Note**   Team System doesn't make the distinction between application architects and infra-structure architects. It's important, however, to separate them into two subroles because one group will know Web services, Web applications, and Windows applications and the other group will know ports, perimeter networks, firewalls, security boundaries, and server configu-rations. Maybe in your organization this is one person, or maybe it's several people.

One thing is clear: architects' needs are different from the needs of project managers. Architects have a need for intuitive design tools that can allow them to achieve productivity, such as generating code. These types of tools are called the Distributed System Designers and are provided solely by Visual Studio 2005 Team Edition for Architects. Using these tools, architects can create one of the following Distributed Application Diagrams (DAD):

- Application diagrams–Represent applications that provide or use services

- Logical Datacenter diagrams–Represent interconnected logical servers that symbolize the logical structure of a datacenter

- Deployment diagrams–Represent the deployment of a specific system into a specific logical datacenter

- System diagrams–Represent application systems, which are composed from other application diagrams

These diagrams, like any good model, tell a story to other team members who might not share the same level of expertise as the architect. Communication with other members of the team, as well as to nontechnical stakeholders of a project, is important, and pictures improve the chances of effective communication taking place. This communication can lead to better collaboration and an increased predictability of success of the project. For example, if a team's architect can accurately diagram the network infrastructure and then demonstrate how the project's application will deploy successfully onto the servers, the operational staff's worries can be alleviated.

What's better is that these architectural diagrams are created in a visual environment, which is interesting and captivates its users. It also tracks just the right amount of information, which has always been the goal of a good model-driven approach. In the past, a big problem with modeling tools has been that they've been very good at documentation but not very helpful for the actual development, deployment, and management of systems. When used properly, Team System realizes all these goals.

Dynamic Systems Initiative (DSI)

A major new initiative by Microsoft and other industry partners, such as Sun Microsystems and Siebel Software, is the Dynamic Systems Initiative (DSI). The goal of DSI is to reduce complexity while increasing communication flow. It's a way to design for the eventuality of a piece of software being deployed or, put another way, to *design for operations*. A key feature of DSI is its visualization of the systems and services and tracking the metadata about each to properly describe it to another system or service. This metadata will allow for one diagram to validate against another, and for the reasons I just mentioned, it's important for application architects to validate their application design against an infrastructure architect's datacenter design.

 Note   Another key factor of DSI designs is that they're always kept up to date. Achieving this level of accuracy depends greatly on the tool and the commitment of the user; but, if the diagrams are not kept up to date, the validation can be worthless.

DSI is geared toward ensuring that the design is correct the first time and that it will deploy into the host environment successfully. But it's more than that–DSI also aims to capture knowledge and lessons learned once an application gets deployed and to apply that knowledge for easier ongoing maintenance. To achieve this, the industry is working to find new techniques for describing these systems using rich metadata about the design, development, deployment, and operational requirements that can be understood and exchanged by various automation tools.

This all sounds great. So where does most of the effort need to occur? Domain experts in various software development areas will need to brainstorm and capture the important metadata about a particular component. This metadata includes settings, constraints, versions, modes, security—in short, everything. Think of the effort as creating a schema (database or XML, whichever one comes to mind when you hear the word *schema*) to describe every type of operating system, application server, and Web server, as well as every major type of application or service that you can build with .NET.

All these DSI models need to be boiled down to common terms or interfaces so that, for example, the settings of a .NET Web Service can be validated against the policy restriction of its deployment environment. As more systems can be fully described using the DSI approach, many more possibilities emerge for building true automation into the entire software development life cycle.

> **Note**   You've probably heard about the futurists who want to give every device in your home or office its own IP address. DSI can be thought of as being similarly aggressive because the DSI visionaries, of whom I am one, would love to have DSI eventually describe every type of system, service, and server in use!

System Definition Model (SDM)

Microsoft's initial DSI offering will surface in Team System. The implementation of this offering will be known as the System Definition Model (SDM). SDM classifies your application and its deployment environment into layers, much the same way that the Open System Interconnection (OSI) model describes a network stack. SDM offers the following benefits:

- Provides a common language to describe the design and configuration for all aspects of a distributed system

- Provides familiar abstractions that make it possible for application and infrastructure architects to communicate on common ground

- Makes it possible for application architects and developers to communicate application requirements in the run-time environment

- Makes it possible for infrastructure architects to communicate application runtime, security, and connectivity requirements that result from policies defined in the deployment environment

SDM defines the following layers (from the top down):

- Application
- Application Hosting
- Logical Machines and Network Topology
- Hardware

Distributed System Designers store SDM information in XML-formatted documents. In addition to this data, SDM documents can also contain graphical information for diagram items and extended data definitions. You can use Distributed System Designers to create and maintain a set of interrelated diagrams and documents that are based on the SDM documents. Typically, the definitions created in one document (for example, application definitions) are referenced by other documents.

Visual Studio Team Edition for Architects includes a solution template that makes it possible for you to create a distributed system solution, which makes Distributed System Designers available for you to design, configure, connect, and evaluate deployment for applications and application systems. As you go through this process, a distributed system solution typically contains or will contain the following items:

- A single application diagram (.ad file)
- One or more system diagrams (.sd files)
- One or more logical datacenter diagrams (.ldd files)
- One or more deployment diagrams (.dd files)
- SDM documents (.sdm files) for externally implemented application definitions
- Projects containing code files, configuration files, other related files, and SDM documents for internally implemented application definitions

Microsoft has a strong commitment to SDM. Visual Studio's SDM integration will continue to improve as we move into Orcas, which is the next version of .NET and Visual Studio. However, the SDM platform also applies to Windows directly, especially going forward into Windows Vista (formerly known as Windows Longhorn). This maturing SDM platform will facilitate the design, deployment, and ongoing operations of systems in Windows, not just Visual Studio.

Critical to this success is for each product team to build an *adapter* that other teams will depend on for design-time validation. The obvious winners here will be Systems Management Server (SMS) and Microsoft Operations Manager (MOM), which could both leverage SDM to make integrators' and administrators' jobs easier.

Note If you're an independent software vendor (ISV), check back regularly for the software development kits (SDKs) and application programming interfaces (APIs) to help build cool SDM tools for Windows. You should bookmark the main Visual Studio Team System site: *http://msdn.microsoft.com/teamsystem*.

SDM SDK

You can download and use Microsoft's SDM SDK to extend the Distributed System Designers in Visual Studio 2005 Team Architect by adding new application, logical server, and endpoint types, as well as additional resources and constraints. You can also add relationships among new and existing concepts.

SDM systems can be used to model types of applications and logical servers. Application models can then be used within Application Designer. These SDM application systems can contain all other SDM building blocks, including SDM resources, endpoints, settings, and other SDM systems. You can author a logical server system that models a server configuration and can be used in Logical Datacenter Designer. The logical server can model hosting SDM application systems and contain settings, endpoints, and resources. By containing endpoints, the logical server system can have communication relationships with other systems. You can create settings on the logical server system that model the behavior of a real server, such as the minimum version of an application or an OS that the server will host.

The SDM SDK provides three command-line tools:

- SDM Command Line Compiler (SdmC.exe)–Responsible for validating the correctness of an .sdm file according to the SystemDefinitionModel Schema

- SDM Manager Generator (SdmG.exe)–An SDK tool that helps developers to build abstract SDM models for use with Visual Studio 2005

- SDM Prototype Generator (ProtoGen.exe)–Generates an initial Distributed System Designer prototype file for an abstract type

 Note   The SDM SDK is part of the Team System SDK.

Domain-Specific Languages

With Team System, Microsoft takes a model-driven approach to software development. Some would refer to this as *visual engineering*. Microsoft, as well as many others in the industry, realize that Unified Modeling Language (UML) tools can take you only so far. UML-class diagrams, for example, don't support many .NET data types or such concepts as properties or static methods on interfaces. You don't see these limitations when you're drawing pictures and printing collateral to hang on your wall, but when it comes to generating code, you'll have to do some tweaking if you stick with UML. What productive .NET development teams require are *Domain-Specific Language* (DSL) tools that are more agile and precisely target the domain in question without any abstraction or the need for tweaks.

> **Note** Microsoft did some research in this area. It asked many developers who use UML which of the standard models they used. As you can guess, use cases were the most popular. After that, it was sequence diagrams. Beyond that, only a small group of developers delved into the other model types.

Before you ask, let me just say, "No, UML is not dead, nor is it going away any time soon." As far as Microsoft's tools go, you can still use Visio for your UML needs, including creating the popular use-case and sequence diagrams.

What Happened to Visio?

This is a very common question. The answer is this: nothing has happened to Visio. In fact, Visio 2003 Professional remains a great way to create UML, Object-Role Modeling (ORM), and network diagrams, all of which complement Team System nicely. Team System's distributed application designers are intended to build very domain-specific, intelligent documents that can interact and be validated against each other. Visio's documents remain fairly static, with only some of them being able to generate code; however, because they are file-based diagrams, they can be uploaded to the Project Portal and referenced by the entire team.

Visio for Enterprise Architects is included in Visual Studio Team Edition for Software Architects and Visual Studio Team Suite. In addition to all the features in Microsoft Office Visio Professional 2003, with Visio for Enterprise Architects you can perform roundtrip engineering on software with the UML Model diagram and on databases with the Database, ER, and ORM Source Model diagrams. Visio for Enterprise Architects is a separate program from Visual Studio.

Here is an example of how you might use the UML support in Visio with your Team System environment:

1. Launch Visio Professional 2003.

2. Create use-case, sequence, and other UML diagrams.

3. Create your class diagrams using UML notation.

4. From Visio, generate C# or Microsoft Visual Basic® .NET code from the class diagrams you created.

5. Add the code files you generated to your Visual Studio 2005 project.

6. Open a class in the Class Designer (which is a new DSL tool).

7. Fine-tune the class for .NET.

> **Note**   If you have Visual Studio Team System for Software Architects or Visual Studio Team Suite and also installed the version of Visio for Enterprise Architects included in those programs, you can create a Visio UML diagram from within Visual Studio. To do this, you will need to create a UML diagram from Visual Studio by opening the project you want to reverse engineer into a Visio UML diagram and selecting Reverse Engineer under the Project—Visio UML menu. Visio will launch to complete the reverse engineering, and you will be prompted with a Save dialog box, in which you can choose an alternative location or rename the diagram prior to saving it.

DSL Tools in Team System

The DSL tools in Team System include the Class Designer (which you will read about later in this chapter in the section "Tools for Developers") and the Distributed System Designers. Regardless of the designer, the tools have a common set of features, such as continuous synchronization and a design-first approach that are tied together by SDM. These tools are the topic of the following sections.

Logical Datacenter Designer

Network and other topology diagrams have historically been of little value to developers or a development effort. In keeping with the principles of SDM, however, the Logical Datacenter Designer will allow network/infrastructure architects to create diagrams of their deployment environments that are more than just pretty pictures. The SDM diagrams will contain important metadata, such as constraints for application architects to test-deploy their applications against. These diagrams are an abstraction of the physical environment—hence the term *logical*. The server prototypes that the architect drags and drops will represent server roles in an actual deployment, so any constraints and settings placed on these servers should be general.

Using the Logical Datacenter Designer, you can create a logical representation of your datacenter. Logical Datacenter Designer enables you to model the placement and connectivity of logical servers and Zones. The logical datacenter diagram provides a logical, rather than a physical representation of the target datacenter. As a result, a physical server with Microsoft Windows Server™ 2003, Internet Information Services (IIS) 6.0, and SQL Server would be represented by three logical servers.

Logical datacenter diagrams can contain the following logical servers:

- **WindowsClient**   A rich .NET Windows client
- **IISWebServer**   An Internet Information Server (IIS) that can run an ASP.NET Web application or service
- **DatabaseServer**   A SQL server
- **GenericServer**   Any other server, such as Microsoft BizTalk®, COM+, MSMQ, Exchange, or another, non-Microsoft server

These logical servers can be placed in *Zones*. A Zone is defined as a kind of boundary, such as a firewall, cluster, domain, or other security boundary. Zones and the logical servers that they contain are subject to communication constraints that are specified on Zone endpoints. Zones are a nice way to place servers in a logical group. Zones can also have metadata and constraints. Figure 3-8 shows logical servers placed into Zones.

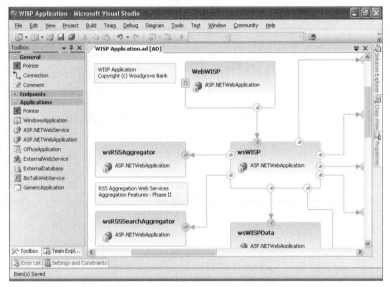

Figure 3-8   Logical servers grouped into Zones

> **Note**   One limitation of a logical datacenter diagram is that they do not support firewalls directly. As the designer, you must use Zones to separate the public and private areas of your network, configure the information flow directions and security of your endpoints, and then add appropriate comments and notes to the diagram to indicate that there is a firewall there.

After dragging and dropping the Zones and logical servers and arranging them appropriately, infrastructure architects will want to set the appropriate settings and constraints. This will ensure that only the correct type of service, version, and security are allowed onto each of their boxes. This process is a way for infrastructure architects to define the policies of their datacenter.

This documentation will become evident when a deployment report is generated. More important, these settings and constraints are required to implement SDM. Application architects can immediately see what the requirements and restrictions are for their software.

Here are some examples of types of settings and constraints:

Zone Constraints

This type of constraint defines the following characteristics:

- The type of logical server that can exist within the Zone

- Versions of .NET runtime that can exist on the servers within the Zone

- Whether there is support for the global assembly cache (GAC) on the servers within the Zone

- IIS settings, such as application-pool restrictions on the servers within the Zone

- Whether the Zone can contain other Zones

Windows Client Constraints

This type of constraint defines the following characteristics:

- Whether the client can run Office applications

- Whether the client can run other generic or Windows applications

Windows Client Settings

These settings define the following characteristics:

- Operating system type, version, build, and service pack (see Figure 3-9)

- Application name and path

- Version of the .NET runtime

- Whether there is a need for the GAC

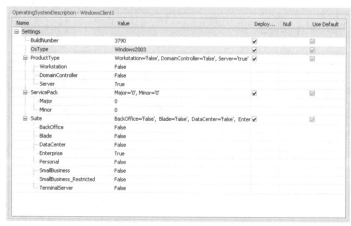

Figure 3-9   Configuring operating system settings

IIS Web Server Constraints

This type of constraint defines the following characteristics:

- The type of application (ASP.NET, BizTalk, external Web application, or other generic application)
- Whether the ASP.NET application requires membership support and related settings
- The type of ASP.NET security (none, forms, Passport, or Windows) and related settings
- The type of ASP.NET session state (off, in-process, state server, SQL server, or custom) and related settings
- Other ASP.NET Web server settings the target application must specify in order to run on this server

IIS Web Server Settings

These settings define the following characteristics:

- IIS server settings, including application pools, Web sites, and their endpoints
- Operating system type, version, build, and service pack
- Application name and path
- Version of the .NET runtime
- Whether there is a need for the GAC

Database Server and Generic Server Constraints

This type of constraint defines the following characteristic:

- The type of application that can be installed on this logical server (external database or generic application)

Custom Settings   Each server type and Zone shape allows you to specify custom settings so that you can track any additional metadata. Figure 3-10 shows an example of a custom setting for a Zone, which specifies that each server placed in the Zone must pass the Baseline Security Analyzer test. This test is a security diagnostics utility that you can obtain free from Microsoft. It tests the integrity and security best practices of most of Microsoft's popular servers.

The final step in designing logical datacenters is to connect the endpoints of the various shapes: Zones to Zones, servers to servers, and servers to Zones. You can think of these endpoints as representing physical ports or communication pathways. These connections convey a workflow of information. They also form another constraint check: consumer endpoint types have to match provider endpoint types for the connection to be allowed. This requirement will keep you from connecting to your database server over port 80 as an HTTP consumer when you really need to connect as a Tabular Data Stream (TDS) consumer using port 1433.

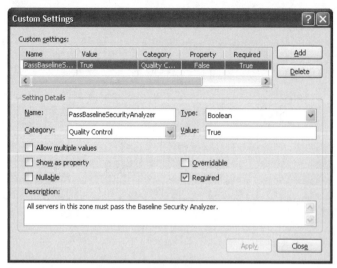

Figure 3-10   Creating a custom setting

Note   You'll need to forget for a moment that SQL Server 2005, the database of choice for building Team System applications, now supports direct connection over HTTP. Maybe the Logical Datacenter Designer will become aware of this fact in a later release.

Here's another example. Let's say you have two shapes on your design surface: an IISWebServer and a DatabaseServer. By default, the outbound client/consumer endpoint on the IISWebServer shape is an HTTP type endpoint, so you cannot connect it to the inbound provider endpoint on the DatabaseServer, which is expecting a different protocol. The solution here is to right-click IISWebServer, add a new client endpoint (as shown in Figure 3-11), and then connect the two endpoints.

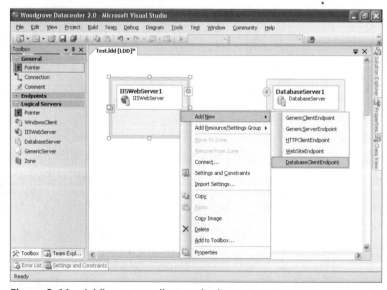

Figure 3-11   Adding a new client endpoint

You'll learn more about the Logical Datacenter Designer in Chapter 5.

Application Designer

Application architects are accustomed to walking up to a whiteboard and diagramming their applications. The diagram usually consists of some squares, some text, and some lines connecting the squares and the text. If these artists are lucky, the whiteboard has the ability to e-mail or print the drawing for later reference. Or maybe someone nearby has a digital camera. The Team System Application Designer provides what I like to call "an intelligent whiteboard," which allows the architect to drag and drop services and applications onto the design surface, configure settings, and then connect the applications and services. If that were all it did, you'd probably call it Visio. Team System, however, is superior to the whiteboard and Visio in several areas: it's a permanent, updateable, version-controlled document part of the team project.

- It can be test-deployed against one or more logical datacenters, with validation.

- It can generate code for the developers to begin implementing the services.

- It can generate a deployment report for the IT operations team.

- It can be saved to the toolbox or as individual systems for reuse in later diagrams.

- It looks really, really nice. (See Figure 3-12.)

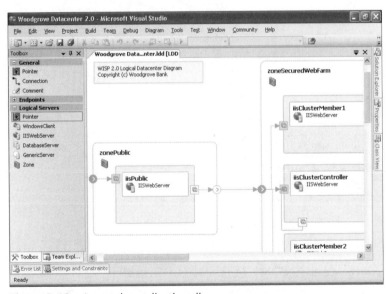

Figure 3-12   A sample application diagram

Application diagrams can contain the following application and service types:

- **WindowsApplication**   A .NET Windows forms application

- **ASP.NETWebService**   An ASP.NET XML Web service

- **ASP.NETWebApplication**   An ASP.NET Web forms application

- **OfficeApplication**   A Visual Studio Tools for Office (VSTO) application

- **ExternalWebService**   A non-ASP.NET Web service (a Web Services Description Language document)

- **ExternalDatabase**   Any database or database server

- **BizTalkWebService**   A BizTalk orchestration exposed as a Web service

- **GenericApplication**   Any other application that isn't already mentioned in this list

> **Tip**   A Distributed System Solutions project can contain only *one* application diagram. If you need to combine information from two diagrams, you'll have to create a second solution, add the application diagram, and then copy and paste the content back into the original application diagram.

After the diagram is built and arranged nicely, the application architect needs to set the appropriate settings and constraints on his or her applications and services. This will document and communicate any special requirements to Team System. This documentation will also surface when a deployment report is generated. More important, these settings are used during test deployment to validate the application design against a predefined logical datacenter diagram, as I've been mentioning throughout this chapter.

For example, if the application architect defines an ASP.NET Web Service that requires version 2.0 of the .NET Framework, this service won't deploy to a server that the infrastructure architect defined to support only version 1.1. When the deployment is validated, this conflict will appear as a validation error, and a resolution will be required. Better to find out about it now, during the early stages of the project!

Here are some examples of types of settings and constraints:

WindowsClient, OfficeApplication Constraints

These types of constraints define the following characteristics:

- Operating system type, version, build, and service pack

- Version of the .NET runtime

- Application name and path

ASP.NETWebService and ASP.NETWebApplication Constraints

These types of constraints define the following characteristics:

- Operating system type, version, build, and service pack

- Version of the .NET runtime

- IIS settings, including application-pool settings

ExternalWebService or BizTalkWebService Settings

These types of settings are provided by the Web Services Description Language (WSDL) document, which Visual Studio prompts you for in a familiar fashion. (See Figure 3-13.)

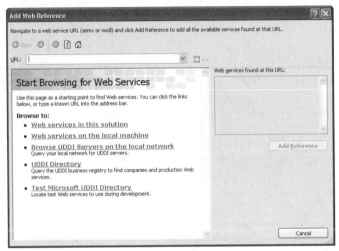

Figure 3-13   Dropping an ExternalWebService or BizTalkWebService prompts you for the WSDL document through Visual Studio's standard Add Web Reference dialog window

GenericApplication Constraints

These types of constraints define the following characteristics:

- Whether the application is a DatabaseServer, GenericServer, IISWebServer, or WindowsClient application

- Operating system type, version, build, and service pack

- Version of the .NET runtime

> **Tip**   If your diagram contains both ASP.NET Web Services and ASP.NET Web Applications, the designer will name them "WebApplicationX," without the distinction. In fact, the only way to tell is by looking at the type and name of the endpoint on the shape. Because of this, I recommend a naming convention such as *wsFoo* and *webFoo* for Web Service and Web Application, respectively.

Similar to logical datacenter diagrams, the final step in creating application diagrams is to connect the shapes: applications to services and services to services. These communication pathways are similar to the lines you'd be drawing on your whiteboard, connecting your squares. As with logical datacenters, these lines convey a communication workflow to the casual observer, but they also document the connectivity requirements of your application. During the test deployment, the success or failure will depend on whether these shapes are still able to communicate with each other within a particular datacenter.

For example, if you design a Windows client and an ASP.NET Web service, connect them in the application diagram, and then try to deploy them onto two separate servers in two separate datacenter zones that don't allow HTTP communication, the validation will fail—as it should.

You'll learn more about the Application Designer in Chapter 5.

Deployment Designer

An architect can use the Deployment Designer to test a deployment of an application diagram against a logical datacenter diagram. As I've alluded to in the previous sections, the two diagrams have to mesh correctly—the settings of the application diagram applications and services have to mesh with the constraints of the logical datacenter diagram, and vice versa.

Once the two diagrams have been completed to the best of each architect's ability and insight, one of the architects, most likely the application architect, will define a test deployment and carry out the validation. Both diagrams will need to be in the same project at this point, and checked out of version control.

Tip To define a test deployment, first open the application diagram and then right-click its designer, or choose the Define Deployment menu option from the diagram menu. At this point, you'll select a logical datacenter to deploy against. (See Figure 3-14.) Remember, a project can contain multiple datacenters, as a real company could have many sites and locations to deploy to.

Figure 3-14   Selecting a logical datacenter to test a deployment against

The Deployment Designer allows an architect to drag and drop the various applications and services, as defined in the application diagram, onto the various servers in the various Zones, as defined in the logical datacenter diagram. The applications and services can be found in the floating or dockable System View window. (See Figure 3-15.)

It really is that easy—drag and drop until all the shapes are bound. If your mouse pointer changes to the "no drop" shape, which is the familiar circle with a line through it, you're not allowed to drop that application or service onto that server.

Figure 3-15   The System View window, which lists all applications and services

> **Tip**   If you happen to get the "no drop" mouse pointer, hover your cursor over that spot for a few seconds and a ToolTip will pop up explaining why you're not allowed to drop the item you're dragging. This is a nice feature.

At some point—either immediately after dropping a service or application or after you've finished all the drops—you should ensure that the correct bindings were used. For example, an IISWebServer can have several inbound or outbound endpoints. If you're lucky, the infrastructure architect named them well, making your job easier because when you bind your applications and services to the server, you need to choose the correct endpoint, as you might have different constraints on them. You can do this by right-clicking on the bound application or service within the logical server and selecting Binding Details. (See Figure 3-16.)

After all your applications and services are bound properly, your final step will be to validate the diagram. I say "final" assuming that all goes well and you didn't receive any warnings or errors. For large-scale, distributed applications deploying to large-scale, distributed environments, this might not be the case the first time you get to this point. You can find the Validate Diagram option on the Diagram menu. If any errors are detected, they'll be listed in the Errors List window, typically at the bottom center of the Visual Studio 2005 integrated development environment (IDE).

> **Tip**   Reconciling validation errors might require the input and collaboration of both the infrastructure architect and application architect. If this happens to be the same person, it's fine. If, however, there are two people involved, I suggest using an eXtreme Programming engagement, in which you "pair program" the final fixes. In other words, both architects sit at the same keyboard and come up with the compromises together so that the application will deploy. Successful deployment could require loosening up the requirements of the application, the datacenter, or both.

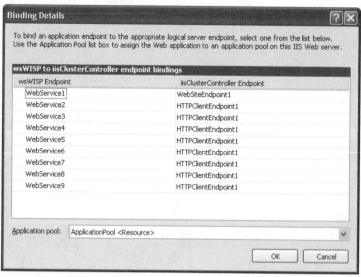

Figure 3-16   The Binding Details window without good naming conventions

Once the validation succeeds, a deployment report can be generated that will serve as a bill of materials to deploy the application. We'll look at this report in more detail in Chapter 10. You'll learn more about the Deployment Designer in Chapter 5.

System Designer

The System Designer can be used to compose and configure pieces and parts of an application diagram into *systems*. A system is considered a unit of deployment and is a configuration of one or more applications and other subsystems. By combining complex applications into a system, you can more easily handle large-scale distributed system scenarios. An application architect can design a complex multi-tiered system as a hierarchy of "nested" systems.

Using System Designer, you can design application systems by composing them from applications or other systems. An application system describes a set of configurations, rules, and policies that apply to its members at deployment. These rules and policies include application settings that you might override as well as those governing connections between and access to members of the system. For example, you can design systems composed from applications that are configured for Internet and intranet use and then create, define, and validate deployment definitions for those systems.

> **Tip**   If you want to connect a system with other applications or systems in other system definitions, you must add at least one proxy endpoint to the definition of that system. A proxy endpoint delegates communication with the system to the application endpoint from which the proxy endpoint is created.

Creating a system diagram allows for more granular deployment, defined independently of the entire configuration shown on the application diagram. In some cases, the settings defined on the application diagram as a whole can be overridden on the same application within a system diagram. In other words, multiple system definitions can be created, each having distinct configurations of the applications defined in the solution. This versatility allows different configurations to be defined for different deployments and perhaps for different logical datacenter configurations. Figure 3-17 shows how two existing ASP.NET Web services can be combined into a system, given a name, and then used directly in future deployment diagrams.

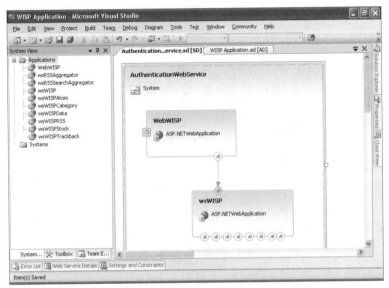

Figure 3-17   Combining two existing services into a system

 Tip   Another way to gain some benefits of designing a reusable system is to simply add a server, service, or application to the toolbox for later use. (See Figure 3-18.) For example, if you know that your company has a standard Web server configuration (Windows Server 2003 Enterprise, Service Packs, .NET 2.0, and certain security configurations), design it once, describe it fully, and then right-click the shape and choose to add it to the toolbox, giving it a friendly name and optionally a graphic image. You can then drag and drop that item later and save yourself some configuration steps.

You'll learn more about the System Designer in Chapter 5.

Figure 3-18   Adding an ASP.NET Web service to the toolbox

Tools for Developers

Let's now focus on the code. Team System provides many new tools specifically for developers, primarily in the areas of version control, class designing, and unit testing.

Source Control Explorer

When working on projects under version control, the Source Control Explorer window will be very important. It shows you all the projects under version control on the Team Foundation Server, based on your permission settings. (See Figure 3-19.) Source Control Explorer has many context menus, which are available with a right-click, as well as a useful toolbar that repeats all the options found by right-clicking.

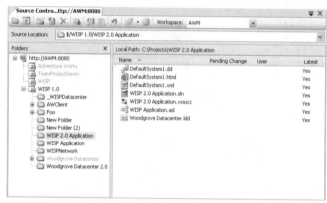

Figure 3-19   Source Control Explorer

All version control functions, shown in the following list, can be performed from the explorer:

- *Get Latest Version*

- *Get Specific Version*

- *Check Out*

- *Undo Pending Changes*

- *Check In*

- *Lock*

- *Unlock*

- *Delete*

- *Undelete*

- *Branch*

- *Shelve*

- *Merge*

- *Resolve Conflicts*

- *History*

- *Compare*

- *Label*

You'll learn more about Source Control Explorer in Chapter 6.

Class Designer

The new Class Designer is another example of a Domain-Specific Language. This designer is not UML-aware, but it does specialize in the construction of .NET classes, which is what you and I both want—a tool that does one specific thing very well. Technically, the Class Designer is not part of Team System. It is part of Visual Studio 2005 Professional, but it is worth mentioning in this section.

One of the last steps that an application architect performs is to implement one or more of the ASP.NET Web services. When implemented, Visual Studio 2005 will create new ASP. NET Web Service projects and prepare the class up to the point of implementation.

Note   The implementation feature is available only in Visual Studio Team Edition for Architects. So, either your architect will need to begin this process, saving the projects to version control for the developers to implement, or the developers will need a copy of the Architect Edition (or Team Suite) to begin implementation themselves.

The Class Designer is a graphical tool, where each class is represented by a rectangular shape. Any properties, methods, fields, and events will be listed on the shape. (See Figure 3-20.) You can expand and collapse the member list, depending on the limitations of your monitor. You can right-click on the shape and add new members, or you can work directly in the Class Details window, which allows you to manage all class members in one easy-to-use grid.

The best part about the Class Designer is that it is tightly coupled with the source code file behind it. In other words, if you have a file named Class1.cs and its class diagram is in ClassDiagram1.cd, they will always be in sync. Changes to one file are instantly seen in the other, and vice versa. There are no reverse or roundtrip engineering steps required—another advantage of a Domain-Specific Language tool.

Tip   Sometimes it can be difficult to find and launch the Class Designer. What works for me is to view all my classes in the Class View window, right-click the class in question, and choose View Class Diagram.

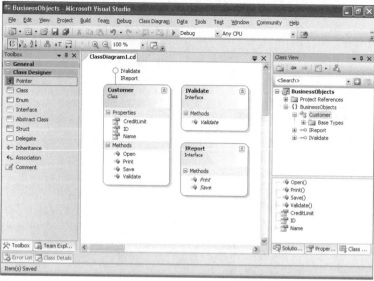

Figure 3-20   The Class Designer

You'll learn more about the Class Designer in Chapter 6.

Pending Checkins

Both the Pending Checkin window and the Checkin window give you a concise list of what has changed in your project during your editing session. You can quickly see which files were checked out and which ones were added or edited. (See Figure 3-21.) If you don't like the flat view, you can change to a tree view—more like the one seen in Source Control Explorer. You can select or deselect the individual check boxes to have full control over what gets uploaded to Team Foundation Version Control.

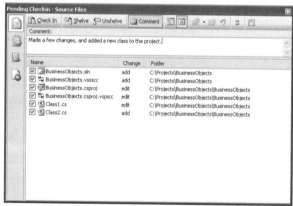

Figure 3-21   The Pending Checkin window

A lot of the functionality of Source Control Explorer is duplicated in the Pending Checkin window. You can check in, shelve, or unshelve. More important, you can associate your check-in with comments, work items, and check-in notes. This is important, because your project manager might have made some of these items mandatory during a check-in.

> **Tip**   If you're unsure what change you made during your editing session, just right-click the item in the Pending Checkin window list and select Compare, against either the workspace version or the latest version. You'll be able to see at a glance what has changed and make your decision on whether to check the file in or undo, reverting back to the original code.

Testing and Quality Tools

Whether or not developers are strictly following test-driven development, they will still need to perform unit testing and code coverage. These tests are too important to ignore altogether. I'm glad that Team System makes it so easy to create and run these tests. I hope that .NET software quality as a whole will improve because of it.

Team System has many testing tools. The following apply to developers:

- **Unit Testing**   Code that exercises your project's methods
- **Code Coverage**   Ensures that the unit tests cover all possible code pathways
- **Static Analysis**   Ensures that your code follows established coding guidelines
- **Code Profiling**   Performance based on binary instrumentation and sampling

You'll learn more about the Developer role and related tools in Chapter 6.

Tools for Testers

Testers are an important part of the Team System family. What they do and what they contribute is perhaps the most important part of the development process. They have the final say over the quality of the software, and they have the responsibility to perform load and stress tests on the applications. Testers do not necessarily perform development tasks, but they do work in tandem with developers. As testers find bugs and performance problems, the developers can diagnose the problems and fix them—a collaboration that is enriched with Team System.

Testers, like developers, are able to build and run unit tests and code coverage tests, but they can also run the following tests, which are unique to their edition of Team System:

- **Load Testing**   Simulate multiple users running your automated tests
- **Web Testing**   Simulate how a user might interact with a Web application
- **Manual Testing**   Step through tasks that you're not automating

- **Generic Testing**   Wrap legacy tests and other external programs
- **Test Case Management**   Used by testers to categorize all their tests

You have many new windows in Team System relating to testing, including the following ones:

- **Test View**   Allows test authoring
- **Test Manager**   Lists tests for execution
- **Test Results**   Displays the outcome of tests for execution
- **Code Coverage Results**   Displays the effectiveness of tests for execution

You'll learn more about the Tester role and related tools in Chapter 7.

Internet Explorer for All Team Members

Regardless of your role in Team System, you'll want to access the Project Portal and view any relevant queries and reports. The portal is also ideal for storage of documents, announcements, discussions, and archived communication between members. With Windows SharePoint Services (WSS), Microsoft allows wide reach via the browser. WSS security allows the administrator to lock down certain lists and certain reports by group or user so that only an authorized user can see the administrator's reports.

> **Note**   Other than the read-only project portal, Microsoft is not providing a Web-based interface for Team System. Although you can upload and edit documents, you can't add or manage work items or make changes to a team project. I suspect that an ISV will extend Team System to provide this functionality because it would close the loop nicely on working remotely.

Command-Line Utilities

Many aspects of Team System are managed by command-line utilities. These are the same tools that Microsoft's internal developers built to use themselves for testing and troubleshooting.

- **TF.exe**   TF.exe is the command-line utility for Team Foundation Version Control system. It enables any user to interact with Team Foundation Version Control (TFVC) from any environment. By passing the appropriate switch, you can perform all the following functions: *Add, Branch, Checkin, Checkout, Delete, Difference, Dir, Get, Help, History, Label, Lock, Merge, Permission, Rename, Resolve, Shelve, Undelete, Undo, Unlabel, Unshelve, View,* and many others.

- **TFSBuild.exe**   TFsBuild.exe is the command-line utility for interacting with Team Build.

- **TFSDeleteProject.exe**   TFSDeleteProject.exe is the command-line utility for deleting unwanted team projects.

Tools by Roles

I feel that it's important to enumerate which tool, designer, and feature will be available by each edition of Team System. This enumeration is shown in Figure 3-22.

| Client, Designer, or Tool | Standard Edition | Professional Edition | Team System | | | | Suite |
			Architect Edition	Developer Edition	Tester Edition	Foundation Server	
Application Designer			✓				✓
Class Designer	✓	✓	✓	✓			✓
Code Coverage					✓		✓
Code Profiler					✓		✓
Command Line Utilities						✓	✓
Deployment Designer			✓				✓
Load Testing					✓		✓
Logical Datacenter Designer			✓				✓
Manual Testing					✓		✓
Microsoft Excel - Work Item Add-in						✓	✓
Microsoft Project - Work Item Add-in						✓	✓
Source Control Explorer				✓	✓		✓
Source Control Migration Tools						✓	✓
System Designer			✓				✓
Team Explorer, TFS						✓	✓
Team Explorer, Visual Studio			✓	✓	✓		✓
Test View					✓		✓
Unit Testing				✓	✓		✓
Web Testing					✓		✓

Figure 3-22 Visual Studio features by edition

Summary

Team System provides a number of tools for members of all roles. Although your particular function might require you to become familiar with only a few of these tools, I thought it important to show you how productive all team members can be when using the tools designed just for them. Not all the tools exist inside of Visual Studio 2005, either. Project managers, for example, might feel more comfortable working within Excel or Project, and these environments are supported as well. The browser serves as the one tool that all core and extended team members can use to monitor a project throughout its life cycle.

Part II
Team System for the Entire Team

In this part:

Chapter 4: Project Managers.. 71
Chapter 5: Architects 93
Chapter 6: Developers.. 125
Chapter 7: Testers 155

This part of the book takes a role-based approach to teaching you Microsoft Visual Studio 2005 Team System. Each chapter will be specific to one of the roles and will focus on the features that apply to that role. I'll present each chapter as though it were a step in the development life-cycle workflow—one possible workflow anyway.

As I said earlier, Team System by itself isn't a methodology or a workflow. It is just a series of tools. Depending on the methodology you choose to implement for a project, however, a workflow can be implied. Each development team will end up using Team System a bit differently. This is to be expected. The work item examples and workflow that I present in this section will be based on the Microsoft Solution Framework (MSF) for Agile Software Development methodology, which is a new methodology created just for Team System. If you choose this methodology, my examples should resonate with how you "visually engineer" your projects, which is to use Visual Studio to orchestrate your software development effort.

Regardless of the methodology you select, these chapters will still provide a valuable example of how Team System can be used by the different roles, and of which tools and features are found in each edition.

Chapter 4
Project Managers

In this chapter:

Organizing the Team. 71
Starting a New Project 72
Managing the Ongoing Project 75
Summary. 91

Project managers can go by many names: product manager, program manager, business manager, stakeholder, analyst, advocate, project lead, team lead, or the lone consultant. Whatever title is used, the responsibility is the same—to see the project through to its successful completion. In other words, the project manager needs to ensure that the project goes live on *time*, on *budget*, *bug free*, and meeting all requirements. It is with the project manager role that we begin the Team System story.

In Team System, the Project Manager role doesn't contribute designs, code, or tests. Project managers remain strictly in the management position and perform such duties as creating and configuring a project, managing work items, managing the content on the Project Portal, and reviewing any generated reports.

Organizing the Team

Before we launch Team System, let's set up the team. I'm assuming that you have a team, you know their names, and, most important, you know what roles each member will play on the team *and* inside Team System. Remember that a team member can play more than one role. For example, Sharon could be both an architect and a developer. As project manager, you need to know all these details before starting a new project—primarily to configure security.

 Note   From a software standpoint, Team System comes in editions specific to the various roles. If you have a team member who plays two roles, such as architect and developer, you'll need to install licensed copies of both Microsoft® Visual Studio® 2005 Team Edition for Software Architects and Visual Studio 2005 Team Edition for Software Developers. Installing a licensed copy of the Team System Suite is another option.

Even team members who don't correlate directly to an edition of Team System will still be able to interact by one of the other client interfaces, such as Microsoft Office Excel®, Microsoft Office Project, or the browser. Anyone in the company who has the correct permission levels can add or edit documents to the project portal.

Note   Team System doesn't provide any Web-based work item support. Only collateral documents uploaded to the portal can be viewed and edited. This might change in future versions. Until then, it certainly is a great opportunity for integration. See Chapter 9 for more information on customizing and extending Team System.

To prepare for the new project, you should know the following information about each Team System member:

- Name

- Windows domain and user ID

- Role that the person will play in Team System (project manager, network infrastructure architect, solutions architect, developer, tester, or observer)

- Which edition of Team System the person has installed (because this will affect what he or she can and cannot physically accomplish)

Tip   I know of several one-man-shop consultants who plan to use Team System. They will most likely decide to install and use Team System Suite. Installing Team Foundation Server might be a way to gain access to the Team Foundation Version Control and Team Build utilities. However, they will still be underutilizing Team System because they won't really be using the collaboration features.

Starting a New Project

You can create a new project from Team Explorer. It's a simple process—if you have all the answers to the questions. Besides the name and description of the project, you'll be prompted to configure the following project areas:

- **Methodology**   Choose between MSF for Agile Development, MSF for CMMI Process Improvement, or any other methodologies that have been loaded into Team Foundation Server

- **Project portal title and description**   The friendly name and description of the Microsoft Windows® SharePoint® Services portal your team will use

- **Source version control folder and branching information**   New folder, branched folder, or no source control

Selecting a Methodology

As I mentioned in Chapter 1, Team System will ship with two methodologies: MSF for Agile Development (MSF Agile) and MSF for CMMI Process Improvement. Depending on the type of project and the characteristics of your team, either methodology might make sense. Each has its own strengths and weaknesses. When creating a new team project, you'll be able to select one of these two methodologies. (See Figure 4-1.) If you have any other custom methodologies installed, they will also be available in the drop-down list here.

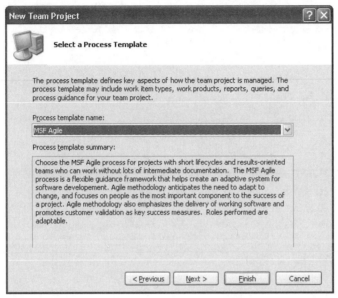

Figure 4-1   Selecting a new project's methodology

Team System's extensibility allows it to be modified and extended as your software development process evolves and improves over time. As your team evolves and matures, its methodology needs might also evolve and mature as well. Team System is designed to support that. With some free time and an understanding of how Team System integrates with a methodology, you can export an existing methodology—MSF for Agile Development, for example. These exported files can be edited to suit your development team's needs. The new files can be imported back into Team System and named something more topical, such as Adventure Works Agile Development.

More info   For more information on MSF for Agile Development, be sure to read Chapter 8. For more information on extending Team System, especially with regard to methodologies, be sure to read Chapter 9.

Configuring the Project Portal

Team System relies on Windows SharePoint Services (WSS) for disseminating information to the extended team. I use the word "extended" here to mean two things: team members who are geographically dispersed and team members who might not play a direct role in Team System. With WSS, integrating members of an extended team into Team System becomes a no-brainer. A team member with permissions can upload, edit, or simply view any type of document hosted in WSS.

> **Note**   Team members must authenticate to Team Foundation Server by way of Windows authentication. This might limit who can work remotely.

Anyone who has used WSS knows it has many collaborative advantages, including the following ones:

- Tight integration with Office 2003
- Document check-in, check-out, and version control
- Configurable security settings
- Customizable Web-part technology

Team System will set up the Project Portal site for you. When you reach that step in the wizard, you'll be prompted for the project portal name and description. Because it's assumed that Windows SharePoint Services is installed on the application tier of Team System, the project creation step will happen automatically. In other words, the Web service being called by Team Explorer will create the WSS site and configure it for you. You don't have to know anything about WSS to make this happen. The URL is provided at the bottom of the dialog box. Just copy it and e-mail it to your team members, letting them know that the portal has been created.

After the wizard has run and the site is created, you may want to customize it for your team. As with any WSS site, you can customize it in many ways. New document libraries can be created from Team Explorer, and documents can be uploaded and managed. Beyond that, you'll need to tweak and customize the portal by using the WSS administrative screens.

Here are some customizations that you might want to perform on the portal:

- Grant any additional, non–Team System users permission to access the portal.
- Add Web parts, such as any third-party reports.
- Change site title and description.
- Redesign the page layout.
- Change the theme.

Configuring Version Control Settings

It's likely that all Team System projects will want to take advantage of the Team Foundation Server version control capability. This capability is enabled by default, but you can choose any of the following options (as shown in Figure 4-2):

- Create an empty version control folder.

- Create a new version control branch.

- Do not create a version control folder at this time.

The default action is to create an empty version control folder, which is nice and safe, but doing this doesn't help start your project in any way. What I mean is that if you can *branch* from an existing project, you'll already have some content from which to work. As I mentioned in Chapter 2, branching is a powerful feature of Team Foundation Version Control. This flexibility is evident when you're creating a team project that is a new version of an existing project, has similar or shared functionality, or must diverge in functionality or focus from its core.

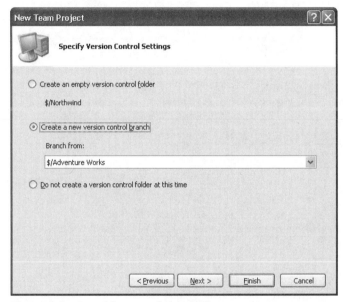

Figure 4-2   Branching an existing project

Selecting the source control option is the last step in creating a new project. The wizard will then begin creating the new project, which includes updating many database structures and copying many templates into the portal. This process can take several moments to complete.

Managing the Ongoing Project

Once Team System has created the project, your architects, developers, and testers can begin contributing diagrams, code, and tests to the project. No additional settings are required. In other words, work can commence immediately. I would, however, recommend configuring security, classifications, and check-in policies before you embark on any software development effort. To further aid your team, you might want to upload any process guidance or other related documents to the portal. As the project goes forward, you might need to tweak some of these settings, especially if new team members arrive or existing team members leave.

Configuring Security

Team System is very secure, which is good, because tight security, even when dealing with trusted developers, is a requirement at many companies nowadays. Financial institutions, government, and any Sarbanes-Oxley-compliant companies will judge a finished product by its security support and the level of security that surrounded its construction. Security is also a good way to protect the team against itself. If you lock down privileged operations to only a select few members, any inexperienced team members won't be able to accidentally change critical information.

Team System can integrate with Active Directory®, so it is able to map Microsoft Windows users and groups directly to its own predefined roles and permissions. Enabling this role-based security is done in two steps. First, you map in the Active Directory users and groups. Then you assign the relevant permissions.

Mapping users and groups to Team System is done by right-clicking the team project inside Team Explorer, selecting Team Project Settings, and clicking Groups. Team System defines both *global* groups as well *project* groups. (See Figure 4-3.)

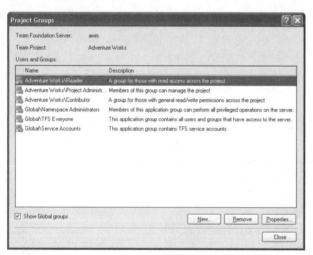

Figure 4-3   Built-in Team System project and global groups

Here are the built-in *global* groups:

- **Namespace Administrators**   Includes members who can perform all privileged operations

- **TFS Everyone**   Includes all users and groups that have access to the server

- **Service Accounts**   Includes Team Foundation Server service accounts

Here are the built-in *project* groups:

- **Project Administrators**   Includes members who can manage the project

- **Contributor**   Includes members who have general read/write permissions across the project

- **Reader**   Includes members who have read access across a project

Tip   Team System allows you to create new project groups so that you can classify your team members any way that you want. These groups can then be assigned whatever permissions you'd like, thus enabling you to create your own customized Team System roles.

The next step is to assign the appropriate Team System permissions to these users and groups. Figure 4-4 shows the level of permissions allowed. Team System's level of security even allows you to secure the state transitions of work item types. In other words, you can specify which team members can log bugs in and, more important, which team members can transition them to fixed or closed.

Note   Team Foundation Server supports Windows 2000 or 2003 native active directory. This environment is required for a dual-server installation. If you want to install Team Foundation Server onto a single-server, an Active Directory environment is not required, and you can simply install onto a workgroup server.

Figure 4-4   Assigning permissions to users and groups

Best Practice   A best practice is to assign permissions to groups of users, and not directly to the individual users. This has long been a best practice in Windows, and it also applies to Team System.

Creating Classifications

Projects can have a hierarchy of *classifications*. These represent generic organization units by which you can classify your work items. You're free to add any classifications or child classifications to build your container hierarchy in whatever way you want it. I recommend good names—names that your team members immediately recognize as applying to them. Classifications are optional, however.

Here are some examples of classifications:

- Design, Code, Bugs

- North America, Europe, Asia

- Top Secret, Secret, Classified, For Official Use Only, Unclassified

- Red, Green, Blue

For example, you could have three geographically separated development teams, all working on the same project. To keep the work items, such as tasks and bugs, partitioned for each team, you could create North America, Europe, and Asia classifications, and then select the respective classification when creating work items.

Creating Iterations

Projects can also have *iterations*, which represent milestones or specific epochs in the project's software development life cycle, as seen in Figure 4-5. Depending on the methodology, Team System creates some default iterations, such as *Iteration 0*, *Iteration 1*, and *Iteration 2*. You should rename these and strive to have very self-evident iteration names, as you cannot associate any additional metadata with them.

Here are some examples of iterations:

- Alpha, Beta, Release Candidate, RC1, RC2, Gold, RTM

- Phase 1, Phase 2, Phase 3

- Proof of Concept, Executive Buyoff, Available to Public, Certified

For example, your project might go through several phases, such as Alpha, Beta, and then release. To keep the work items, such as tasks and bugs, partitioned for each phase, you could select the respective iteration when creating work items.

As you can see, the iterations are very flexible. They are just names. To fit your organization and methodology, you can have as many as you want and name them whatever you want. As you move through Team System, any work item you create can be associated with a classification and an iteration.

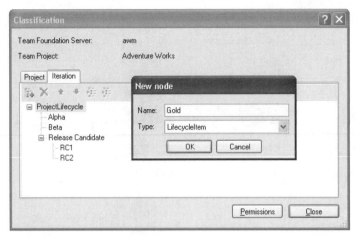

Figure 4-5   Creating iterations for the various phases of your project

Security can be applied to either classifications or iterations. In other words, you're able to lock down by user or Team System role who has permission to do what within these classifications and iterations. Figure 4-6 shows the level of permissions you can assign. Refer to the online documentation for the specifics of each permission.

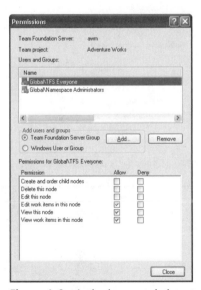

Figure 4-6   Assigning permissions to a classification or iteration

Setting Check-In Policies

One of the most powerful features of Team System is its support of *check-in policies*, which give the project manager, architect, or lead developer a great deal of control over the project and its team. Keep in mind that when used properly, these policies can result in better quality code being checked in; however, developers can get lazy and bypass the policies or revolt altogether if placed in an environment with too many policies. Diplomacy and psychology should be used when introducing new policies to your team. These discussions, however, are beyond the scope of this book. Figure 4-7 shows a project with the Clean Build and Work Items policies enabled.

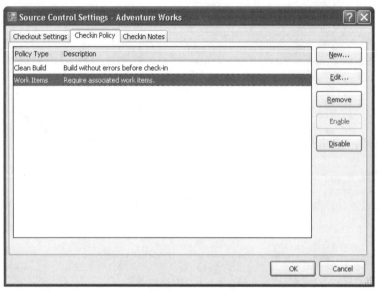

Figure 4-7   Enabling a project's check-in policies

Here are some check-in policies that Team System supports:

- **Clean Build**   The code must be error free before check-in is allowed.

- **Static Analysis**   The code must pass a static analysis test before check-in is allowed.

- **Testing Policy**   The code must pass one or more tests before check-in is allowed.

- **Work Items**   The code must be associated with one or more work items before check-in is allowed.

- **Notes**   One or more notes (such as reviewer's name, issues, status, hours, and so on) must be associated with the code before check-in is allowed.

- **Custom**   Custom check-in policies can be created as well. Be sure to read Chapter 9 for more information.

> **Note**   Project managers can also decide whether a project needs the ability to have multiple users checking out the same files at the same time. This is an advanced feature, but one that Team System supports very well with its merging technology. The ability for multiple users to check out and work on the same file is not appropriate for every team. In my opinion, training on the types of conflicts that can occur and hands-on experience resolving conflicts should be required before a team tries to use this feature.

Uploading Documents and Other Assets

Team System relies heavily on WSS for disseminating information to the distributed team. As I've already mentioned, a number of application clients interact with Team System, but none is more ubiquitous than the browser. The developers whom I've met are constantly online, searching for sample code or downloading guidance. Microsoft knows this and, as an acknowledgment, has even integrated the browser into the start page of Visual Studio. The project portal, however, is more than just a nice-looking site. It's a fully managed WSS portal, written in ASP.NET and fully configurable and customizable. Anyone who has used WSS knows it has many collaborative advantages over other, non-managed sites.

By default, Team System uploads process guidance documents based on the methodology selected. (See Figure 4-8.) This is just one way that the portal can empower the team—by providing how-to and best-practice documentation for the actual construction of the software.

> **Note** As you might expect, this documentation can be customized, improved, and associated with the methodology template so that future Team System projects will contain newer, more focused documentation. Chapter 9 discusses how to do this.

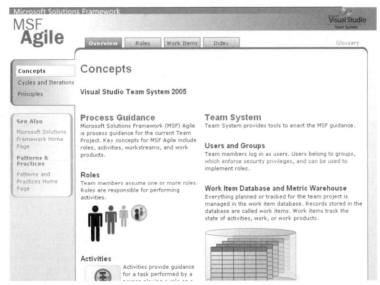

Figure 4-8 Default process guidance documents available through the project portal

Here are just a few examples of other documents you can upload to the project portal:

- **Business documents** Bids, estimates, accounting spreadsheets, functional specifications, team contact information

- **Technical documents**   Technical specifications, UML diagrams, database designs, graphical representations of current systems, other Microsoft Visio® diagrams

- **Guidance**   Best-practice examples, whitepapers, how-to guides

Adding and Managing Work Items

I think of work items as being the *currency* of Team System—that is, work items enable the collaboration and the "development commerce," if you will. In other words, these documents represent the communication packets traveling from teammate to teammate. Work items can be tasks, bugs, risks, scenarios, Quality of Service (QoS) requirements, or any other type defined by the methodology you're using. Because the team will be looking to the project manager to kick things off, he or she must be an expert in creating and assigning work items to initiate and maintain the workflow.

A work item is just a database record that Visual Studio 2005 Team Foundation Server uses to track the assignment and state of work. The MSF for Agile Software Development process defines five work items to assign and track work:

- **Scenario**   Defines a single path of user interaction within the system

- **Quality of Service (QoS) requirement**   Documents characteristics of the system, such as performance, load, availability, stress, accessibility, serviceability, and maintainability

- **Task**   Work that needs to be done

- **Bug**   A potential problem that exists or has existed in the system

- **Risk**   Any probable event or condition that can have a potentially negative outcome on the project

 More info   Please see Chapter 8 for more information on MSF for Agile Software Development and these work item types.

The MSF for CMMI Process Improvement process defines seven work items to assign and track work:

- **Bug**   A potential problem that exists or has existed in the system

- **Change Request**   A proposed change to some part of the product or baseline

- **Issue**   An event or situation that may block work or is currently blocking work on the product

- **Requirement**   What the product needs to do to solve the customer problem

- **Review**   Results of a design or code review

- **Risk**   Any probable event or condition that can have a potentially negative outcome on the project

- **Task**   Work that needs to be done

> **More info**   Please see Chapter 8 for more information on MSF for CMMI Process Improvement and these work item types.

Choosing the Best Work-Item Client Application

To add and manage work items, the project manager—or any team member for that matter—will need to use one of the three client applications that I mentioned in the previous chapter: Visual Studio 2005, Microsoft Excel, or Microsoft Project. Most developers feel at home inside Visual Studio 2005. They enjoy its do-anything attitude, meaning that they get 100 percent of the Team System features and capabilities. Visual Studio 2005, however, makes a terrible spreadsheet, and its Gnatt chart capabilities are also lacking. I think you see my point—each application has its own strengths and weaknesses. For more information on how to decide which client application is best for you, please refer to the previous chapter.

Adding Scenarios

In MSF for Agile Software Development, a *scenario* records a single path of user interaction through the system. As that user attempts to reach a goal, the scenario records the specific steps that he or she will take in attempting to reach it. Some scenarios will record a successful path; others will record an unsuccessful one. When writing scenarios, you should be as specific as possible. There are an infinite number of possible scenarios for all but the most trivial of systems, so it is important to be discerning in deciding which scenarios to write.

Scenarios begin in the Active state. The business analyst or project manager creates the scenario, provides a descriptive title, and fills in the description field with as much detail as possible about the scenario. (See Figure 4-9.) When the scenario is fully written, the business analyst assigns it to a lead developer. The scenario remains in the Active state while it is being implemented. The lead developer coordinates efforts with other developers to implement the scenario.

During a project's life cycle, a scenario can be any of the following states:

- **New**   A scenario is activated as a new scenario when it is first created.
- **Active**   Scenarios begin in the Active state. The business analyst creates the scenario, provides a descriptive title, and fills in the Description field with as much detail as possible about the scenario. When the scenario is fully written, the business analyst assigns it to a lead developer. The Specified field is set to Yes, and the scenario remains in the Active state while it is being implemented. The lead developer coordinates efforts with other developers to implement the scenario.

- **Resolved**   When the scenario is implemented in code, the lead developer sets the state to Resolved. The lead developer also assigns the scenario to a tester so that testing can begin.

- **Closed**   The tester closes a scenario if it passes its tests. A scenario is also closed if it is Deferred, Removed, or Split into more scenarios.

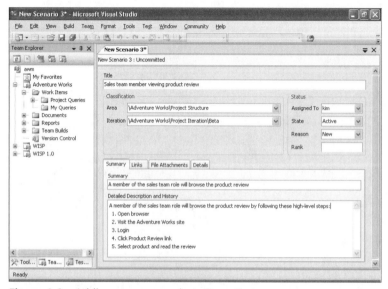

Figure 4-9   Adding a new scenario to Team System

During a scenario's life cycle, a scenario may make any of the following state transitions:

- New to Active–Occurs when a new scenario is first created.

- Active to Resolved (Completed)–Occurs when the development team completes writing code for the scenario and the lead developer assigns the scenario to a tester.

- Active to Resolved (Split)–Occurs when further review indicates that the scenario is too large or that it needs more granular definition.

- Active to Resolved (Deferred)–Occurs if it cannot be implemented in the current iteration. A scenario can be deferred because the team does not have enough time or because blocking issues were discovered.

- Active to Resolved (Removed)–Occurs if it is no longer deemed necessary to implement.

- Resolved to Closed (Completed)–Occurs when the tester indicates that it has passed its tests.

- Resolved to Closed (Split)–Occurs because further review indicated that the scenario was too large or that it needed more granular definition.

- Resolved to Closed (Deferred)–Occurs because it could not be implemented in the current iteration.

- Resolved to Closed (Removed)—Occurs because it is no longer deemed necessary to implement.

- Resolved to Active (Test Failed)—Occurs if the scenario fails to pass any tests and the tester must return the scenario to an active state and reassign it to the original lead developer.

- Closed to Active (Reactivated)—Occurs because of a change in functionality.

Adding Quality of Service Requirements

In MSF for Agile Software Development, a Quality of Service(QoS) requirement documents characteristics of the system, such as performance, load, availability, stress, accessibility, serviceability, and maintainability. These requirements usually take the form of constraints on how the system should operate.

> **Note** QoS requirements are not the same thing as *requirements*. MSF for Agile Software Development doesn't directly help with the gathering, synthesizing, or storing of software requirements. A project manager could work around this by using another methodology or Excel to maintain a list of requirements and map them to other Team System work items. Another option would be to customize Team System and add a requirement work item type.

The QoS requirements can be created in the QoS requirements list found in the requirements folder in the document library or by using the new work item menu in Team Explorer. The business analyst or project manager creates the requirement, provides a descriptive title, and fills in the description field with as much detail as possible about the requirement. When the requirement is fully written, the business analyst or project manager assigns it to a lead developer. The requirement remains in the Active state while it is being implemented. The lead developer coordinates efforts with other developers to implement the requirement.

During the project's life cycle, a QoS requirement can change to any of the following states:

- **New**   A QoS requirement is activated as a new requirement when it is first created.

- **Active**   QoS requirements begin in the Active state. The business analyst creates the requirement, provides a descriptive title, and fills in the Description field with as much detail as possible about the requirement. When the requirement is fully written, the business analyst assigns it to a lead developer.

- **Resolved**   When the QoS requirement is implemented in code, the lead developer sets the state to Resolved. The lead developer also assigns the requirement to a tester so that testing can begin.

- **Closed**   The tester closes a QoS requirement if it passes its tests. A requirement is also closed if it is Deferred, Removed, or Split into more requirements.

During a QoS requirement's life cycle, a requirement may make any of the following state transitions:

- New to Active–Occurs when a new QoS requirement is first created.

- Active to Resolved (Completed)–Occurs when the development team completes writing code for the requirement. The lead developer assigns the requirement to a tester.

- Active to Resolved (Split)–Occurs when further review indicates that the requirement is too large or that it needs a more granular definition.

- Active to Resolved (Deferred)–Occurs if the requirement cannot be implemented in the current iteration. A requirement could be deferred because the team does not have enough time or because blocking issues were discovered.

- Active to Resolved (Removed)–Occurs if it is no longer deemed necessary to implement.

- Resolved to Closed (Completed)–Occurs when the tester indicates that it has passed its tests.

- Resolved to Closed (Split)–Occurs because further review indicated that the requirement was too large or that it needed more granular definition.

- Resolved to Closed (Deferred)–Occurs because it could not be implemented in the current iteration.

- Resolved to Closed (Removed)–Occurs because it is no longer deemed necessary to implement.

- Resolved to Active (Test Failed)–Occurs if the QoS requirement fails to pass any tests and the tester must return the scenario to an active state and reassign it to the original lead developer.

- Closed to Active (Regression)–Occurs if a regression test indicates that the requirement is no longer passing.

- Closed to Active (Reactivated)–Occurs when a QoS requirement's assigned iteration begins.

Adding Tasks

Probably the most understandable and commonly used Team System work item is the *task*. A task work item simply communicates the need to do some work. Each role will get tasked to do different things. For example, a developer uses development tasks to assign work derived from scenarios or QoS requirements to component owners. The tester uses test tasks to assign the job of writing and running test cases. A task can also be used to signal regressions or to suggest that exploratory testing be performed. Finally, a task can be used generically to assign work within the project. On the work item form, certain fields are used only in cases when a task relates to a particular role.

A new task work item can be created whenever new work is identified that needs to be done. To create a new task work item, use the new work item menu in Team Explorer. Initially, the state, or status, of a task is automatically set to Active. An Active task indicates there is some element of work to be done. All tasks should be assigned to an owner and a discipline if they are development or test tasks.

During the project's life cycle, a task can change to any of the following states:

- **New**   A new task work item can be created whenever new work is identified that needs to be done. There are two types of tasks. Development tasks identify development work to be done as part of implementing scenarios, QoS requirements, or architecture. Test tasks identify testing to be completed. Tasks can also be used to identify work outside of these two areas.

- **Active**   When a new task is created using Team Explorer, the state, or status, is automatically set to Active. An active task indicates there is some element of work to be done.

- **Closed**   A closed task means that no further work is to be done for the current product version. A development task is closed after the code changes have been integrated. A test task is closed when all the tests are complete for that area.

During the project's life cycle, a task may make any of the following state transitions:

- New to Active—Occurs when a new task is first created.

- Active to Closed (Completed)—Occurs when there is no further work to be done.

- Active to Closed (Deferred)—Occurs if the task cannot be implemented in the current iteration. A task can be deferred because the team does not have enough time or because blocking issues were discovered.

- Active to Closed (Obsolete)—Occurs if the work that the task represents is no longer applicable to completion of the product.

- Active to Closed (Cut)—Occurs if the functionality for that task is removed from the product.

- Closed to Active (Reactivated)—Occurs when a QoS requirement's assigned iteration begins.

Adding Bugs

I'm pretty sure you know what bugs are. Some teams refer to them as "defects." Whatever term you use for them, Team System bugs are work items that indicate a potential problem exists or has existed in the system. The goal of creating a bug work item is to accurately report bugs in a way that allows the reader to understand the full impact of the problem. The descriptions in the bug work item should make it easy to trace through the steps used when the bug was encountered, thus allowing it to be easily reproduced. The test results should clearly show the problem. The clarity and understandability of this description often affects the probability that the bug will be fixed.

As bugs are detected in your software product, they must be documented as quickly as possible so that developers can resolve them. When you discover a new bug and enter it using Team Explorer, the bug work item is automatically set to an Active state. An Active bug indicates that a problem exists and must be addressed. Bugs can be discovered and documented as a result of a build failure or other causes, such as those discovered by developers, testers, or users.

> **Tip**   Before creating a bug work item, you should query existing bugs to be sure the bug you discovered hasn't already been reported. You can do this from Team Explorer by browsing the Active Bugs list of work items, or by creating a new query for bug work items by title, date, iteration, and so on.

During the project's life cycle, a bug can change to any of the following states:

- **New**   As bugs are detected in the software product, they must be documented as quickly as possible so that developers can resolve them.

- **Active**   When you discover a new bug and enter it using Team Explorer, the bug work item is automatically set to an Active state. An active bug indicates that a problem exists that must be addressed.

- **Resolved**   A bug is in the Resolved state when it has been addressed by a developer or during triage. A bug is resolved as either Fixed or As Designed.

- **Closed**   A closed bug means that no further work is to be done for the current product version. A bug is closed after the resolution has been verified.

During the project's life cycle, a bug may make any of the following state transitions:

- New to Active (New)—Occurs when a new bug is first created.

- New to Active (Build Failure)—Occurs as a direct result of a build failure.

- Active to Resolved (Fixed)—Occurs when the changed code is checked in.

- Active to Resolved (As Designed)—Occurs if the bug describes an expected condition or behavior of the system.

- Active to Resolved (Deferred)—Occurs if the bug will not be fixed in the current iteration. It will be postponed until it can be reevaluated in a future iteration or version of the product.

- Active to Resolved (Duplicate)—Occurs if the bug describes the same problem as another bug.

- Active to Resolved (Obsolete)—Occurs if the bug is no longer applicable to the product. For example, if the bug describes a problem in a feature area that no longer exists in the product, it is obsolete.

- Active to Resolved (Unable to Reproduce)—Occurs if the developer cannot reproduce the bug on his or her computer.

- Resolved to Closed (Fixed)—Occurs when the author of the bug has verified that the fix is in place in a build.

- Resolved to Closed (As Designed)—Occurs if the bug author agrees that the bug describes something that is intentional by design.

- Resolved to Closed (Deferred)—Occurs if the bug author agrees that the bug should be deferred.

- Resolved to Closed (Duplicate)—Occurs if the bug author confirms that the bug describes the same problem as another bug.

- Resolved to Closed (Obsolete)—Occurs if the bug author agrees that the problem described is no longer applicable to the product.

- Resolved to Closed (Unable to Reproduce)—Occurs if the bug author is unable to produce a working example of the bug or provide more specific instructions for reproducing the bug.

- Resolved to Active (Resolution Denied)—Occurs if the resolution is unacceptable.

- Resolved to Active (Wrong Fix)—Occurs if the fix was incorrect.

- Resolved to Active (Test Failed)—Occurs if a test demonstrates that the bug still exists.

- Closed to Active (Regression)—Occurs when a regression test indicates that the bug exists again.

Adding Risks

An essential aspect of project management is to identify and manage the inherent risks of a project. A *risk* is any probable event or condition that can have a potentially negative outcome on the project in the future. A risk work item documents and tracks the technical or organizational risks of a project. When concrete action is required, these risks can translate into tasks to be performed to mitigate the risk. For example, a technical risk can set off an architectural prototyping effort. In this case, the project manager or another team member would create new Task work items, linking them back to the original Risk task item or items. The linking of these work items is important to establish a proper work item lineage for management.

The team should always regard risk identification in a positive way to ensure team members contribute as much information as possible about the risks the team faces. The environment should allow individuals identifying risks to do so without fear of retribution for their honest expression of tentative or controversial views. Teams creating a positive risk management environment will be more successful at identifying and addressing risks earlier than teams operating in a negative risk environment.

A new risk work item can be created whenever a new risk is identified. These new work items should contain a title and description that clearly states the potential adverse outcome. The potential impact should be selected. New risks can be created by any team member and should be assigned to the person who will track the risk until it is closed or reassigned. To create a new risk work item, use the New Work Item menu in Team Explorer. An Active risk indicates there is some potential unrealized event that could affect the project. All risks should be assigned to an owner.

During the project's life cycle, a risk can change to any of the following states:

- **New**   A new risk work item can be created whenever a new risk is identified. These new work items should contain a title and description that clearly state the potential adverse outcome. The potential impact should be selected. New risks can be created by any team member and should be assigned to the person who will track the risk until it is closed or reassigned.

- **Active**   When a new risk is created using Team Explorer, the state is automatically set to Active. An active risk indicates there is some potential unrealized event that could affect the project.

- **Closed**   A risk that is closed is no longer a threat to the project. However, a risk that was closed during an iteration may be worth discussing in the iteration retrospective.

During the project's life cycle, a risk can make any of the following state transitions:

- New to Active—Occurs whenever a potential risk may affect the project.

- Active to Closed (Mitigated)—Occurs when some actions are performed ahead of time to prevent the risk from occurring altogether or to reduce the impact or consequences of its occurring to an acceptable level.

- Active to Closed (Inactive)—Occurs when the probability of the risk occurring drops low enough to be negligible.

- Active to Closed (Transferred)—Occurs when the risk can be moved outside the project. The risk has not been eliminated, but it is no longer in the scope of the current project. Example methods of transferred risk include moving the risk to the next release, using external consultants, or purchasing a component instead of building it.

- Active to Closed (Accepted)—Occurs when a risk is such that it is simply not feasible to intervene with effective preventative or corrective measures. The team elects simply to accept the risk to realize the opportunity.

- Active to Closed (Avoided)—Occurs because of a change to the project or the risk itself. The risk may have failed to materialize, so the project can stop tracking it.

- Closed to Active (Regression)—Occurs when a risk reappears.

Summary

In Team System, the project manager is both the technical and functional administrator of the project. He or she is responsible for the creation, configuration, and ongoing maintenance of the project. In other words, the project manager launches and manages the project by creating and assigning work items—such as scenarios, QoS requirements, and tasks—setting up policies and constraints, and maintaining the project's status.

Chapter 5
Architects

In this chapter:

The Architect Role. 94

Infrastructure Architect 94

Application Architect 95

DSI, SDM, and DSL Revisited 96

The Distributed System Designers 96

The Logical Datacenter Designer 100

The Application Designer. 107

Settings and Constraints. 115

The System Designer. 117

The Deployment Designer 119

What's Next? 123

Summary. 124

Customers have been telling Microsoft for some time that many of the CASE tools they bought in the 1980s and 1990s did not add sufficient value to the development process. Selling points of the tools failed to materialize, and even good products were swamped by over-promised technology.

If the models that the CASE tools supported did not reflect the code and other implementation artifacts, they quickly became irrelevant. If the models were used to generate code, they typically got out of sync after the developers added other code around the generated code. Even products that did a good job of "round tripping" the generated code eventually overwhelmed developers with the complexity of solving this problem. These problems were often exacerbated because CASE tools tried to operate at too high a level of abstraction relative to the implementation platform beneath. This forced them to generate large amounts of code, making it even harder to solve the problems caused by mixing hand-written and generated code.

Despite these issues, there is a belief among those involved in software development that somehow modeling can be applied to make our lives easier. Team System's vision is to change the way developers perceive the value of modeling: to shift their perception that modeling is a marginally useful activity that precedes real development to the recognition that modeling is an important mainstream development task, not an activity primarily focused on documentation. When models are regarded as first-class development artifacts, developers write less conventional code because more powerful application abstractions can be employed. Model-driven development is thus inherently more productive and agile. Moreover, others involved in development—from business analysts, architects, and designers to network staff and system management specialists—will perceive modeling as adding value to the tasks for which they are responsible. When models span development and run-time activities in this way, communication between people can be optimized and traceability can be enabled across the life cycle in any direction. We hold that making modeling mainstream in this way can ultimately change the economics of software development and ensure that software systems meet the needs of a business.

> **Note**   This approach to model-driven development is part of an initiative at Microsoft called Software Factories.

The Architect Role

Microsoft® Visual Studio® 2005 Team System actually identifies two separate architect roles: the *infrastructure architect* and the *application architect*. On your team, this might be one person or it could be several. In practice, architects can have other roles as well. They might be project managers, lead developers, or the only developer. Regardless of a team's organization, either architect role in Visual Studio 2005 is served by the one edition: Visual Studio 2005 Team Edition for Software Architects.

So, what is an architect? When it comes to architects of this type, it can be hard to define, but here is one possible definition: *an architect is someone who puts together the structure or structures of a system, whether it is a network, datacenter, or software system.* One thing is for sure: architects must be experts in the areas of maintenance, performance, compatibility, and security because their guidance will affect each of these areas. In addition, architects must represent these systems using a notation that is easily understood by all users of the designs.

This chapter introduces you to the architecture support features in Team System.

> **Note**   There are many layers of architecture to an enterprise-scale application. I recommend visiting the Microsoft patterns and practices Web site and downloading the *Enterprise Library,* which is a collection of great .NET application blocks for helping with specific architecture guidance. You can find it at *msdn.microsoft.com/patterns.*

Infrastructure Architect

Of the two architect types that Team System identifies, I'll begin with the infrastructure architect, who designs and documents the datacenter and network infrastructure. This architect understands and models the application's logical datacenter, including its hardware, communication types, pathways, firewalls, and security constraints. Although not *directly* related to the software development effort, these models are critical to the success of an application because the application must be validated against these constraints to prove that it can be deployed to that environment. This concept is known as *Design for Deployment*.

The infrastructure architect, in conjunction with IT operations, will use the Logical Datacenter Designer in Team System to model the environment. Before using this tool, the infrastructure architect should have an understanding of the datacenter environment, including some of the following key points:

- The types of application Hosts (Web server, database server, and generic) in the datacenter

- The versions of operating systems and .NET on each server

- The firewalls or communication flow restrictions between the servers (HTTP, TDS, or generic)

- The protocols allowed into and out of each server and Zone

- Any other constraints for each server and Zone (including custom constraints)

 Note   The infrastructure architect role might be known by other names in your company: network architect, technical architect, network security architect, enterprise architect, information system architect, operations analyst, or systems architect.

Application Architect

This architect type plays a somewhat larger role in Team System by defining the application's connected systems as an array of connected Web services, Web applications, Microsoft Windows® applications, and other external databases and components. Most of the Distributed Systems Designers in Team Edition for Software Architects are for the application architect's use, including the Application Designer, the System Designer, and often the Deployment Designer. Each of these tools will be discussed in this chapter.

Before beginning the application design effort, the application architect should have a general understanding of the application architecture. The designers will be used just as whiteboards are used: to develop the design iteratively and incrementally, capturing a design as it is formulated. The architect may not start off with the complete design in mind, but should at least have some insight into a few key points:

- The number and types of applications (Web services, database, or Windows)

- The versions of operating systems and .NET required to execute

- The communication flow restrictions between the services (HTTP, TDS, or generic)

- Any other settings for each service and Zone (including custom settings)

> **Note**   The application architect role may be known by other names in your company: software architect, solution architect, Web services architect, and even .NET architect.

DSI, SDM, and DSL Revisited

Going back to what I mentioned in Chapter 3, the Dynamic Systems Initiative (DSI) and the System Definition Model (SDM) are important initiatives that will enable the development of your product, as well as Microsoft products, to be dramatically simplified and more automated. This is especially true in regard to deployment and ongoing operations and maintenance.

Visual Studio 2005 provides an extensible modeling platform on which Domain Specific Languages (DSLs) can be implemented. Since DSLs are visual languages used to define requirements and generate parts of a solution, they are a natural fit inside of Visual Studio. ISVs can create custom designers on this platform as well, integrating their DSL tools into Visual Studio 2005. This modeling platform includes support for UI integration, extensible drawing surface (such as routing and auto-layout), artifact generation, constraint checking, user guides to resolve issues, and in-memory graphing.

Visual Studio 2005 Team Edition for Architects is the first suite of designers based on this modeling platform. It will include the Distributed System Designers and the Class Designer.

The Distributed System Designers

The Distributed System Designers are a set of design tools in Visual Studio 2005 Team System Edition for Software Architects that help reduce the complexity of developing and deploying service-oriented applications.

Application architects visualize their service-oriented applications, and developers work with the generated code while keeping the code changes synchronized with the visual design. Infrastructure architects create logical abstractions of their datacenters. Prior to actual deployment, these architects validate the application design against the constraints of the logical datacenter design. Reports generated from this validation help to document the application's deployment.

There are four Distributed System Designers:

- **Logical Datacenter Designer**   This designer creates diagrams of interconnected application Hosts. These Hosts represent the logical structure of a datacenter for the purpose of communicating those aspects of the datacenter architecture that constrain the design and configuration of the application.

- **Application Designer**   This designer allows developers and architects to define applications that will be configured into systems for deployment.

- **System Designer**   This designer composes applications into systems, for deployment and reusability.

- **Deployment Designer**   This designer describes a deployment of a system to a logical datacenter, which is accomplished by binding applications within the system to logical servers (application Hosts) modeled in the logical datacenter diagram.

Logical datacenter diagrams and application diagrams can be created independently, by different users, and in any order. When starting a new software project, it might make sense to begin with the logical datacenter diagram. You would start with this diagram because, more than likely, that infrastructure will already exist or your company will already have established Windows versions and policies in place. I realize that this isn't the case for all environments. Not as common are the environments in which the company knows what the application architecture is first and then designs the datacenter and all constraints to accommodate. This would be a great company to build software for, wouldn't it? In either case, you'll need to ensure that *both* the logical datacenter and application diagrams have been created before using the Deployment Designer.

Note   In the past, the tools typically used by architects to design and document a datacenter didn't integrate well with the tools used by application architects and developers. Visual Studio 2005 Team System breaks this mold.

Security

The Distributed System Designers will support constraining and validating your design against many different security models, both Microsoft and industry recognized, including the following:

- Internet Information Server (IIS) Security

- ASP.NET Security

In addition, for each Host and service component relationship, Team System has enabled pre-built constraints, such as ensuring that an application component requiring Windows authentication will deploy only to an IIS server that supports Windows authentication. You can also author user-defined constraints as well as specify custom settings for the security requirements of your own organization. Your simple and custom constraints may be validated by the Distributed System Designers.

Interoperability

A popular architecture choice today is one of a service-oriented architecture (SOA). These types of architectures are built on loosely coupled, autonomous, service-based applications communicating via well-defined messages and often across trust boundaries. In the future Microsoft will be shipping a variety of technologies to make it easier for you to build and manage these types of systems and to extend the capabilities of the underlying platform. Until then, we can still implement solid SOA architectures by creating ASP.NET Web services.

Unified Modeling Language (UML)

Many people who read the views of Microsoft on model-driven development assume that the emphasis on Domain Specific Languages somehow equates to an anti-UML position. This assumption is not true. Before UML, there was an unproductive diversity of modeling approaches, and their convergence into UML 1.0 was a significant step forward in using models in software development. However, for whatever reasons, the existence of UML and UML-based tools has not significantly changed the way developers build applications. Nor has it significantly contributed to developer productivity. In fact, Microsoft ships one of the most-used UML tools, which is based on Microsoft Visio®. Anonymous surveys of customers and developers have shown that a very small population claims to use UML tools in support of their tasks; most usage clusters around use cases and class diagrams. On top of that, only a tiny fraction actually uses UML tools to generate code.

This fact was one of the driving forces behind the model-driven development tools in Visual Studio Team Edition for Software Architects. Microsoft really wanted to take tasks that developers and architects find difficult and provide ways for modeling tools to add value and assistance.

> **Note**   In fact, developers at Microsoft are enthusiastic supporters of UML notation and diagrams. A walk around the developers' offices in any corridor reveals whiteboards covered with UML class diagrams and sequence diagrams. Developers use UML notation in specification documents and in many other diagrams prepared for presentations.

To support the need for developers to produce documentation and conceptual sketches, Microsoft will continue to ship the UML toolset with Visual Studio 2005. For instructions on how to generate code from your Visio UML diagrams and make use of it in your Visual Studio 2005 project, refer to Chapter 3.

UML diagrams are rarely a point-perfect compliable program source. That's a key difference for developers. Any artifact that contributes to actual software development must be capable of digital manipulation. Source code has a well-defined syntax and a comprehensible semantics, and can be manipulated consistently by compilers, debuggers, and refectory programs. To be useful to developers, a model must have the same status as source code. A model must also have a precise syntax, a comprehensible semantics, and well-defined mappings to source code or other well-defined models. It must be more than just documentation.

A diagram created with Team System's Application Designer is not just documentation, although it can serve that purpose. Instead, it allows a developer (or architect) to focus on one aspect of the system, such as the connectivity between services in a service-based architecture. The architect can design this aspect of the system before building projects,

WSDL files, code, and schemas, or he or she can ask the tool to document connectivity between services if those artifacts already exist.

Custom Assemblies

The Application Designer is used for modeling the structure of the applications. This structure is made up of deployable units of functionality. The connections between these applications are made via communication protocols supported by the applications. If custom assemblies are part of the application, they are simply deployed with the application, as long as they are properly referenced in the project. You won't see them referenced on the diagram. Microsoft is considering adding a feature for a future release that will allow you to drill into the implementation of an application.

 Note Although it's not technically a Visual Studio 2005 Team System tool, the Class Designer can be used to design any class or service you want. You'll learn more about the Class Designer in the next chapter.

Other Languages

Visual Studio 2005, as you are aware, supports numerous languages—many more than Microsoft itself produces. With regard to Visual Studio 2005 Team System, Microsoft has targeted features toward what it believes is the audience most likely to use them in association with building Web services. In other words, the application diagram will support implementing Windows applications, Web applications, and Web services in Microsoft Visual Basic® and Microsoft Visual C#®. The Class Designer supports these languages as well. Other languages can be used in your Visual Studio solution as referenced Web services or existing code libraries (assemblies).

Existing Code Libraries

You can reuse any existing code or code libraries inside the Application Designer, as long as you wrap them up as a Web service. If this is too much effort, or if your application architecture doesn't call for Web services, you can leave the code libraries and not model them on the design surface. They won't be directly referenced, but they will be referenced by any project you build using Visual Studio. If you are wrapping existing libraries as Web services, you can simply drag and drop an ASP.NET WebService application prototype or an ExternalWebService prototype onto the design surface.

Web Services, J2EE, BizTalk Server, and SQL Server

Interaction with existing Web services can be modeled by adding External Web Services to the application diagram. You must specify the location of the WSDL file that describes each Web service. You will then be able to connect other applications to it. Connecting an application to an external Web service will result in a Web reference being generated in code. Keep in mind that this Web reference won't automatically update if the underlying Web service ever changes. You can update it from the diagram using the right-click menu on the application, however.

Within the Application Designer, you can also model existing J2EE services as external Web services. You'll need to have access to the J2EE service's WSDL document.

Microsoft BizTalk® applications are also callable as Web services. This takes advantage of the fact that BizTalk 2004 and 2006 can easily expose their orchestrations as ASP.NET Web services. These Web services provide the WSDL documentation automatically. You model a BizTalk application by using the BizTalkWebService application prototype.

While there is no native support for Microsoft SQL Server™ 2005 Web service access you can use the External Web Service prototype to describe access to these services. You would not use an External Database prototype in this case.

The Logical Datacenter Designer

The infrastructure architect's primary task is to model the network and datacenter onto which the application will be deployed. Using Visual Studio the architect will define the metadata and configuration requirements by using the Logical Datacenter Designer. Specifically, this means defining the following characteristics:

- Types of servers (application Hosts)
- Communication pathways between Host (server endpoints)
- Types of communication boundaries (Zones)
- Communication connection points (zone endpoints)
- Types of services enabled
- Configuration of application services
- Adding or removing setting resources to logical servers and endpoints

Creating Logical Datacenter Diagrams

Logical datacenter diagrams are created independent of the application-development process. In other words, the infrastructure architects using Visual Studio 2005 Team System might not necessarily be doing any coding on the project itself. It is important to design these diagrams before the application development gets underway. The application architecture must be vetted against the logical datacenter diagram to ensure that it will deploy. The more time the architect spends accurately designing the network diagram, the more complete it will be for this and future application-development efforts.

Note Every project will be different. In some cases, the logical datacenter diagram may be developed in tandem with, or even after, the application diagram. This would occur in cases where an infrastructure is being configured for a specific application. Regardless of the order, the logical datacenter diagram must be completed before any validation can be performed.

At a high level, here are the steps to create a logical datacenter diagram:

1. Create a new Distributed System Solution project.

2. Select the Logical Datacenter as a template.

3. Design your logical datacenter by adding and configuring the appropriate Host's logical servers (application Hosts), adding and configuring the appropriate endpoints, and connecting those endpoints.

Tip When you create a new project, Visual Studio will name the logical datacenter diagram the same name as the project. This isn't always what you want. What I like to do is delete this .ldd file and add a new logical datacenter diagram to the (now empty) project, but this time I can specify a more meaningful name.

You can add the following shapes to your diagram:

- **Zones** The boundaries—such as domains, perimeter networks, or other isolated security areas

- **Endpoints** The communication gateways into or out of the Hosts logical servers and Zones, including both client- and server-side gateways (Web site, HTTP, database, and generic)

- **Hosts** The various application Hosts (IISWeb, database, Windows, and generic)

Zones

Zones are a logical container of Hosts. Zones do not necessarily map to anything specific in the datacenter, and only serve as a method of encapsulation. This encapsulation allows the architect to essentially hide the servers, ports, and pathways contained within the Zone, while exposing only a minimal number of public ports. This is similar to the concept of design classes in .NET—you have private members exposed through well-controlled public methods. Zones can represent a boundary, such as a firewall, VLAN, or security networks. Zones convey to the developer that they are about to cross a boundary (security, physical, network, and so on).

Here are a few examples of what Zones can represent:

- Internet

- VPN

- Perimeter network (also known as DMZ, demilitarized zone, and screened subnet)

- Firewalls

Note   Remember, a Zone doesn't have to represent a physical border or trust boundary. A Zone can be any logical collection of Hosts as well.

From a diagramming standpoint, you should strive to design your datacenter using Zones if possible. They force you to hide your sensitive servers and ports, only revealing a few public access points. Some other examples of this type of encapsulation include a hardened database Zone and an intranet Web portal Zone. Both of these examples can contain embedded Hosts and connection pathways, but expose only a minimal number of ports to the other clients and servers.

Here are the steps to create a Zone:

1. Drag a Zone onto your diagram.
2. Name the Zone using its property window or by changing it directly in the designer.
3. Specify other properties, settings, or constraints.
4. Add Hosts to the Zone
5. Add, edit, or remove any of the Zone endpoints.

Zones can also contain other Zones. You might use this capability to define your complicated datacenter in an easy-to-read way. For example, suppose you have a secure Zone, and within that zone, you have a corporate intranet Zone and a secure data Zone. Both inner Zones are considered secure.

When you decide that your datacenter diagram needs to have a Zone removed you can simply delete it. If your Zone isn't empty and contains Hosts, you have the option of just deleting the Zone. This will leave the Hosts that were contained in the diagram. You can also choose to delete all the contained Hosts as well as the Zone. Figure 5-1 shows you these deletion options. You can delete multiple Zones at the same time by selecting them all first.

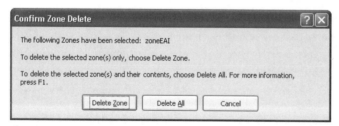

Figure 5-1   Deleting Zones

Tip   You should think carefully before deleting any Hosts or other components of your diagram. This is especially true if you've already validated applications against these diagrams. Changes at this point could adversely affect a successful deployment.

Endpoints

When you initially drag and drop a Zone onto the diagram it has one inbound endpoint, represented by an inward-pointing arrow, and one outbound endpoint, represented by an outward-pointing arrow. These endpoints are usually on opposite sides of the Zone. Typically, Zones need at least one inbound endpoint so that you can connect them to a client application or Host. Zones can also have an outbound endpoint which will allow it to communicate with other servers or Zones.

> **Tip**   When configuring Zone endpoints, remember that the communication flow can be inbound, outbound, or bidirectional. This setting is extremely important, especially when communication flow will be behind networking hardware or software that will physically constrain the flow. You want to ensure that the diagram matches the actual datacenter.

After defining the direction of the endpoint, you should define any constraints. The first type of constraint is to specify what type of Host or application can communicate. This is where the real value of the logical datacenter diagram is set. By specifying the types of connections that can be made to and from these endpoints, as well as any additional constraints (such as the security method, IP port number, and so on), you're actually specifying what type of traffic your Zone can support. This detail is essential to ensure an environment that is secure but still capable of running the application.

Endpoint constraints affect only what passes into and out of the Zone; they don't affect what is restricted inside the Zone. If you want to further constrain the endpoints between Hosts in a Zone, set the appropriate constraints on their endpoints. Also, when creating the Zone endpoint constraints, keep in mind the constraints of the physical servers inside the Zone. For example, don't block the physical port 1433 when the servers inside of that logical Zone must communicate using that port number.

You will learn more about settings and constraints later in this chapter.

Clients and Servers (Hosts)

You are allowed to have empty Zones on your diagram, but this is only beneficial for documentation purposes. More than likely, your Zones will contain Host servers and interconnecting communication pathways.

Here are the various server prototypes you can add to the diagram:

- **DatabaseServer**   A server hosting a database
- **IISWebServer**   A Web server that hosts ASP.NET Web applications
- **WindowsClient**   A desktop machine in the enterprise, representing an end-user client application

■ **GenericServer**   A server of an unspecified type in the datacenter, which you can
extend to represent a custom server type

> **Note**   There's no direct correlation between logical servers and physical machines. One
> logical server can be implemented on several physical machines (as in a Web farm), and many
> logical servers can be implemented on a single physical server (as with a Web server and da-
> tabase server running on the same hardware). This flexibility of what the logical datacenter
> represents means that you don't have to buy a complete Web farm datacenter for each of
> your developers just because that's the environment that the application will eventually get
> deployed to. The logical datacenter is flexible enough to represent a smaller QA environment
> as well as the scaled-out production environment.

To add Hosts to your Zone, you can drag any of the server prototypes from the toolbox
(shown in Figure 5-2) and drop them inside the Zone. You can also right-click the Zone,
select the *Add New* option, and then position the newly added Host manually. Just like
Zones, these Hosts can also have settings, constraints, and endpoints.

Figure 5-2   Logical Datacenter Designer toolbox

> **Note**   A frequently asked question is whether the Logical Datacenter Designer can *probe*
> for the servers on the network and determine their configurations and constraints automati-
> cally. A few years ago, Microsoft had a similar feature called AutoDiscovery, in its Visio 2002
> Network Tools edition. Future releases of Windows Management tools may offer this capa-
> bility to Team System, providing the ability to generate a logical model from the physical
> model. Today, there is support for importing IIS settings into your IISWebServer Host.
> Figure 5-3 shows the dialog box that appears when you right-click an IISWebServer Host and
> select *Import Settings*.

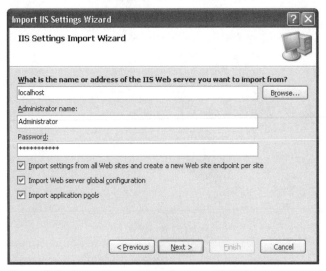

Figure 5-3   Importing settings from an IIS Web server

Connecting Endpoints

Once you've added Hosts to the diagram, connect them to indicate which communication pathways exist. There are several ways to do this:

- Hold down the Alt key while dragging from one Host or Zone to another.
- Right-click the Host or Zone and use the *Connect* option.
- Use the connection tool from the toolbox.

Here are the various endpoint types:

- **DatabaseClientEndpoint**   A consumer of a database connection
- **GenericClientEndpoint**   A consumer of a nonspecific connection
- **GenericServerEndpoint**   The provider side of a nonspecific connection
- **HTTPClientEndpoint**   The consumer side of an HTTP connection
- **WebSiteEndpoint**   The provider/server side of an HTTP connection
- **ZoneEndpoint**   A communication endpoint on the edge of a Zone

Note   Notice that there is no DatabaseServerEndpoint. This absence is by design because you cannot delete the default DatabaseServerEndpoint on a DatabaseServer Host. Therefore, you never need to add one back. You also cannot add additional DatabaseServerEndpoints.

> **Tip**   If you're having difficulty lining up the endpoints and connection of two services let the designer do it for you. Simply right-click the connection line and then select *Redraw Connection*. This should tidy things up. If you're good with a mouse, you can also route the connections and move the endpoints manually.

Figure 5-4 shows a Zone containing an IIS Web server that has the properly configured and connected endpoints.

Figure 5-4   An example of a logical datacenter diagram containing a Zone

Reusing Custom Server Prototypes

As you create and configure logical servers, you might find that you want to reuse these Hosts on other diagrams. This makes sense, especially when you have a standard configuration for your IIS Web servers with a specific version of Windows, .NET, and security. If this is the case, you can create your own custom prototypes and save them to the toolbox. Right-click the item, or a group of items, and use the *Add to Toolbox* feature. Specify a friendly name and a graphical bitmap image to represent the toolbox item. Visual Studio will save the host as a Logical Datacenter Designer prototype file (.lddprototype). You will be prompted for the file name and path.

> **Tip**   These prototypes are saved in a proprietary format rather than XML, so they are not easily edited. Any changes have to be made by using the designer and then saving a new prototype.

You are allowed to save the following as prototypes to the toolbox:

- Logical server
- Group of servers
- Zone
- Group of Zones

Later when you're editing a diagram, you can locate your new Host under the Logical Servers section in the toolbox and drag it onto your design surface. It will have all the same settings and constraints that you gave it initially, and you can change any to suit the new datacenter if need be.

Note   These prototypes are saved to a folder on your hard drive. By default, this is found under \Common7\Tools\DesignerPrototypes\Prototypes. It is possible to save your proto-types to other folders or drives, as long as you edit the registry and add those paths to the list that Visual Studio searches when populating the toolbox. By default, the registry location is \HKLM\SOFTWARE\Microsoft\VisualStudio\8.0\EnterpriseTools\DesignerPrototypeFolders. There is a value named *PrototypesFolder1*, which contains the preceding default path. You can add additional string values with additional paths here.

Tip   By default, any Hosts or Zones that you add to the toolbox will appear under the Logical Servers section. Use the Add Tab feature by right-clicking in the toolbox to add a new tab. You can then drag and drop your toolbox items onto that new tab to organize your toolbox. As shown in Figure 5-5, I have created a new tab called Logical Servers (Custom). If you want to share your Zones and Hosts with other architects, copy the .lddprotype file to a shared folder, and other users can download them to their machines.

Figure 5-5   The Logical Datacenter Designer toolbox with a custom CertifiedIISWebServer prototype

The Application Designer

The application architect's primary task is to define the application's architecture, including its applications, services, and communication pathways. Using Visual Studio, the architect will define the metadata and configuration settings by using the Application Designer. Specifically, this means defining the following characteristics:

■   Types of applications (applications, services, or databases)

- Communication pathways between applications (connections and endpoints)

- Constraints and settings

The focus of the Application Designer is to assist in the development of SOA applications. This means that you are primarily modeling ASP.NET Web services and the applications that consume them.

> **Note**   Many of the actual steps to create an application diagram are the same as those to create a logical datacenter diagram.

Creating Application Diagrams

Application diagrams can be created before any coding has started. This allows application architects, who may not be involved with the detailed implementation of a system, to use Visual Studio 2005 Team System to work on the design ahead of time. Designing these diagrams before application development gets underway allows the application architecture to be vetted against one or more logical datacenter diagrams, ensuring that it will successfully deploy. Issues caught early with the architecture are easier and less costly to fix than if coding has commenced. After a design has been validated the Application Designer will generate a skeleton implementation with projects, code, and configuration files that precisely match the design.

At a high level, here are the steps to create an application diagram:

1. Create a new Distributed System Solution project.

2. Select the Distributed System as a template.

3. Design your application by adding and configuring the appropriate application types, adding and configuring the appropriate endpoints, and connecting those endpoints.

> **Tip**   One of the coolest features of Team System is the ability you have to simply add an application diagram to an existing solution and have it reverse engineer your code. This will generate the respective applications, endpoints, and connections on the diagram. Try it!
>
> A solution can contain only one application diagram. It can, however, contain multiple logical datacenter diagrams, system diagrams, and deployment diagrams. This is because an application diagram is solution-scoped, as it can contain many applications that would be other projects under the solution. For example, you might want separate logical datacenter diagrams to represent separate eCommerce, B2B, and intranet hosting portions of a datacenter.

Here are the various types of application prototypes that you can add to your diagram:

- **Applications**   Windows, Microsoft Office, ASP.NET Web applications, or generic applications

■ **Services**   An ASP.NET Web service, BizTalk Web service, or external Web service

■ **Database**   An external database

In addition, you have other elements in the toolbox that you can add to your diagram:

■ **Endpoints**   A Web application, Web service, or generic endpoint

Applications, Services, and Databases

The Application Designer toolbox (shown in Figure 5-6) contains application prototypes that you use to design applications. Each of these prototypes describes a preconfigured version of a base application type. Dragging a prototype onto the design surface creates an application definition of the base type that is configured as described by the prototype. Application Designer comes with a standard set of prototypes (listed above). You can create your own custom prototypes from applications that you have added and configured on the design surface. See the section in this chapter titled "Reusing Custom Application Prototypes" for more information.

Figure 5-6   The Application Designer toolbox

You work with the Application Designer by dragging application prototypes onto the design surface and connecting the resulting application to define the connected system. You can right-click the design surface, select the *Add New* option and choose from the list of available prototypes. Then you position the newly added application manually.

Some of these base application types, such as ASP.NET applications and Windows applications, support round-trip developing with code. This means that the application design can be implemented, which is to say that code can be generated. Once implemented, changes made to the code are reflected back in the designer, whereas changes made in the designer are also reflected in code. This is a great development feature, especially when the architect and developer are two separate people sitting at two separate keyboards. This is known as *code round-tripping*.

Config round-tripping is also supported and is similar to code round-tripping, but it applies to changes made to the web.config. Initially, you might not have a web.config file in your project—one is generated only if you make some configuration settings in the Application Designer, such as a security setting. You could also add one manually to your Web project. After that, any changes to the web.config file will be reflected in the SDM properties and therefore in the Application Designer, and vice versa.

> **Tip**   You can also create your own custom prototypes by using the SDK.

Endpoints

Applications communicate through endpoints. For two applications to be connected there must be a provider endpoint at one end of the connection and a consumer endpoint at the other end. You can add additional provider endpoints directly to applications that support them either by dragging them from the toolbox or by right-clicking an application and selecting *Add New*. Be sure to pick the right endpoint type. To create consumer endpoints you connect an application to a provider endpoint. This creates an endpoint of the right type and configures it with the URL of the target in one go. (This is described in the following section.)

There are four application endpoint types, each of which has provider and consumer forms:

- **WebServiceEndpoint**   A SOAP-based Web service endpoint. These endpoints also show up on External Web Services and can be used on any other custom application type that supports Web services connectivity, such as a SQL Server 2005 Database.

- **WebContentEndpoint**   An HTTP-based Web content endpoint for accessing files other than Web services.

- **DatabaseEndpoint**   Defines a connection to a database.

- **GenericEndpoint**   An endpoint of unspecified protocol.

> **Tip**   To keep your diagram clean, delete any endpoints that you won't be using. You can hide the labels by right-clicking the endpoint and choosing *Hide Label*, or by just deleting the label.

Connecting Endpoints

After you've added applications to the diagram, connect them to indicate which communication pathways exist. There are several methods for doing this:

- Hold down the Alt key while dragging from one application to another.

- Right-click the application and use the Connect option.

- Use the connection tool from the toolbox.

Tip To tidy up the connections, try right-clicking each connection and then selecting *Redraw Connection*. You can also manually reroute a connection by selecting the connection and then dragging individual line segments into place.

Figure 5-7 shows three ASP.NET Web applications and the properly configured and connected endpoints.

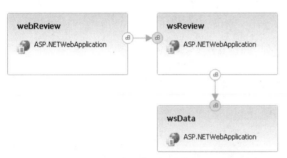

Figure 5-7   An example of an application diagram

Reusing Custom Application Prototypes

As you create and configure applications, you might find that you want to reuse the same—or similar—application definitions in other solutions. Perhaps you have a standard configuration for an ASP.NET application, or maybe a standard set of operations that all Web services should offer. If this is the case, you can create your own custom prototypes and save them to the toolbox. Right-click the item or group of items and use the Add to Toolbox feature. Specify a friendly name and a graphical bitmap image to represent the toolbox item in the toolbox. Visual Studio will save the application as an Application Designer prototypefile (.adprototype). You will be prompted for the file name and path.

Tip These prototypes are saved in a proprietary format rather than XML, so they are not easily edited. Any changes would have to be done by using the designer and then saving a new prototype.

You are allowed to save the following as prototypes to the toolbox:

- Application

- Group of applications

- Endpoint
- Group of endpoints

Later, when you're editing a diagram, you can locate your new application under the Applications or Endpoints sections in the toolbox and drag it onto your design surface. It will have all the same settings and constraints that you gave it initially, and you can change any of them to suit the new application if need be.

> **Note**   This form of reuse is based on propagating a copy of the application or endpoint specifications and is very different from reusing an application implementation complete with code. An implemented application can be reused by including it in multiple systems. Systems are not intended to be used in other application diagrams; they serve as an efficient way to deploy many related applications together. You'll learn more about systems and the System Designer later in this chapter.

You can save these prototypes to custom locations on your hard drive and then edit the registry to enable Visual Studio to find them. Refer to the "Reusing Custom Server Prototypes" section previously in this chapter.

Implementing the Classes

When I hear the word *implement*, I usually envision the process of adding all the code to the class so that it's complete, can be compiled, and can be used by the application. In other words, implementing a class means to construct it. Therefore, it would be safe to say that although the application architect architects a Web service, it's the developer who implements it. This is how the workflow in Team System is set up . . . almost.

In practice it's the architect who gets to use the Implement feature in Team System because that feature is available only in the Team Edition for Software Architects. The architect can right-click a Windows application, Web application, Web service, or Office application and Team System will generate the stub code. What's even better is that Team System supports an *Implement All Applications* feature, which will generate all the projects and template code for every respective application and service in the diagram. (See Figure 5-8.) This code can then be checked-in to source control, and one or more task work items can be created. This lets the developers know that there's some starter code out there, ready to implement.

> **Tip**   This is a perfect situation in which you may want to install the Team Developer and Team Architect editions together, or Team Suite, on the developer's desktop. For the architect who develops, or the developer who architects, having both editions would be very productive.

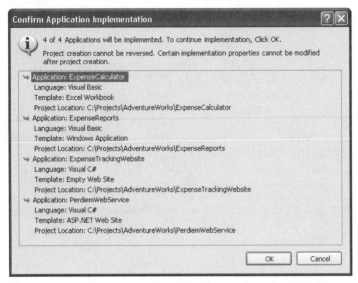

Figure 5-8   Implementing all applications and services at once

Let's not get too far ahead of ourselves here. Before using the productive implement function the application architect might need to specify a few things for the application or service. After you implement the projects there's no going back. Some properties are immutable and cannot be changed. You would have to delete everything and start over. So slow down and plan first. The following properties can and should be set first. (See Figure 5-9.)

- Default Class namespace
- Language
- Name
- Project (location)
- Template

By default, the implementation is very basic. It's just a skeletal structure, or stub code that gets generated. This is just enough for the architect to take a cursory look, change a few namespaces, reference a few assemblies, add some comments, check it into version control, and then send it on its way to the developers. Figure 5-10 shows the new project that is created.

Tip   Team System allows you to customize these templates. Notice in Figure 5-9 that the Template drop-down control includes an option for Custom. You can define your own custom template, which could be a starter application or an application template that defaults to your company's best practices.

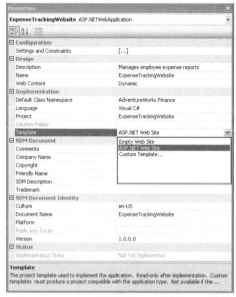

Figure 5-9   Setting implementation properties in the Application Designer

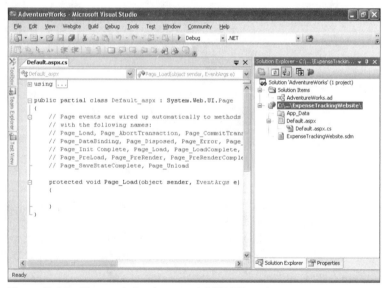

Figure 5-10   The newly implemented ASP.NET project

Team System will also create a System Definition Model (SDM) document, and associate it with the newly created project. This document describes the ASP.NET Web application (or whatever application you implemented). This file is created from the detail that was previously stored in the application diagram. This SDM document will be saved and associated with the Visual Studio project. If you double-click the SDM document it will simply take you back to the application diagram (assuming you have it available in your solution). If, instead, you right-click the document and open it with the XML editor, it will look like the document shown in Figure 5-11. Seeing descriptive XML like this makes you appreciate what SDM and DSI are accomplishing. It also makes you value the designers and their ability to distract you from all of that detail.

Tip   If you are interested in learning about the inner workings of these documents, the schema is documented in the SDK. The SDK also provides examples on how to populate model data.

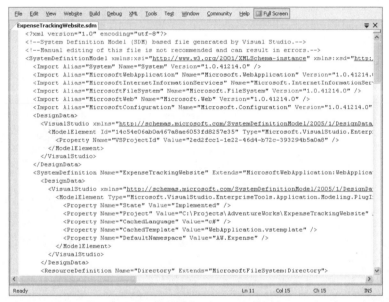

Figure 5-11   The SDM document that is created when you implement an ASP.NET Web application

More Info   For more information about SDM and its association with the Microsoft Dynamic Systems Initiative (DSI), refer to Chapter 3.

Settings and Constraints

Almost every Host and application placed on a logical datacenter diagram, an application diagram, or a system diagram can have settings and constraints configured. Constraints define requirements that must be satisfied during deployment. For example, a constraint can be set on an application, which dictates the logical server onto which it can be hosted. Servers in a logical datacenter diagram can be restricted in many ways to properly model the policies that exist in that datacenter. A constraint might require or restrict certain types of communication. Examples include requiring specific security aspects or barring a certain application type altogether.

There are three primary types of constraints:

- **Implicit**   Based on the element being used

  Example—IIS Servers intrinsically allow only certain file extension mappings. For example, if the .soap script map were removed from the Web server, the Web service bound to a Web site would not be supported. Implicit constraints are the same as built-in constraints in that there is no user interaction required to enable and fire the constraint. Other examples include securing of ASP.NET applications to be compatible with IIS settings.

- **Predefined**   As defined by the designer

  Example—A constraint controls whether an ASP.NET application can be hosted on a specific Host.

- **User-defined**   Created by authoring one or more settings to form a constraint

  Example—Only ASP.NET Web services built by the user named Cory can be hosted on a specific Host.

Note   New constraints can be authored with the SDK.

Logical server constraints can also advertise the capabilities of the server. Predefined constraints can be used to specify the operating system and the .NET Framework versions available on a server. A server can be constrained so that certain application types are not permitted to deploy. Other constraints might specify that a specific feature of an application is required, such as specifying that only the ASP.NET SqlProvider be used for Role and Membership in ASP.NET applications. All of this is important documentation, both for the team members and for Team System's designers. In other words it's important for architects, developers, and especially the IT professionals who will be deploying the application to understand configuration issues and to have a readable document. You will learn more about the deployment report later in this chapter.

Note   All constraints will be evaluated using the Deployment Designer, ensuring that the application can be properly hosted on the corresponding Host.

The Settings and Constraints Editor (shown in Figure 5-12) is used to define various element attributes included in each diagram: *logical datacenter*, *application*, and *system*. In other words, this is the same editor used by all of the Distributed System Designers. The Settings and Constraints Editor is normally docked below the bottom edge of the main designer. If it isn't visible, it can be displayed from any diagram element's context menu.

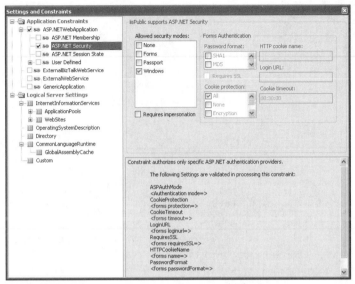

Figure 5-12   The Settings and Constraints Editor

The System Designer

The System Designer is another of the Distributed System Designers. Although seemingly an optional tool, it is arguably at the heart of the entire suite. When you deploy a distributed application system, you actually deploy a configuration of applications. The applications you deploy need to be configured and connected in a carefully considered way. In doing so, you will achieve both the functional goals of the system and realize a successful deployment. The important point is that you actually deploy a configured use of the applications and not the applications themselves. This is easier to think of if you imagine needing to deploy the same system into two datacenters where each requires a different configuration. In this case, you need to provide different customers with a slightly different configuration of the same basic functions.

A *system* is a description of such a configuration. You might think the application diagram is the center of the design process, but it is simply a foundation on which to design systems. The Application Designer is used to design the applications and how they can be connected. The system diagram, however, defines how they should actually be connected. The system diagram represents the architectural view of the systems as they will look in your datacenter. Although the application diagram may well include applications that are an artifact of the development process (such as test harnesses or stubs of services), these applications will be excluded from the system that is to be deployed.

It's also important to recognize that a system is not required to be a fully self-contained business application. Systems can selectively expose the behavior of the applications they comprise, so they are composable. Systems can then be created as reusable configurations, composed of applications or other systems that allow you to construct architectures with nested subsystems.

For example, an architect might want to group two ASP.NET Web services into a security system. This is done because those Web services implement authentication and authorization. To create a system, the application architect just needs to highlight one or more applications in the Application Designer, right-click one of them, and choose *Design Application System*. Visual Studio will prompt for the name of the system (as shown in Figure 5-13) and then open the System Designer, allowing the architect to arrange the constituent applications and override any additional settings.

To selectively expose the behavior of a member application in the system, you can select the endpoint to expose, and from the right-click menu select *Add Proxy Endpoint*. This adds a proxy endpoint on the system that is delegated to the application endpoint. If you now create another system and add it to the system you just built, you will see the proxy endpoint that you just created and be able to connect this to other applications or systems as required. A final system diagram is shown in Figure 5-14.

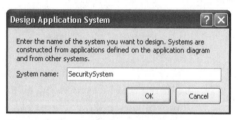

Figure 5-13   Naming your new system

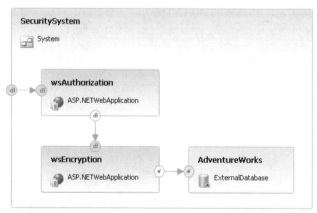

Figure 5-14   The System Designer

The Deployment Designer

The Deployment Designer is typically the final Distributed System Designer that you will use in a given iteration. This designer will allow you to perform a pre-deployment verification step, called a *trial deployment*, in which you validate the deployment of your application against a specific logical datacenter. During this process, settings and constraints will either fit together nicely or clash and generate warnings and errors.

To create a deployment diagram, you must have a completed application diagram and at least one logical datacenter diagram completed as well. Right-click the application diagram and select *Define Deployment*. Visual Studio prompts you for the logical datacenter onto which you want to deploy your application. (See Figure 5-15.) In other words, choose the datacenter against which you validate your application.

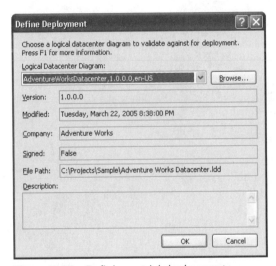

Figure 5-15   Defining a trial deployment

Tip   If you created a system diagram, you can right-click that diagram and define the deployment.

Using the Deployment Designer is quite easy. You just drag an application from the System View—which provides a list of all the applications in your application diagram—onto the appropriate Host server in the logical datacenter. Repeat this process until all your applications are bound. Figure 5-16 shows the Deployment Designer with two of the three applications bound to the public and private IIS server Hosts, respectively. Only the wsReview ASP.NET Web service remains unbound.

The designer will provide visual feedback via tooltips that indicate the compatibility of the application on the logical server. This will guide you to appropriately bind the application to a valid server. The feedback also checks for compatible endpoints (communication capabilities), and hosting restrictions enabled by the model.

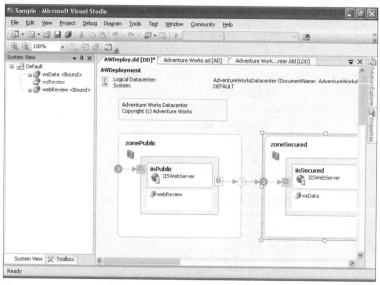

Figure 5-16 Binding applications to a Host

Validating the Deployment

Much of the deployment validation is done as you are dragging and dropping your applications from the System View window onto the Logical Datacenter Designer surface. Right away, the simple communication rules are enforced. For example, if you try to drag an application that requires HTTP access onto a Host that doesn't support that type of endpoint, it won't drop. Instead, you'll get the "no drop" mouse pointer (a circle with a line through it). This occurs because communication can flow only between certain connected endpoints and is restricted to using only the same *type* of communication paths that are in the datacenter model.

Tip If Visual Studio stops you from dropping your application onto a Host and gives you the "no drop" pointer, just hover your cursor over that Host for a second or two and a tooltip will pop up, indicating what the problem is. More than likely, the Host doesn't have the right kind of endpoints and you'll need to return to the Logical Datacenter Designer to make some adjustments.

Deeper constraint violations won't be apparent until a validation is performed. Remember that much finer policies can be created using the Settings and Constraints Editor, in both the Logical Datacenter Designer and the Application Designer. Individual elements in the diagrams can be provided with constraints that further restrict the behavior and capabilities of applications deployed in the datacenter. These constraint violations won't surface as you are dragging and dropping, but they will occur later when you actually validate the diagram and review the errors and warnings.

To perform an explicit validation, you need to right-click the deployment diagram and then choose *Validate Diagram*. Make sure all your applications are bound correctly and no implicit validation errors or warnings occurred. The validation process will compile all the related documents and then provide a list of errors and warnings. (See Figure 5-17.) No errors or warnings means that your application will deploy successfully to the datacenter.

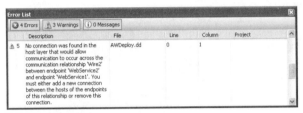

Figure 5-17　Deployment errors and warnings

 Note　Some items in the error list can be double-clicked, taking you directly to the offending application or Host. Make your changes according to both the guidance of the error message and that of your organization. What I mean is, don't let the tool override your constraints. Errors and warnings sometimes mean that the infrastructure architect and application architect need to meet and talk, compromising where necessary.

Generating a Deployment Report

The deployment report is simply an XML document that can serve whatever purpose the team might have. It can be transformed or used as input for some other process, such as scripting a deployment. Team System also generates an HTML report for reference. It contains the following information:

- Inventory of all systems, including names and types

- Resources for each of the systems, including assemblies, executables, directories, resource files, endpoints, and web.config files

- Server settings, including versions, domain controller, terminal server, IIS settings, application pools, .NET versions, and GAC settings

- Embedded diagrams (optional)

The report serves as a bill of materials report for the deployment team. It enumerates all the servers and services. Figure 5-18 shows an example of the report as it is in XML format. Figure 5-19 shows the same report as HTML, suitable for presentation and communication with IT professionals and architects.

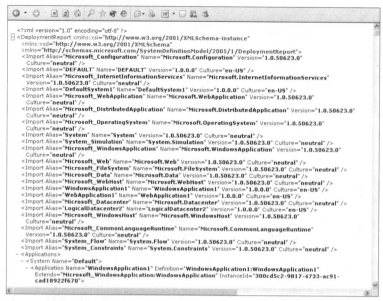

Figure 5-18   Sample deployment report (XML)

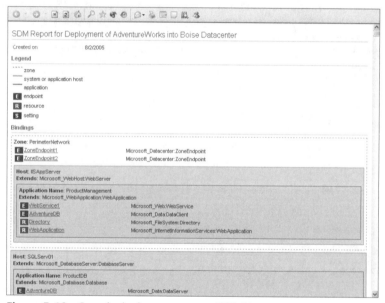

Figure 5-19   Sample deployment report (HTML)

Tip   Look for a file named DeploymentReport.xsl. It contains the XSL template that converts the XML deployment report into the nice-looking HTML report. Feel free to edit this .xsl document to customize the deployment report. By default, this template is found in \Common7\ Packages\SDM\XSL\1033 (for US English).

Both the XML and HTML documents are generated from the trial deployment created using the Deployment Designer. Team System provides you with some options when generating the report, such as including the diagrams, owners, binaries, source code, and other content files. When generated, all these files are copied to a specified folder, maintaining a structure of all the files. For troubleshooting, you might also want to run the report, asking to see only exceptions. Figure 5-20 shows the various reporting options that are available.

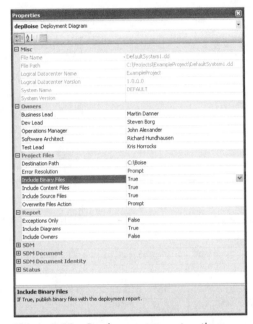

Figure 5-20   Deployment report options

> **Note**   Microsoft has said that a future version of Team System will allow the deployment report to be used as input for automated deployment, possibly integrating with Microsoft Operations Manager (MOM) and Systems Management Server (SMS).

What's Next?

At this point, the architects have created their respective diagrams and validated them against each other, producing a deployment diagram and a resulting deployment report. Now it's time to get the developers online to implement the various applications and Web services and proceed with the construction of the software. The deployment report, which serves as a bill of materials, can be sent to the IT operations teams to prepare them for the deployment phase, which occurs later in the life cycle.

Are the architects done with Team System? This depends on your project and your team. I would say that the infrastructure architect is probably done with this iteration at this point and will return to Team System only if there is a need to alter the logical datacenter diagrams. This is a definite possibility with today's agile project methodologies.

> **Tip**   Because not everyone on your team will have a copy of Visual Studio 2005 Team Edition for Architects, you should save a few printed screen images, such as the deployment report (with embedded diagrams), to the project portal for all the team members to refer to. I recommend saving the deployment report as a single Web Archive file (.mht) so that all the graphics are embedded into a single file. This makes uploading to the portal easy and maintains the fidelity of the report. You'll need to ensure that all your team members have at least version 5.0 of Microsoft Internet Explorer.

As for the application architects, because they are more aligned with software than hardware, they will likely continue to use Team System and assist with the project throughout its life cycle. Does this mean that they'll assist in the coding efforts? Maybe. Again, it depends on the team and the project.

Summary

Intelligent and productive modeling tools are what every team needs. In Team System, both the infrastructure and application architects will use the Team Edition for Software Architects to gain access to the various Distributed System Designers. The architects will create logical datacenter diagrams and application diagrams. Team System improves the communication between these two architects, which is critical because there can be many constraints to document and adhere to. From these two diagrams, a successful deployment can be agreed upon and validated. From this process, the developers can proceed by implementing the various Web services and IT operations and can prepare for the deployment by studying and scripting over the generated deployment report.

Chapter 6
Developers

In this chapter:

Viewing Work Items 125

Implementing the Web Application or Service 127

Version Control 130

Integrated Testing 136

Team Foundation Build 145

Reports 151

Impact on Code Development 153

Summary 154

Arguably, in any software development project, developers perform the key role. Not so long ago, before software development became a profession, developers often worked alone—renegades slinging code in a darkened room. Later, as software became more complex, developers worked in teams, planning an application over coffee, Coke, and pizza.

Today, software is far more complex, requiring well-organized teams of people, from architects to testers. In this environment, structure becomes very important. Microsoft® Visual Studio® 2005 Team System can be a critical tool to assist in providing that structure.

Visual Studio 2005 Team System provides an entire suite of tools for developers. These tools help the developer create more efficient, less buggy, and cleaner code in less time. Some of the Team System tools geared toward developers include a Class Designer to assist in developing well-structured class diagrams graphically, unit testing tools, code coverage tools, static analysis tools, and even profiling tools. All the work performed using these tools can also be tracked by associating the work done with a work item.

Viewing Work Items

In a development life cycle build using Team System, the primary method for initiating action is a *work item*. Depending on the structure of the development team, a developer might be assigned a task from the development manager, an application architect, a senior developer, a tester, a fellow developer, or even the developer himself.

Work items are the mechanism by which members of the team track items of interest to the development life cycle. The first type of work item that most people are exposed to is a task. This work item simply assigns work to some member of the development team. That task can then be commented on, tracked, reported on, and closed out when it is complete. The types and names given to work items generally depend on the methodology being used. Microsoft Solutions Framework (MSF) 4.0 for Agile Software Development, for instance, includes Task, Quality of Service (QoS) Requirement, Risk, Scenario, and Bug. Other methodologies may implement different work item types, which allows for a large amount of flexibility in the way a team develops code. Work items are also extensible, allowing for easy custom creation of work items specific either to a custom methodology or even tailored to a specific development project. For instance, a development team might create a "Critical Bug" type of work item for bugs that are discovered in software that has already been shipped, or a "Security Bug" work item type that tracks the discoverability, reproducibility, exploitability, affected users, and discoverability (DREAD) of the security flaw. Reports could then be generated that could aggregate and rank the security risks of the software in its current state of development.

Work items, then, are the base tracking mechanism in any Team System project, and the work items can be of many different types. As a developer, you'll be exposed to hundreds or thousands of work items throughout any given project; unfortunately, many of them will be tasks.

Besides the many different types of work items, there are also many different ways of viewing the work items that have been tasked. Inside Visual Studio, the primary way to view work items is to use the Work Items Project Queries. There are several default queries created inside the project. These queries are determined by the development methodology used. For instance, in the MSF 4.0 for Agile Software Development methodology, there are queries that return the currently active bugs, all the work items assigned to the currently logged-in developer, all tasks, and all bugs. There are also several other built-in queries. You can also create your own query to view particular work items of interest. In fact, if the development methodology has been modified to include new types of work items, you can create a custom query to ensure you stay on top of your assigned work items.

Custom queries are created by adding them to the My Queries folder. (See Figure 6-1.) When you add a query, you can choose from a variety of selection criteria, including who assigned the work items, who the items are assigned to, whether or not the items have attachments, the current status of the item, and many other criteria. In fact, you can even query work items based on the number of files that were attached to the work item!

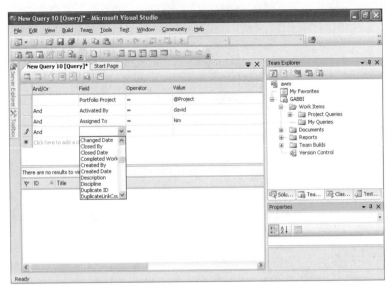

Figure 6-1   Creating a new work item query from Team Explorer

Implementing the Web Application or Service

After being tasked to develop some business functionality, the first action a developer will need to take is to create a structure from which to build the code. Depending on the version of Visual Studio 2005 Team System you're using, you might or might not have the ability to automatically generate the code for a Web application or Web service inside of Visual Studio. Visual Studio 2005 Team Edition for Software Architects includes a graphical tool called the Application Designer, which can be used to graphically architect a solution. With a simple right-click, code can be generated from the tool that includes the entire appropriate infrastructure. The application connection diagram can be seen in Figure 6-2.

A very cool feature of the application diagram is that you can set many settings and constraints on each of the components. For instance, you can constrain a Web service to run only on a machine that supports Internet Information Server 6 and .NET Framework version 2.0. You can also specify which language should be used when generating the code skeleton from the application diagram.

If you're using Visual Studio 2005 Team Edition for Software Developers, you won't be able to create code from the architectural diagrams. If that's the case, you'll need to depend on the architect to have generated the appropriate skeleton code for you. However, if you have Team Edition for Architects installed or are using the Team Suite edition, you'll be able to do everything the architect is able to do, including generating skeleton code from the application diagram. Either way, at some point you might have a basic, skeleton code structure with all the appropriate connection points to other services already defined.

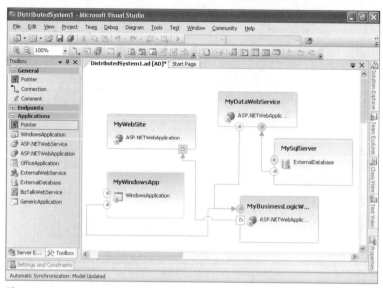

Figure 6-2   An application diagram

After you have the appropriate skeleton code, you then must implement the business logic and desired functionality. If the architect has generated the code skeleton, the first step is to check out the code from version control. You can then begin implementing the actual code.

There are a few cases where you might actually be creating your own framework. Primarily, this is when you're designed a class, or set of classes, that will be compiled into a dynamic-link library (DLL). Although there are no architectural designers to aid in the building of a DLL as a whole, you can use the Class Designer to work on individual classes and interfaces.

Using the Class Designer

There are a couple different ways to create code in Visual Studio 2005 Team System. You can write code as text or you can graphically create code using the Class Designer. The Class Designer provides a graphical interface for creating code. Unlike a "round trip" code engineering tool that generates code from a graphical representation and can, in turn, modify the graphical representation when the code changes, the Class Designer *is* the code. It's a purely graphical representation of the code structure. Although the difference between these two different methods might seem small, conceptually there is a great deal of difference. First, the text itself is treated as the code and the graphical representation is treated only as a representation. This mistakes the text of the code as the code itself, but in fact it's the only possible representation of the code. Although traditionally software code has been represented by text, this is by no means a requirement, and the conceptual step of treating code as functionality and having many possible representations of that functionality is one of the reasons why the Class Designer is important.

The Class Designer itself is technically not an exclusive part of Visual Studio 2005 Team System; it's also included in the other versions of Visual Studio 2005. As such, we might be taking a little detour discussing it here. However, it's so useful for developing code that we need to talk about it!

The Class Designer has many excellent features that can improve both the speed of development and the quality of the resulting code. Seeing the code visually allows you to quickly ensure that there is a clean relationship between the classes and that the class inheritance hierarchies are of a reasonable depth. In addition, you can use graphical features to create new classes, add new properties and methods to those classes, and set up relations between classes.

To get to the class diagram, you can either add a new one to the project or simply right-click the project and select View Class Diagram. Figure 6-3 shows a simple class diagram of a *Dog* class, an inherited *Beagle* class, and also an *Owner* class that is related to the *Dog* class. Note that the connection between *Owner* and *Dog* is an association relationship, and it has a label with the word "Dog" above it. The Class Designer was smart enough to know about the relationship between the two classes, based on an examination of the classes. The *Owner* class has a public property called *Dog*, which references a private instance of the *Dog* class. This property was automatically generated when the association was made!

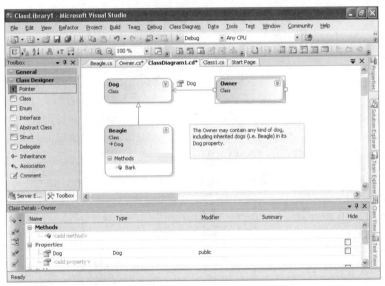

Figure 6-3   A simple class diagram created using the Class Designer

Another powerful feature of the class diagram is the ability to quickly use the Object Test Bench. The Object Test Bench is a fast tool to create an instance of a class so that you can test its features easily, without having to whip up a quick Microsoft Windows® application and some lines of code to create an instance and call it. Simply right-click on any class diagram, and choose the Create Instance menu item. You are then prompted to name the soon-to-be-created instance. (See Figure 6-4.)

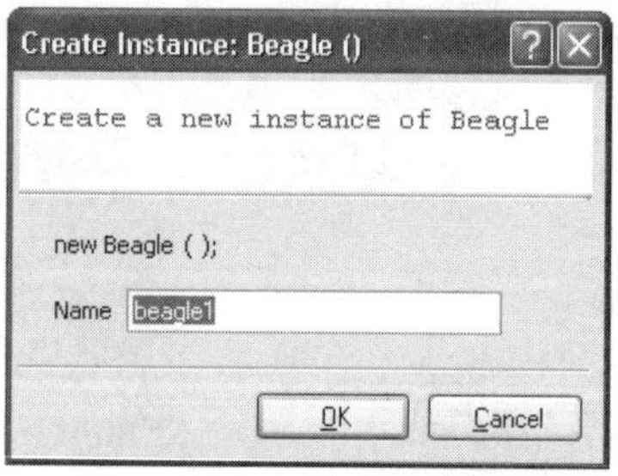

Create Instance: Beagle ()   ? X

Create a new instance of Beagle

new Beagle ( );

Name beagle1

OK   Cancel

Figure 6-4 Naming the instance

You can now use the Object Test Bench to call any of the methods on the class. In Figure 6-5, you can see how easy it is to graphically call the *Bark* method on the *Beagle* class. Prior to the *Bark* method actually being invoked, you get the option to specify any input parameters that are necessary. In the case in Figure 6-5, there are no parameters, so the *Bark* method can execute without additional information. The return value can then be saved as a value in the Object Test Bench so that it can be used later, possibly as an input to another method call.

Figure 6-5 Using the Object Test Bench to implement methods

The Class Designer also allows you to do a fair amount of refactoring directly inside the graphical interface. For instance, back in Figure 6-3, there was an inheritance hierarchy with a *Dog* class. If you wanted to extract an interface from the *Dog* class, you would simply right-click the *Dog* element, choose Refactor, and then select Extract Interface. A wizard then walks you through a few steps, allowing you to select which elements of the *Dog* class you want to be included in the interface. The interface is then created in code, and your *Dog* class is changed to reflect an implementation of the created interface.

There are a few other things to mention about the Class Designer. As noted previously, it's a part of Microsoft Visual Studio 2005 Standard Edition, not just Team System, so many people will have access to it. In addition, it's not a Unified Modeling Language (UML) diagram tool. The Class Diagram uses a very easy to learn and convenient graphical representation of code that helps maximize the development speed and quality of class code.

Version Control

Any development project that involves more than just creating some simple demo code has a critical need for some sort of version control. In the Microsoft world, this has generally meant using Microsoft Visual SourceSafe® (VSS). Although VSS was a very useful tool, many enterprise customers chose to use a third-party version-control system instead. Many of these tools allowed developers to use more advanced features than were available in VSS.

With the introduction of Microsoft Visual Studio 2005 Team Foundation Server and Team System, Microsoft has provided an advanced, full-featured, enterprise version-control system that is able to handle the most complex development tasks. It handles tasks such as code branching and merging with far more reliability than VSS did. It also includes new features such as code shelving, which allows developers to place their unfinished code in the repository without actually checking it in. It also provides different types of locks when checking out files from version control. You can decide to not lock the code at all, allow others to check out code but not check in code, or lock other developers from even checking out the code at all. (See Figure 6-6.)

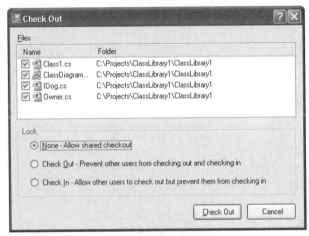

Figure 6-6   Checking out code

One of the major features of Team Foundation Server and Team System is that it allows the creation of version-control check-in policies. These policies can warn developers if they are trying to check in code that violates some stated policy. These policies can be defined by an administrator and include rules such as the following:

- The source code must have been reviewed by a senior developer.

- Unit tests must have covered more than 80 percent of the code.

- There are no violations of the corporate naming convention guidelines.

Associating Check-Ins with Work Items

When you check in code, it can be associated with a work item. This allows developers to track their work as it relates to their assigned tasks. When code is related to a check-in, it's also reported to the Team Foundation Server. This system allows reports to be generated that track code churn, bugs, and the progress made toward project completion.

You can even define a check-in policy to ensure that every piece of code added to the version-control system is tied to a particular work item. This best practice ensures that project managers, architects, and other stakeholders can use the built-in reports to understand the progress being made in the various areas of the project.

To associate a check-in with a work item, you simply begin the check-in process. First, you need to select the files you want to check in. (See Figure 6-7.) You then associate the check-in with a work item by clicking the Work Items icon on the left-hand side of the wizard. You can then search for the appropriate work item to associate with the check-in. Once you select the appropriate work item, you can ensure that the Checkin Action is set to Associate. (If the code you wrote resolves the work item, you can instead select Resolve.)

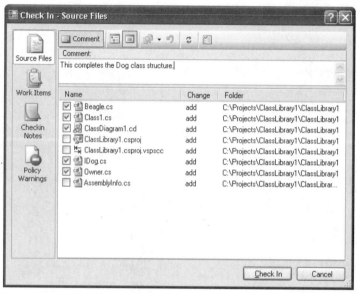

Figure 6-7 Checking in code

Associating a check-in with a work item allows the progress of the project to be tracked more closely, and it allows other developers to easily find code relating to certain features of the system. (See Figure 6-8.) This is especially true if you relate the code to a Quality of Service (QoS) Requirement or a Scenario work item.

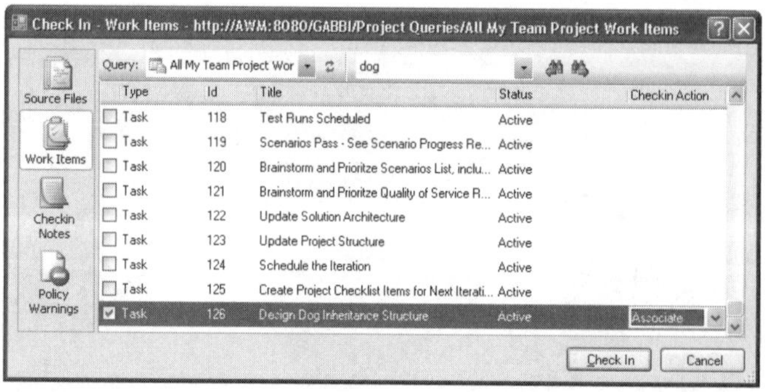

Figure 6-8 Associating a check-in with a work item or multiple work items

You might also choose to associate more than one work item with a particular check-in. In fact, in many situations you will be associating a piece of code or an architectural diagram with as many as three or four different work items, possibly more. For instance, your code may solve a particular bug that has been reported, so it clearly needs to be associated with that work item. In addition, it is likely that the code was related to a particular feature of the application, or possibly a QoS Requirement so it will also be associated with that work item. Finally, you may have responded to the bug by a task created automatically by Team Foundation Build. You should associate your check-in with that task so it gets reported as being completed.

Version Control Explorer

You can choose from a number of tools to access the source control inside Visual Studio. You can go to the File menu and select the Source Control item. (See Figure 6-9.) You can also use the Source Control Explorer window. (See Figure 6-10.) The Source Control Explorer window allows you to see all the available projects and individual files. You can also add new files to version control, get the latest versions, and even compare two different source-code revisions.

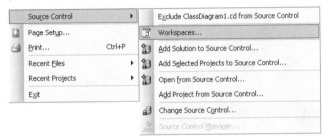

Figure 6-9   Accessing version control from the main menu

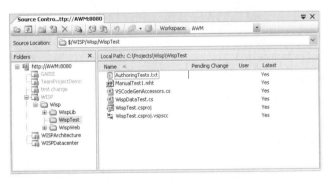

Figure 6-10   Using the Source Control Explorer

Pending Check-Ins

In addition to using the Source Control Explorer, you can use the Pending Check-ins window (available by choosing View and then selecting Pending Check-ins menu item). This window allows you to check in existing code, shelve and unshelve code, associate work items with the check-in, and perform other source-code-related tasks. The user interface is nearly identical to the wizard interface shown in Figures 6-7 and 6-8.

Pending check-ins are a way for you to determine which code you currently have checked out of version control. They also alert you to which code is stored only locally, which is valuable information because any changes made to locally stored code since check-out have not yet been uploaded to the server. A failure of your local system, then, could result in code being lost. Shelving your code can help prevent that from happening.

Shelving and Unshelving

Shelving code allows a developer to place his or her code on the version-control server, but it doesn't force a developer to do an official check-in. This process can ensure that your code is safely tucked away without requiring you to fully check in your code.

In many version-control systems, you simply check in your code, even in an unfinished state, and check it out later for the fixes. However, because of the possible check-in policies mentioned earlier, you might be unable to check in your code because it is not yet ready to pass the policies. In this case, you can simply shelve your code because shelved code doesn't have to pass any of the source-code-control check-in policies.

To shelve your code, simply select the items to be shelved in the Source Control Explorer window and click the Shelve button. You then provide the shelved code with a Shelveset name so that it can be unshelved as a group later. The code is then shelved. To unshelve your code, simply click the Unshelve button in the Source Control Explorer and select the Shelveset you want to unshelve. (See Figure 6-11.)

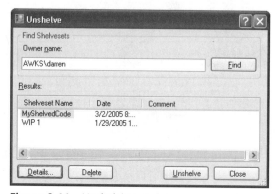

Figure 6-11   Unshelving code

When unshelving code, you might have a conflict with code that you have changed locally, because shelved code doesn't prevent you from editing the files that were shelved. (This allows you to shelve multiple versions of the same code if you want.) In that case, you'll be informed of the conflict and presented with options for resolving the conflict. (See Figures 6-12 and 6-13.)

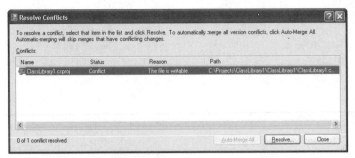

Figure 6-12   Resolving conflicts

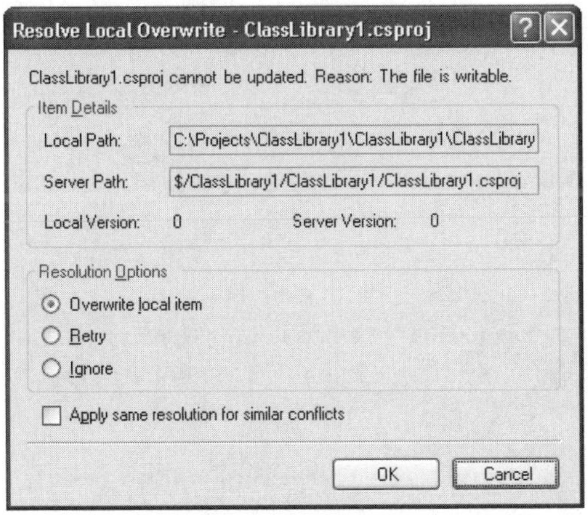

Figure 6-13   Resolving a local overwrite conflict

Shelving and unshelving open up many new possibilities for developing code. If a customer doesn't know what type of user interface design to choose, a developer can come up with several different versions of a window or Web page, each one having a different look and feel. Each version could then be shelved separately, and when the customer came in, the versions could be unshelved in turn and demonstrated, without affecting the remainder of the code.

Another use of shelving is dealing with the unavoidable need to fix a bug, right when you're in the middle of developing a new feature. With shelving, the feature you're working on can be directly shelved, leaving your code in the previous state (before you began working on the feature). You can then go back and fix the bug. When the bug is fixed, you can unshelve the code and continue work on your new feature. As long as the bug wasn't found in the code you were editing or writing for the new feature, you don't need to do anything. If it was, you are prompted to resolve any conflicts that occurred.

In the case of bug fixes, code shelving can be a lifesaver. Because the code for the new feature is likely incomplete and will not pass the check-in policies, you can simply put it to the side easily and continue working. You can also pass shelved code to another developer to look over, possibly for a security check or to help out with a particularly nasty bug.

Version Control Check-In Policies

Check-in policies are used to ensure that the code checked in to version control passes a set of minimum standards. Generally, senior developers or architects will specify the policies to ensure that the enterprise developers follow the appropriate coding guidelines when designing, building, and refactoring code. These check-in policies can also be enforced against unit tests that are checked in to the system as well.

Using check-in policies opens up a whole new frontier in code quality. The capability of an organization to programmatically enforce a comprehensive and tailored set of policies can ensure that developers build good, solid code that has far fewer bugs, is more secure, and is far more maintainable. Later, we'll discuss using code analysis to check code for hundreds of well-known security, reliability, maintainability, and performance rules, as well as check for the presence of several well-tested best practices. Developers can be forced to implement these configurable best practices and rules before their code will be allowed to be checked in to version control.

Integrated Testing

One of the greatest benefits in Visual Studio 2005 Team System is the addition of integrated testing. Testing has steadily grown more popular over the past few years, and an increasing number of developers are using a development methodology that encourages the strict use of testing.

Visual Studio 2005 Team System provides numerous testing support pieces for the developer. First and foremost is the integrated unit-testing capabilities. Unit tests allow developers to create code that will be used to test the quality and completeness of their production code. Visual Studio 2005 Team System can create unit-test skeletons and test projects with only a few mouse clicks or keystrokes.

The ability to generate unit tests isn't the only testing feature available in Visual Studio 2005 Team System, however. You can also run a suite of unit tests while looking to see the amount of code that is covered by those tests. This process is referred to as *code coverage testing*, and it allows you to see, by line, which areas of the code were tested by the unit tests that were run and which weren't.

Static analysis testing is also available. Static analysis tests allow a developer to analyze his or her compiled code for common errors and poor programming practices. For Microsoft .NET developers using Microsoft Visual Studio .NET 2003, static analysis testing has been done by using a plug-in such as FxCop to perform static analysis on the code. The ability to do static analysis is now built into Team Edition for Developers, allowing developers to quickly and easily get concrete recommendations for improving code with a minimum of effort.

Finally, developers are able to profile their code for performance. Profiling allows them to see where their application is spending the majority of its time, determine how long methods are taking to execute, and identify performance bottlenecks in their application.

Test-Driven Development

One of the primary development trends in testing is the use of Test-Driven Development (TDD). TDD puts testing front and center in any development methodology. In fact, in TDD, unit tests (explained in further detail later) are developed to test the functionality of a piece of code before that code is actually written. This process has several benefits, including confidence in the condition of your code, ease of refactoring, reduction in the amount of time spent debugging, and the uncovering of flaws in the architectural design of the system. There are many other benefits to TDD, and I highly recommend learning more about it if you plan on doing professional code development.

When developers are first exposed to TDD, they often balk at implementing it, thinking that it's an incredible waste of time to write all those unit tests just to test a simple piece of functionality. However, the benefits of TDD often quickly overcome the initial resistance.

For me, the most important benefit is confidence—confidence in your code. When you have a suite of unit tests that effectively test your code, you can be confident that your code will compile and run with a very low likelihood of errors. Thus, when a customer asks to see a demonstration of the code in its current state, you don't need to spend hours running through your code checking out possible locations for errors and fearing that something might go wrong. Instead, you can simply run the suite of unit tests against your code, ensuring all of them pass. When they do, the code can be compiled and demonstrated or delivered.

Another major benefit to TDD is the ability to confidently refactor code. Refactoring involves changing existing code to improve its design. Try as we might to create loosely coupled code, in any nontrivial software development project there will always exist strongly coupled objects or methods. This strong coupling can make it extremely dangerous to change the structure of the code, because a change in one area of the code can affect another area. At times, these effects aren't entirely clear and might not be caught in compile-time checks. Thus, many developers avoid making clear improvements in their code for fear it will break the fragile structure that has been built. With a suite of unit tests that cover the code, refactoring can be done with confidence. If some area of the code is affected by the change, it will fail the unit tests when the suite is run. By examining the unit test that failed, the developer can find exactly where the problem exists, and either roll back their refactoring or make a change in the affected code.

Another enormous benefit is the drastic reduction in time spent debugging. Granted, as a developer using TDD, you'll have spent a good deal of time building unit tests; however, much of that time is compensated by the reduction in debug time. It's said that developers spend 60 percent of their time in design, 30 percent of their time in development, and 80 percent of their time debugging. Although this is said tongue in cheek, that sentence holds some truth for many developers. Debugging always takes far more time than originally planned, regardless of the complexity of the code. TDD reduces (although it doesn't eliminate) the time spent in debugging. It does this by clearly indicating the location of a problem. If a test suite has been developed and the code has been run and has failed, the location of that failure is immediately apparent. All you need to do is visually examine the results of the unit tests. The failed ones will be highlighted in red. Because a single unit test covers only a relatively small piece of functionality, the location of the error becomes almost immediately apparent. And because a unit test is testing a single path through the code, you also know the nature of the failure. This amount of information is critical to quickly fixing the code. Many developers I've talked with say that the debugging tools they used so heavily in the past are now rarely used. It's easier to determine the exact nature and location of a code failure by looking at a failed unit test than it is by stepping through code in a debugger.

Finally, an often overlooked benefit of TDD and unit tests in general is that they can reveal flaws in the architecture of the system. Some unit tests can admittedly be difficult to write, but if a unit test requires a lot of thought to design so that it works properly, that might be an indication of poor design. Quite often, difficult unit tests reveal tight coupling between elements of a design. This tight coupling might be intentional, but in most cases it reveals poor design. The code and the design can then be refactored. And because you already have a suite of unit tests, you can refactor with confidence. Thus, TDD can assist in the design of a system rather than just testing the system.

There are a few best practices for using TDD. The first is the mantra "red/green/refactor," which defines the steps to developing a piece of functionality. If you write a test designed to fail and run it, it should fail. That's the red. You then write just enough code to make the test pass, which earns it a green designation when it passes. Finally, you refactor your code to clean it up prior to moving to the next piece of functionality. Another good practice is to ensure that all your test cases for a particular piece of functionality encapsulate the requirements of the code. That is, there shouldn't be any explicit requirements for a piece of code that aren't checked by the unit tests. That doesn't mean, however, that you must write unit tests to test trivial code. For example, simple properties that contain no validation logic do not normally need to be unit tested.

Unit Testing

To build clean, well-structured code, the developer needs some mechanism to ensure that the code written runs effectively. One solution is for the developer to write a piece of code and then run the application to see whether it works the way it should. The developer then moves on to the next piece of code, never coming back to test that functionality until it's close to the release date. You probably know someone who codes like this. And you might even be guilty of it yourself! Unit tests are a way to automate that method of testing so that the tests can be run repeatedly as the product is developed.

Unit tests involve designing a series of test cases that test whether the business logic is functioning correctly and whether inputs produce the expected outputs. To be complete, many unit tests might test the same piece of function code to ensure that all the branches and internal code flow are tested. We'll see how Visual Studio solves this problem when we talk about code coverage later. Because unit tests test basic functionality at the method level, they are considered to be a developer's responsibility and not the responsibility of the testing staff.

The support for unit testing runs deep in Team System and it gives developers the ability to quickly generate unit tests and unit test projects directly from a code skeleton. It's as simple as right-clicking a method and selecting Create Tests. (See Figure 6-14.) A test project is created, and a fully built skeleton of a unit test is generated for you. The unit test will be set up to return Inconclusive, and all the appropriate inputs and outputs are generated. You can then add the test code that will be used to test the functionality of your code. Often you'll need to create several unit tests to test one method. This is generally done by copying and pasting the previously created unit test. Although this frustrates many developers—specifically, those who believe Team System should automatically generate a larger number of unit tests—remember that a great deal of overlap often exists between two unit tests that test the same piece of code. Thus, one test can be fleshed out completely, and a copy/paste/edit of that test will often result in far less effort than editing a newly created skeleton.

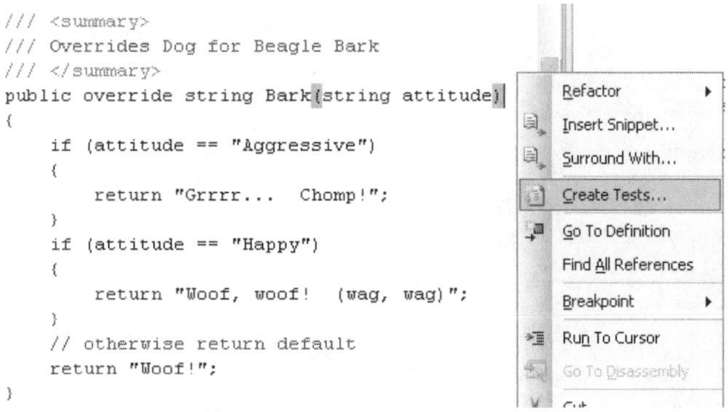

Figure 6-14   Creating a unit test from code

Once you've selected to build a unit test, a wizard guides you through the remaining steps. You can select which tests you'd like to generate, as well as which language the test project should be created in. (See Figure 6-15.) If you want, you can also change the defaults by clicking the Settings button. Doing this allows you to change how the projects and tests are created and named. (See Figure 6-16.)

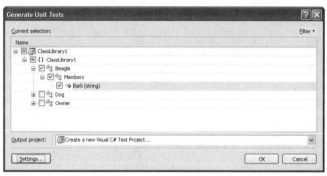

Figure 6-15   Generating unit tests for class members

Test Generation Configuration

Naming options

File Name: [File]Test.cs

Class Name: [Class]Test

Method Name: [Method]Test

General

☑ Mark all test results Inconclusive by default

☑ Enable generation warnings

☐ Globally qualify all types

☑ Generate tests for items that already have tests

☑ Enable doc comments

[OK]   [Cancel]

Figure 6-16   Configuring default unit test options

Once the unit tests have been generated, they can be edited to test for the desired functionality. Figure 6-17 shows a completed unit test for the *Bark* method on the *Beagle* class.

```
/// <summary>
///A test case for Bark (string)
///</summary>
[TestMethod()]
public void BarkTest()
{
    Beagle target = new Beagle();

    // TODO: Initialize to an appropriate value
    string attitude = "Aggressive";

    string expected = "Grrrr...  Chomp!";
    string actual;

    actual = target.Bark(attitude);

    Assert.AreEqual(expected, actual, "Bark did not return the expected value.");
}
```

Figure 6-17   The completed unit test on the Bark method

Finally, the unit tests are executed. This is done either in the Test Manager window or the Test View window. Both windows can be seen in Figure 6-18. From either of these windows, you can execute selected unit tests. In addition, the Test Manager window allows you to create groupings of tests that should be run together.

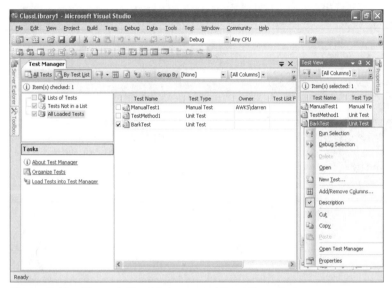

Figure 6-18   The unit Test Manager and Test View windows

Finally, when you've executed the tests, the Test Results window pops up and shows you the results of your test. (See Figure 6-19.) Hopefully, all your tests will have passed after you have built the code to implement those tests. Don't forget that although we demonstrated building tests for code that already existed, it's a best practice in TDD to build tests first for just the code skeleton and then actually implement the code.

Figure 6-19   Unit test results—passed!

Code Coverage

Writing unit tests is a critical tool for creating solid, quality code. However, developers need one additional tool to be sure that enough unit tests have been written. The code coverage tool built in to Team System provides a simple method to verify that the created unit tests are testing as much of the code as possible.

One of the nicest features of using the code coverage tool is that it demonstrates dramatically which areas of your code were not covered by the unit tests. After looking at the statistics that show how much code was covered, you can simply open the text view of your code to see every uncovered line highlighted in red and every line of code that was executed by a unit test highlighted in green. It's not just the complete methods that show up in red or green. The code coverage tool will highlight un-followed paths through the code inside of a method as well. For instance, you might test a path through an *if* statement but fail to test the path through the *else* portion. It will also highlight *try-catch* blocks that were not tested.

> **Tip**   The red and green code coverage indicators provide immediate and dramatic feedback. Reports are also important, in that they summarize the information on a broader scope and can provide even more useful information.

To run the test, ensure that code coverage is enabled for the DLL you want to test. You can do this by editing your current test run configuration file, which you'll find in Solution Explorer. Once code coverage is enabled, you can re-execute your unit tests to show how much of your code was covered. The Code Coverage window gives a summary of the results.

Once you've run your tests, you can also look at the code directly. The code covered by our single unit test will be only the first few lines and will be highlighted in green. The remaining code in the *Bark* method will be highlighted in red and is therefore not covered by our current set of unit tests.

Code coverage is a very useful tool; however, be aware that although a line of code is covered by a test, the test isn't necessarily sufficient to fully stress the code. For instance, you might have a unit test that tests an *AbsoluteValue* function that passes in a positive integer. This test would cover the code, but it would not test for a case in which a negative integer was passed in! Make sure that the tests you've written not only cover the code, but test all the required functionality of the solution as well.

> **Note**   Load testing is another type of test, specifically for the testers in your organization. These types of tests can be used to stress test your unit tests. You will learn more about this kind of test in Chapter 7.

Static Analysis

Creating quality code often involves analyzing code for known defects. In Visual Studio 2005 Team System, this is done through the use of static analysis. The static analysis tool found in Team System that analyzes .NET code is an evolution of FxCop. The static code analyzer runs against compiled code, looking for a large number of known defects and poor programming practices. In addition, it can be used to enforce corporate naming conventions.

The rules used by the static analyzer are fully extensible, and it's possible to add a new rule relatively quickly. It's also possible to enable and disable rules that will be run against the code. For instance, you might choose not to run the rules that enforce naming conventions but be very interested in the results of the tests that check for known security issues. Finally, you can choose whether a violation of a rule generates a warning or a compile time error. For coding conventions that absolutely must not be violated, using an error is the best practice and is one of the easiest to implement. Setting a violation of code analysis to an error, coupled with the built-in check-in policy that prevents code from being checked in unless it has compiled without error, result in an easy-to-implement yet very powerful technique for guaranteeing a certain level of code quality.

To use static analysis, it must first be enabled. It is enabled in the Project Properties window, under the Code Analysis tab. (See Figure 6-20.) Notice that you can enable and disable rule categories or even individual rules.

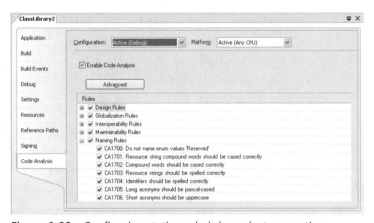

Figure 6-20   Configuring static analysis in project properties

Once you have the project set up for code analysis, all you need to do is recompile your application. This will cause the static code analyzer to run. The results can then be seen by looking at the Errors window. If a particular line of code caused the error, double-clicking the error in the Error window will open the appropriate code window and bring you to the offending line of code. In addition, the results are saved to CodeAnalysisLog.xml. Opening this file will show all the issues discovered during the compilation. (See Figure 6-21.) You can use this file to compare compilations across time.

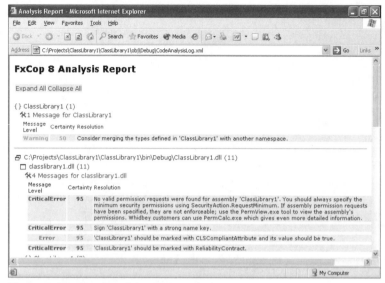

Figure 6-21   Results of the static analysis test

Profiling

After the code has been written, tested, and checked for known defects, it's time to profile your code. *Code profiling* is the process of analyzing how your code executes and where the majority of time is spent inside your code. Code profiling enables developers to measure the performance of an application and identify performance-related issues in the source code. You might have some relatively small method that is executed so often that the majority of time spent executing your code is spent in that method. Conversely, you might have a large, slow method that is called so infrequently that optimizing the performance of that code is virtually worthless. Determining where to spend valuable development time is critical!

To determine where to spend your time improving your code, you can use one of the two profiling engines built into Visual Studio. The two profiling methods are *sampling* and *instrumentation*.

In the sampling method, the profiler interrupts a running application at periodic intervals to determine which function is being executed. The profiler keeps track of the number of times that it was in that function by incrementing a counter. It also looks at the stack trace to determine which functions were called prior to that method. By interrupting the application hundreds, thousands, or millions of times, a statistical view of the application is generated. Although this method is not deterministic, it's a fairly reliable method of determining where an application spends the majority of its time. Once the application is stopped, a report is generated that provides the profile data.

The instrumentation method is more intrusive than the sampling method. In this method, the profiler inserts enter and exit probes into specific functions of an application.

These functions are now monitored when the application runs. The probes capture the deterministic performance metrics for the functions. This means that you get information about how long a method takes to execute. This method also provides a relatively complete numeric look at how often various methods are called. Once the application is stopped, a report can be generated based on the data gathered by the instrumentation profiler.

Determining which profiling engine to use is somewhat of an art, but there are good rules of thumb. The sampling method is far less intrusive than the instrumentation method, and thus allows the application to run at more normal speeds. It doesn't, however, provide a complete look at the data. For instance, although you can see how often the code appears inside a particular method, you cannot determine how long that particular piece of code takes to execute. Thus, the sampling method is often used as a first look at an application. With it, a developer can quickly determine where to focus attention in the short term.

The instrumentation profiles, on the other hand, provide for very specific performance metrics. However, this is very intrusive. This makes it appear as though the application is crawling when it is executed. Therefore, this method takes much longer to run enough functionality to fully profile the application. Thus, you'll generally use the instrumentation profiler at fewer intervals than the sampling profiler. However, the instrumentation profiler provides more specific and reliable information than the sampling method, and thus is an excellent tool to use at critical intervals during the development process.

Load testing should also be mentioned. It's somewhat related to profiling in that it deals with software performance. Load testing can also determine when an application might see a serious degradation of performance, or break altogether due to a peak number of requests per second or total number of users. This is highly useful for capacity planning, especially when a project starts to get popular with the users. In load testing, a developer tests the performance of an application when it's stressed by the expected average number and expected peak numbers of users. This form of testing is not available in Team Edition for Developers, only in the Team Edition for Testers and Team Suite editions of Visual Studio 2005 Team System.

Team Foundation Build

In addition to writing and running various quality and performance tests, another facet of the software development life cycle that often applies to developers is that of building the application(s). To have a successful software development life cycle project, it is important to employ an automated build system that should support the ability to build the software project at scheduled intervals as well as the ability to revert back to a previous build. A typical build scenario requires the need to execute tasks other than compilation only; for example, running unit tests as part of the build and deploying the compiled bits to a central location. Prior to Team System, this proved very difficult, if not impossible, to support in Visual Studio.

Open source tools, such as Nant, made a splash in the development community in their ability to support complicated build processes. Nant is a build tool framework that executes builds based on a set of instructions and tasks defined in an XML-based script. A task might include getting the latest source code from the source code repository, executing a set of unit tests, or copying files from one location to another. Nant was successful as a build tool because it had the ability to execute tasks, in a defined sequence, other than just compilation. The true reason why it was such a success, however, was because it was extensible. If a particular task didn't exist to support a step in your build process, you had the opportunity to create it and plug it into the Nant build framework. With its strong community backing, Nant provided a significant number of tasks to support complex build scenarios.

MSBuild is Visual Studio's new build engine that is very similar to Nant. As with Nant, MSBuild executes builds based on a set of instructions and tasks defined in an XML-based script. MSBuild is also extensible and supports a wide range of tasks to build your .NET solutions. The difference between Nant and MSBuild is that MSBuild is supported by Microsoft and will ship with the .NET Framework and eventually the OS. Team Foundation Build takes the MSBuild engine and extends it into a full build automation system.

Team Foundation Build is a flexible and extensible build automation system that forms a tight integration with the Team System tools. Team Foundation Build executes builds that are defined by a combination of scripts defined under a structure called a Build Type. You can define a number of build types for your Team Project to support various scenarios such as full builds, partial builds, nightly builds, incremental builds, and so on. Team Foundation Build includes an easy-to-use wizard interface to create your initial build types. The build type definition lays out a sophisticated build process that includes the following steps:

1.   Get source files from version control

2.   Run static analysis

3.   Compile sources

4.   Execute unit tests

5.   Update work items

6.   Calculate code coverage

7.   Calculate code churn

8.   Generate build reports

9.   Drop binaries into predefined location

> **Note** If all of your requirements are not fully supported by the default build type, you have the opportunity to modify and extend the process to fit your needs. Be sure to read Chapter 9 for more information.

At the conclusion of a build, Team Foundation Build produces a comprehensive report that outlines the general health of the build. Some of the items reported might include the changesets included in the build, errors and warnings from the compilation process, unit test results, code coverage, and static analysis results. As your project progresses over time, the combination of build reporting data allows you to monitor and track your product quality from the early stages of development to the day you deploy your application. With its integrated features and comprehensive reporting capabilities, Team Foundation Build provides a richer implementation model for building .NET applications over other tools such as Nant.

Build Type

Utilizing Team Foundation Build for your build process begins with the creation of a build type, which is a set of files that combine to define the conditions under which a solution or set of solutions is built. The build type maintains a set of parameters that informs the build service how to perform the build. These parameters include information such as which solution or set of solutions to build, which solution configurations to use, what build machine to use, where to perform the build, where to copy the build output to, what tests to perform (if any), and whether or not to perform code analysis.

Creating a Build Type

Creating a build type begins by invoking the New Team Build Type Creation Wizard. (See Figure 6-22.) This wizard can be launched from the Team Build node in Team Explorer or from the Build menu. The first step in creating a build type is defining a name for the build type, for which Team Foundation Build will uniquely identify this build with the other build types defined for your Team Project.

Build types are defined to build a solution or set of solutions in your Team Project. The solutions that are available to be included in a build type are the ones that exist in the version-control system for your Team Project. Figure 6-23 shows the Solution Selection page of the wizard. Solutions are listed based on a selected workspace. After a workspace has been selected, the solutions found within that workspace are listed. You have the option to select one or more solutions to participate in this build. The solutions will be built based on the order they appear in this list. Solutions that depend on one another should be placed in the correct order. For example, if Solution1 depends on Solution2 to be built before it, you must move Solution2 to the top of the list by highlighting Solution2 and using the arrows to position it within the list.

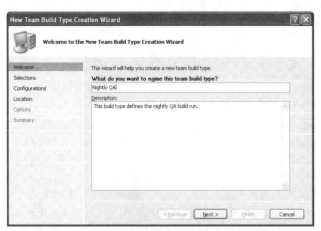

Figure 6-22   New Team Build Type Creation Wizard provides an interface to defining the build steps and parameters needed to perform a build

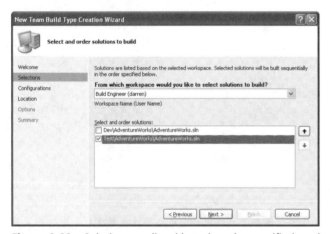

Figure 6-23   Solutions are listed based on the specified workspace, and selected solutions are built sequentially based on the order they appear in the list

A Visual Studio solution maintains one or many configurations that define various parameters and have a direct effect on how projects within the solution are built. Each configuration has a sole purpose in determining how the underlying compiler compiles the projects within the solution. These configurations define items such as conditional compilation constants and acceptable warning levels. Typical configurations that exist in any given Visual Studio solution are Debug and Release.

After the solutions have been selected for the build type, you have the opportunity to select which configurations of the selected solutions should be processed. (See Figure 6-24.)

The Team Foundation Build Service is a Windows service application that accepts requests from the Team Foundation Server to execute a specified build type. A build machine is defined as a machine in your build lab that is running the Team Foundation Build service. Figure 6-25 shows the page in the wizard in which you specify the build machine that will be responsible for executing the defined build type. You also specify a build directory that exists on the build machine. This build directory is the location that the build service will first synchronize the source files to and then execute the build against. A Universal Naming Convention (UNC) share called a drop location is specified as well. The drop location is where all of the built binaries and log files are copied to after the build has completed.

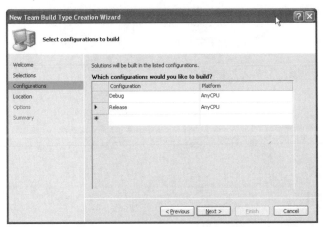

Figure 6-24   Select the configurations that should be processed for the defined build type

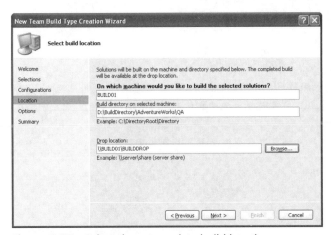

Figure 6-25   Select the appropriate build location

> **Note**   Both the build directory and drop location must have significant permissions for the build to execute successfully. The user assigned to run the Team Foundation Build Service must have write access to each directory and write access on the share permissions for the drop location.

A successful build isn't one that just compiles; it should compile as well as pass a number of tests to verify the functionality performs as expected. A Build Verification Test (BVT) typically consists of a broad variety of unit tests that are used to verify the overall quality of a build. Figure 6-26 shows the list of options to include in your build process, including running tests and performing code analysis.

All the test metadata files defined in your Team Project are available for selection. After a test metadata file is selected, you can then choose which test lists to run as part of the build. In addition to running tests as part of the build, you also have the option of running code analysis, which checks conformance to design rules defined within your Team Project. The test results and code analysis results are collected and combined in the final build report.

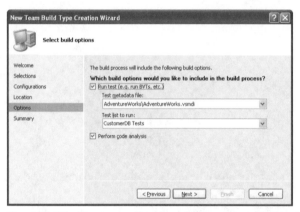

Figure 6-26   You can optionally select to run a set of tests or perform code analysis

Executing a Build

To execute a build, click the Build menu inside Visual Studio and select Build {Team Project Name}. This displays the Build Configuration dialog box, in which you have the opportunity to select which build type you want to run. After you select a build type and click Build, a request is sent to the Team Foundation Server, which in turn sends the request onto the build machine specified in your build type. You can track the results of your build request or view the results of prior build requests on the Team Builds screen. (See Figure 6-27.)

Name	Build Status	Build Quality	Completed On
Nightly Build Verification_050802.00001	Failed	Unexamined	8/1/2005 5:09:...
Nightly Build Verification_050801.00001	Failed	Unexamined	8/1/2005 3:41:...
Build QA_050729.00001	Failed	Under Investigation	7/28/2005 5:0...
Build Dev_050725.00001	Successfully Completed	Lab Test Passed	7/25/2005 12:...

Figure 6-27   Build results are shown with their status along with the date and time they were completed on

Viewing the Build Results

The Team Builds screen displays the build requests that have been processed, with their status and the date and time of completion. Builds that have completed will have a status of either Successfully Completed or Failed. To view the results of a build, double-click the particular build run you want to view. The build report then displays. (See Figure 6-28.)

Figure 6-28   The build report shows how your build fared

The build report displays a number of items, including the status of the build, the build machine on which the build was executed, the time the build started and completed, and the links to the drop location and the build log file. The build report also links the associated work items and changesets, as well as the results from any optional test runs and code coverage analysis.

Reports

Developers, as well as every other stakeholder in a project, need to understand how to use the reporting capabilities of Team Foundation Server. Team Foundation Server automatically analyzes much of the data that is generated by the development process, including metrics gathered directly on the code that developers check in and out of version control.

These reports cover everything from a simple list of all the current bugs in the project, all the way through to sophisticated tools that analyze how often the code base is changing, as well as many reports in between. Each report is geared to a different audience or to provide different data. A Bug List report is very useful for looking at bug details and understanding where effort should be expended next. The report is not at all graphical, however, and it's difficult to get a broad understanding of where the project is heading. A Bug Rates report, on the other hand, shows graphically the progress being made in eliminating bugs. (See Figure 6-29.)

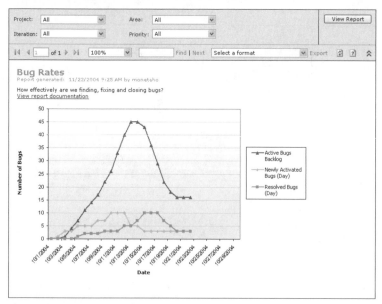

Figure 6-29   An example Bug Rates report

Developers should be intimately familiar with virtually all of the reports. The My Bugs report shows the developer which bugs they are currently assigned to, and the Builds report shows the results of builds that have been run against the entire code base. If automated builds are run every night, it's good practice for a developer to check this report every morning to see whether the project is still building correctly, or if some tests failed and the code needs to be fixed.

> **Note**   Remember that one developer's code might inadvertently break other code that has already been checked in, and this problem might not show up until all the tests are run during a nightly build.

The Test Result Details report can show more details about the tests that failed during a nightly build, and the Quality Indicators report can show areas that need attention.

Reports can be viewed in a number of ways. Most likely, developers will view the reports right from within the Visual Studio integrated development environment (IDE). To do that, simply use Team Explorer and open up the Reports folder under the project that you're working on. The entire list of reports is available there. Double-clicking any of the reports opens up the report in a new window inside the work area.

You can also view the reports by going to the project portal and clicking on the Reports link of the Quick Launch bar located to the left of the Web page.

Note   Because the project portal is built using Microsoft SharePoint® technologies, it is very easy to configure for each individual project, so the link to the reports might appear elsewhere on the site if it has been reconfigured. Be sure to read Chapter 9 for more information on customizing and extending the project portal.

Impact on Code Development

When developers first learn of check-in policies, code analysis, unit testing, and test-driven development, they often despair that they will never be able to be as productive as they were when they could just develop without restrictions. In some cases, developers have legitimate worries. If a developer is a superstar and only rarely creates a bug, why should unit tests have to be built to verify and cover the code? The developer will argue that building unit tests and having to deal with check-in policies will halve the amount of code that can be created.

These restrictions placed on developers by their project managers, architects, and senior developers serve an important purpose, however. Even if every individual developer writes fewer lines of code each day, the project will likely be completed earlier than it normally would have been without these restrictions. This paradoxical result is easily explained. Even superstar coders end up creating code that, by necessity, interacts with the code created by other developers. Although everyone strived for loose coupling, it can never be completely achieved. That coupling means that a change in one person's code can break the code created by another, or at the very least, break a feature that depended on a particular interface. This means more debugging and more testing, both of which take up a considerable amount of time, especially if the issues are discovered late in the development life cycle.

When developers are restricted to following best practices and a particular development methodology, they might feel less productive and more restricted at first. After all, they have to fulfill a number of tasks that may not seem directly related to implementing customer features. However, most developers soon learn that these restrictions actually allow them far more flexibility than they were accustomed to because a strong unit test harness and good practices allow them to make desired changes in their code (refactoring) without having to worry that their changes will create undetected breaks in code somewhere else in the system. If, during refactoring, some code is broken, it will show up immediately when all the unit tests are run, allowing developers to actually become more productive and have considerably more freedom. In an ad hoc development process, developers were tied very tightly to existing code and existing interface, mostly out of fear because (as most developers are aware) making a change to an interface usually involved considerable time tracking down all the impacts in the code. And even then, some impacts were missed, only to be found late in the development life cycle—either by testers, or more upsettingly, by users.

An analogy is car brakes. Why do you put brakes on a car? Is it so you can drive more slowly? NO! You put brakes on a car so you can drive faster more safely. If you lost the brakes on your car, chances are you wouldn't drive very fast at all (only as fast as your fenders could easily handle). That's where we are in software development without a process. With brakes, we can drive far faster because we're confident in our ability to slow down quickly when circumstances warrant. When we develop with a process, we're more like a car with brakes: We can develop faster with the knowledge that if we make a mistake or something changes, we can recover easily, quickly, and safely. After only a few months of development within a smoothly running process, most developers are converts.

The problem is that historically, the process has been very difficult to integrate smoothly. Instead, process was often implemented outside of the development environment, forcing developers to leave their IDE and enter data about what they just did. Nothing is as frustrating to a developer as reentering data or entering data in a different package that could have easily been tracked without any effort if their environment supported it. This is where Visual Studio Team System is so valuable. By integrating process smoothly, inside of the developers' preferred tool, developers can focus on writing code, not on reporting on what they've done. Visual Studio Team System also makes it easy to adopt a process because the integration with the code development area is outstanding.

Summary

Visual Studio 2005 Team System is a great tool for developers. It provides a vastly expanded tool set over previous versions of Visual Studio, especially as those tools relate to the developer. After developing code using tools found in Visual Studio Team Edition for Developers, you'll likely find it difficult and unpleasant to go back to any other development environment.

Using Visual Studio Team Edition for Developers, in conjunction with other role-based editions of Visual Studio 2005 Team System, can dramatically increase the productivity of an enterprise coding team, and Team System will definitely assist you in becoming a more productive developer.

Chapter 7
Testers

In this chapter:

Viewing Work Items 156

Managing Tests 157

Testing in Visual Studio 2005. 159

Test Results and Tracking Bugs 170

Summary. 172

Microsoft® Visual Studio® 2005 Team System is the first version of Visual Studio to include a suite of testing tools designed specifically for testers. These tools support testing throughout the entire software development and maintenance life cycles. In the past, testers have typically relied on third-party products to create and execute tests. Organizations have had to implement custom processes and solutions to coordinate defect tracking and resolution between developers, testers, and managers. This chapter explores the features of Microsoft Visual Studio 2005 Team Edition for Software Testers that support testers in their efforts to create and run tests, record test results, delegate failed tests back to developers, monitor test statistics, and publish test reports.

It's important to recognize that there are many types of testers, and even more types of tests, involved in software development. Before I discuss the specific tools in Team Edition for Testers, we'll look at some of these types of tests, as well as their varying requirements. One common method used to visualize these categories, called the "V" model, is shown in Figure 7-1. This model associates each phase of software refinement, from the justification of a business case to the construction of individual development artifacts, with a class of testing. Testing scenarios addressed directly by Team Edition for Testers are surrounded by a dashed box.

Notice that unit testing is not included as one of these scenarios. This is because unit testing, as well as other testing-related activities such as code coverage and profiling, is generally performed by developers. Developer-centric testing features are addressed in detail in Chapter 6.

Integration and system testing focus on the interaction between various parts of a system. They also verify that the application meets operational requirements such as performance and scalability of both the code base and system infrastructure. For example, an online commerce application might have a shopping cart subsystem and a customer profile subsystem. Although the classes and components in each subsystem are tested individually with unit testing, you would also need to ensure that changes to a user's profile that are made during a cart check-out process are handled correctly. In addition, you would need to verify that the check-out process continues to perform acceptably as the user load increases and as the amount of persisted data in the user profile data store increases over time.

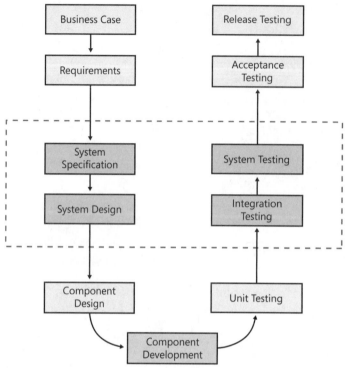

Figure 7-1   The "V" model, which illustrates the relationship between the phases of development and testing

The rest of the chapter will examine the specific tools provided by Team Edition for Testers to address these types of issues. You will also see how Team Edition for Testers provides a predictable and flexible environment for collaboration between developers and testers throughout the product development life cycle.

Viewing Work Items

The testing process starts with a tester creating a test for some aspect of the system. The trigger for this activity will generally be a new work item. This would typically be a task and might possibly be accompanied by a notification from the alert system. Based on the work item's requirement, the tester will create the appropriate kind of test and include it in an appropriate test list. In some cases, the tester might need to create and assign a new work item for another team member to review the test. After the new work item is reviewed, the tester can run the tests, record any defects, and then close out the work item(s).

This section examines how testers can create and manage their tests and then examines each type of test.

Managing Tests

Team Edition for Testers provides a variety of ways to view and manage your tests:

- Test Manager—the primary user interface (UI) for testers
- Test View—a lightweight, focused view of specific tests
- Test Project—a Visual Studio project acting as a test container
- Test Results—where all test results are displayed

Test Manager

Test Manager is typically a tester's primary UI when it comes to creating, locating, running, and managing tests. It provides a highly customizable view of all the tests in the system that supports standard grouping, sorting, filtering, and column-selection features. In Figure 7-2, you can see that Test Manager provides a single interface for all types of tests. Test Manager also allows you to define custom test lists so that you can manage and run tests as a group. For example, Figure 7-2 shows two lists defined on the left that contain the tests for the Shopping Cart and User Profile application subsystems.

You have the flexibility to create categories around any criteria. For example, you might create one list that contains a critical unit test that runs as part of a build-verification process that runs hourly. You can also add additional columns to the Test Manager display to show important information, such as the test owner, priority, and links to any associated work items.

You can find Test Manager by clicking Windows—Test Manager under the Test menu.

> **Note** One piece of information that is not available in Test Manager is the status of any currently executing tests. You can view test execution status—Pending, In Progress, Passed, or Failed—in the Test Results window, which we'll discuss in more detail later.

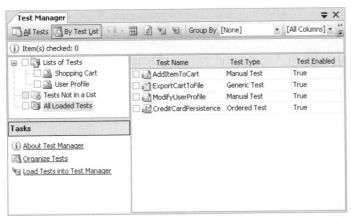

Figure 7-2 Test Manager provides a powerful interface for locating, organizing, and running tests

Test View

Although Test Manager provides comprehensive access to all loaded tests, sometimes you might want a simpler view that provides lightweight access to just a focused subset of tests. Test View provides exactly that experience. Figure 7-3 shows Test View displaying some tests. You can run, debug, open, or delete individual tests from Test View. You can also add new tests, but you cannot view or manage lists.

You can find Test View by clicking on Windows—Test View under the Test menu.

Figure 7-3   The Test View window presents a simplified interface to manipulate specific tests

Test Projects

Visual Studio 2005 Team System introduces a new project type called a *test project*. Test projects are designed to provide a familiar container to hold one or more tests. Although testers should not have to interact directly with a test project often, it's still important to understand that all team system tests belong to a project. Perhaps the greatest benefit of this design is that test projects the test they contain can be stored in Visual Studio 2005 Team Foundation Version Control just like any other project artifact. This means your tests get all the benefits of version control, such as revision auditing, versioning, and rollback. This applies to all test types, not just unit tests. For example, if someone incorrectly modifies the HTTP request in a Web test, you can always find out who made the change and even retrieve a previous version of the test from Team Foundation Version Control. Figure 7-4 shows Solution Explorer with a test project.

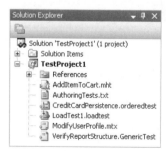

Figure 7-4   A test project and its files in Solution Explorer

> **Tip**   Although testers certainly can open tests from Solution Explorer, they'll likely feel more comfortable using Test Manager.

Testing in Visual Studio 2005

Visual Studio 2005 provides many types of tests for testing your application's functional and operational requirements. This section examines some of these types in detail.

Authoring Tests

Creating a test in Visual Studio 2005 begins by invoking the new Add New Test Wizard, which can be launched from various windows, including Test Manager, Test View, and even the code window. Figure 7-5 shows the Add New Test Wizard and test types available to a C# Test Project. Any new test can be associated with an existing test project or be placed in a new C#, Microsoft Visual Basic®, or C++ test project.

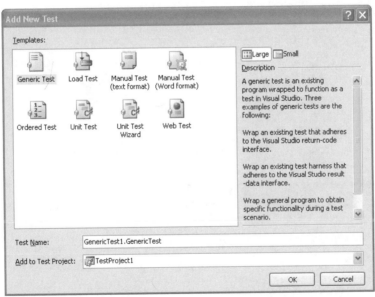

Figure 7-5   The Add New Test Wizard, which presents various test types to add to your test projects

Visual Studio 2005 Team Edition for Testers supports many types of tests:

- Unit—a programmatic test that calls class methods and verifies the return values (discussed in Chapter 6)

- Manual—used by a test engineer rather than automated by Visual Studio

- Generic—allows existing testing applications to be wrapped up in Visual Studio

- Web—makes calls to any HTTP application to verify its functionality

- Load—executes simultaneous and repeated tests for any automated test, such as unit, web, generic, or ordered

- Ordered—allows you to set up an ordered list of tests to be executed sequentially

Each test type has an associated designer, and in some cases a wizard, to guide you through the creation steps.

Manual Tests

Integration and system testing are generally performed by testers in a Quality Assurance (QA) group. Integration and system tests typically consist of scripted instructions that a tester follows to exercise specific features and integration points within an application. These scripts usually take the form of text documents stored in some repository. They are called "manual" tests because a human tester must manually execute each step in the script and record the results. Because the tools and repositories used for manual testing are typically separate from those used for automated unit testing, developers and testers end up learning and managing two separate processes for running tests and tracking bugs. Visual Studio 2005 Team System solves this disparity by treating manual tests as first-class project artifacts and fully integrates them into the test-running and defect-tracking systems.

Manual tests are implemented as either plain text files or Microsoft Office Word documents. Figure 7-6 shows the default Word document provided for new tests. You can choose not to use the default document, though, and create your own templates instead. Visual Studio 2005 automatically launches Word when a new manual test is created so that test writers can work with a tool they're familiar with. In addition, you can apply the importing features in Word to ease migration of existing test scripts into Team System.

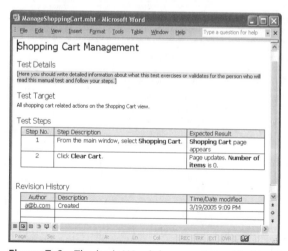

Figure 7-6   The basic Word document provided by Team System for use with manual tests

If you decide to create a text-based manual test instead of using Microsoft Word, you will be presented with this template to edit:

```
To the Test Author

This template provides a structure you can use to create a manual test.

** What is a manual test? **

A manual test is a description of test steps that a tester performs. Typically, manual
tests are used when the test steps are difficult or time-consuming to automate, or cannot
be automated--for example, to determine a component's behavior when network connectivity is
lost. Visual Studio 2005 Team Edition for Software Testers treats manual tests the same as
automated tests. For example, it displays manual tests in the Team Test windows. It also
tracks manual test results the same way it tracks automated test results, and displays them
in the Test Results window.

** Using this template **

Modify the "Test Title" text to provide a two- to three-word description of your test. Under
the "Test Details" heading, describe what this manual test will verify. For "Test Target",
describe the specific functionality that this test will exercise. In the "Test Steps" table,
describe exactly what steps to take, and in what order, to complete the test. For each step,
state the result that the tester should expect. The "Revision History" table lists the
changes made to the test, who made the changes (an e-mail alias is often used), and when
each change was made.

----------

Test Title:

(Enter the test name here.)

Test Details:

(Provide the tester with detailed information about what this test exercises or validates.)

Test Target:

(Describe the functionality that is being tested.)

Test Steps:

(Provide the tester with step-by-step instructions that explain how to complete the manual
test.)

Step No.      Step Description                    Expected Result

Revision History:

(Record the revisions that you and others make to this test.)

Author        Change Description          Time/Date modified
```

Testers begin the process of executing a manual test by running it from within Test Manager, just as with any other type of test. Visual Studio launches the manual test runner, which displays the test script and provides input options to record the results of the test. (See Figure 7-7.) The test run result information is maintained in the Team Foundation Server database separate from, but associated with, the test script. The status of the test remains Pending until the tester saves the results with either Pass or Fail. Upon completion of the process, a work item can be created for a failed test result and assigned to a developer.

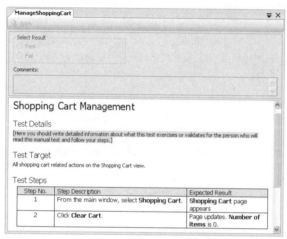

Figure 7-7   Running a manual test in Test Manager to ensure that test status and results are captured by Team System and included in team and managerial reports

Generic Tests

Generic tests provide a mechanism to integrate with existing automated testing technologies or any other technologies that do not integrate directly into Visual Studio 2005. For example, you might have an existing tool for automating user interface testing. Although Visual Studio 2005 Team System does not provide its own mechanism for Windows Forms testing, you can create generic tests that wrap your existing testing tool. This feature allows you to execute the tests and record the results in Visual Studio with the rest of your tests.

There are three categories of tools that you can wrap up into generic test:

- A test that adheres to the Visual Studio return code interface
- A test harness that adheres to the Visual Studio result data interface
- A generic program to obtain specific functionality during a test scenario

One scenario where generic tests can be useful is in the automated testing of install and uninstall scripts. You could create a generic test that invokes the installation program with a particular set of parameters. If the test passes, you know the program installed successfully. A second generic test could run the uninstall program. If the test passes, you know the uninstall program ran without error. You could then run a third test, either unit or generic, that verifies that the application was fully uninstalled by checking registry entries, directory structures, and so on.

Figure 7-8 shows the Generic Test Designer. At a minimum, you must provide the executable to invoke. There are many other optional settings, such as command-line arguments, additional files to deploy with the test, and environment variables.

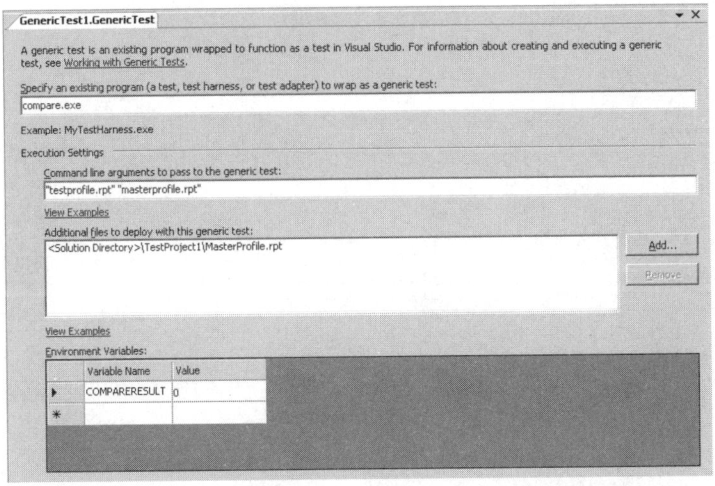

Figure 7-8   The Generic Test Designer, which provides many options for defining how to invoke the external resource

In addition, you can specify some interesting behaviors of the generic test. For example, you can set the working directory, capture the redirection of the test's standard output/error streams, choose to display the testing application, set time-outs, and specify a summary results file. Figure 7-9 shows these additional settings.

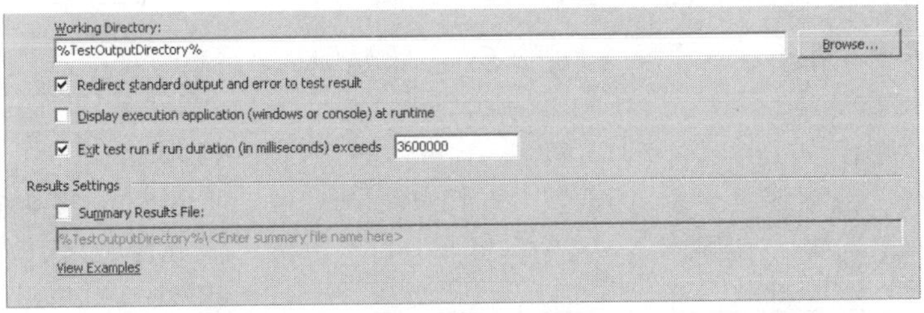

Figure 7-9   Additional settings that you can specify for a generic test

This example shows a test that will execute an application that compares two files and returns their differences. The wrapped-up application, compare.exe, is a hypothetical third-party tool that specializes in comparing text files. A previous report creation test created the testprofile.rpt file, and we expect the testprofile.rpt file to be identical to our masterprofile.rpt file that is part of the solution and deployed with the test. When the test runs, any output from compare.exe will be included in the test results and any return code other than 0 will be recorded as a failure.

Figure 7-10 shows the results of a failed generic test that used ping.exe to attempt to ping an irresolvable Host. All results are captured in the Team Foundation Server database and automatically made available to the developer assigned to fix the defect, as well as other team members who have the appropriate permissions.

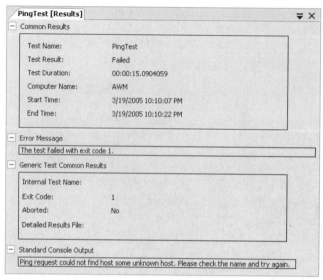

Figure 7-10   Test output from a failed generic test (Notice that both the standard error and output information were redirected to the test harness and captured by Visual Studio.)

Web Tests

Without an automated system, when a tester wants to test a specific page of a Web site, such as a search page, he or she would have to follow a manual script to navigate to the search page, enter a query value into a field, submit the page, and evaluate that the return page contains the expected results. Each time changes are made to the search system, a tester will need to manually re-execute the test. A Team System Web test allows you to automate the testing of Web-based interfaces by recording browser sessions into editable scripts. You can then add value to the scripts with features such as validation and data binding. These scripts become persistent tests that can be run at any time, individually, in groups, or as part of a load test.

> **Note**   If you used the Application Center Test (ACT) that shipped with Microsoft Visual Studio 2003, the Web test should be familiar to you.

When you create a new Web test, Visual Studio launches the Web Test Recorder, which is simply Microsoft Internet Explorer extended with a utility that records each HTTP request sent to the Web server as the tester interacts with the application. Figure 7-11 shows the Web Test Recorder in the middle of a session where the user is testing the search feature of a Web site. You can pause the recorder if you need to perform an action that should not be captured as part of the script. You can end the recording session by clicking the Stop button, at which point Visual Studio will open the test in the Web Test Designer.

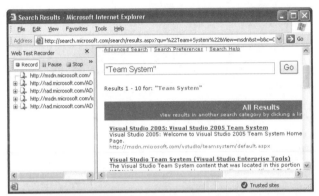

Figure 7-11   The Web Test Recorder, which automatically captures all requests in a browser session

The Web Test Designer allows you to examine and modify a Web test by exposing the details of each HTTP request, including its headers, query string parameters, and post parameters. You can even create and insert entirely new requests from scratch, as well as get (query string) or post (form) parameters, file upload parameters, transactions, validation rules, and comments. Taken together, these features let you modify your test as requirements change, without forcing you to re-record the entire script. Figure 7-12 shows the Web Test Designer for the recorded test described earlier with some of the various nodes expanded.

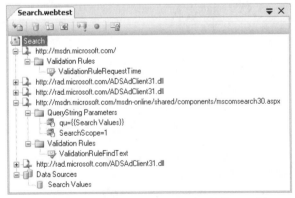

Figure 7-12   The Web Test Designer, which provides access to the details of each request and allows you to add validation and data binding

Typically, you write tests, especially Web tests, not just to test the load of the system but to validate that the execution provided the expected results. Web tests allow you to validate your results by attaching validation rules to requests. Although these rules appear in the designer attached to HTTP requests, they're actually used during execution to validate the HTTP response returned for that request. In Figure 7-12, you can see that validation rules have been applied to two requests. The first rule verifies that a response is received within a specified amount of time. The second rule verifies that the response contains some expected value or expression. You configure validation rules through the Properties window.

Visual Studio 2005 Team Edition for Testers provides the following built-in validation rules:

- *ValidationRuleFindText*—verifies the response contains (or doesn't contain) some specific text; supports regular expressions and case sensitivity

- *ValidationRuleRequestTime*—verifies the response is received in a specified amount of time

- *ValidationRuleRequiredAttributeValue*—verifies that an attribute of a tag is a certain value; supports case sensitivity

- *ValidateRuleRequiredTag*—verifies that a certain tag exists; supports a minimum occurrences value as well

In Figure 7-12, you can also see a Data Sources node at the bottom. Web tests support the ability to data-bind request parameters, such as query-string parameters or form-post parameters, to data sources so that the test uses different values each time it's executed. For example, if you were to run this search test multiple times, perhaps as part of a load-testing scenario, it would be much more valuable if different search terms were used with each execution. You can enable exactly this behavior by defining a data source that points to a column in a database table and binding the appropriate request parameter to that data source. In Figure 7-12, you can see that the "qu" query string parameter on the request to the search component is bound to the "Search Values" data source. Each time this test is executed, the runner will select another value from the data source to use as the search term. You can configure the binding to retrieve values randomly or sequentially.

The Web Test Runner, shown in Figure 7-13, displays the results of executing a Web test. For each top-level request, the list view displays its validation status, HTTP status, response time, and transferred bytes. You can drill into each request to view the details of all dependent requests, or you can select a request and view its details in the tabs on the bottom half of the screen. The Web Browser tab displays the response as rendered in Internet Explorer, and the Details tab displays information regarding any validation rules and exception information. You can see in Figure 7-13 that the first request failed to return a response in the time defined by the validation rule. Also notice that there are links for defining client characteristics such as browser type and network bandwidth. We'll discuss client profiles in more detail in the Load Tests section.

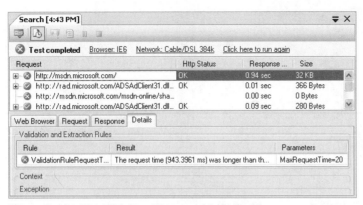

Figure 7-13   The Web Test Runner, which provides convenient access to all the details of a test run

Load Tests

Load tests allow you to simulate an environment where multiple users are interacting with an application simultaneously. The primary purpose of load testing is to discover performance and scalability bottlenecks in your application prior to deployment. It also enables you to record baseline performance statistics that you can compare future performance against as the application is modified and extended. Of course, to analyze performance trends over time you must have a repository in which to store all the performance data. Visual Studio 2005 Team Edition for Testers provides robust design tools, a high-performance execution engine, and a reliable repository for creating, running, and analyzing load tests.

The creation of a load test starts with you running the New Load Test Wizard. This wizard steps you through the process of defining a load test scenario. A scenario includes definitions of the load profile, test mix, user profile, browser mix, network mix, counter sets, and run settings. An example of the results of running the New Load Test Wizard is displayed in Figure 7-14.

The test mix defines which tests are included in the load and how the load should be distributed among them. These tests must have already been created by this point. You can include any automated test type—that is, anything other than manual tests. You then define what percentage of the total load should be executing each test.

The load profile defines how the runner should apply the load to the application. For example, you can select Constant Load, in which case the runner immediately starts with a full load as defined by the maximum user count setting. This option is useful for testing peak usage and system stability scenarios, but it does not help in examining a system's scalability. For scalability scenarios, you can select Stepped Load, which allows you to specify a starting user count, step interval, step user count, and a maximum user count. The runner will increase the load by the step user count after each step interval until the maximum load is reached. With a stepped load, you can examine how performance of various parts of the system changes as user load increases over time.

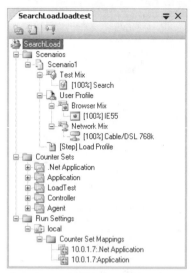

Figure 7-14 The Load Test Designer, which allows you to modify the results of running the New Load Test Wizard

For Web tests, User Profile allows you to define the browser and network types the runner should simulate. Again, you can define multiple types and assign a distribution percentage to each. Browser types include various versions of Internet Explorer, Netscape/Mozilla, Pocket Internet Explorer, and smartphone profiles. The available network types range from various dial-up speeds through LAN connections.

After defining your profiles, you have to decide which information is important for you to collect during the load test and which machines to collect it from. You do this by creating Counter Sets, which are a collection of Microsoft Windows® performance counters, and applying them to specific machines. Advanced users can even define threshold rules and apply them to specific counters. This feature allows the runner to show threshold violations in the test result data. Creating these sets can be a complicated task, as it requires a thorough understanding of the various platform counters: .NET, IIS, and SQL. However, Team System provides some default Counter Sets to simplify the creation of basic tests.

The final step in defining your load test is to specify the test's Run Settings. These settings govern how the runner will execute the test, such as how often it will sample the performance counter data, how it will handle errors, and log test results. You can also specify the total run duration and the maximum number of errors to log details for. These settings are also where you specify which database or XML file the test results should be saved in.

When you run a load test, Visual Studio will display the performance counter data in real time in the Load Test Runner. Figure 7-15 shows a load test in progress. You can add and remove counters from the graph as the test is executing. The Counter's tree view will also display warning and error indicators when a threshold is passed on a particular counter.

In Figure 7-15, you can see that a counter in the Overall group has passed a threshold that represents some key performance indicator. All the data captured by the runner is then logged to a database and made available through Team Services reports to managers and team members.

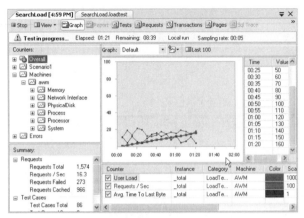

Figure 7-15   The Load Test Runner displaying load test results in real time

Visual Studio 2005 Team Edition for Software Testers Load Agent

Microsoft sells a separate product, apart from the Visual Studio 2005 Team Edition for Testers, to enable organizations to simulate more users and more accurately test the performance of the Web applications and servers. The Load Agent is licensed per processor and is used to generate load on a Web farm and simulate as many as 1,000 users per processor.

The Load Agent is composed of two pieces:

- Team Test Load Agent—the load front end
- Team Test Load Controller—the controller, running remotely, and called by the front-end

Ordered Tests

An ordered test is simply a container that holds a list of other tests and guarantees a specific execution order. You can create and execute ordered tests.

Before creating an ordered test, you must have other tests available to include in the ordered test. After selecting the test(s) you wish to group together, you can change their execution order by using the up/down arrows on the far right side of the designer. (See Figure 7-16.) You can add the same test multiple times to the same ordered test. When you do this, the test will be run as many times as it appears in the ordered test, in the order listed.

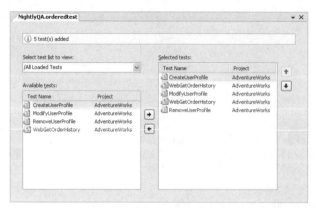

Figure 7-16 The Ordered Test Designer being used to create a QA test run

Tip Ordered tests can contain other ordered tests. You can use this to your advantage by constructing smaller, more focused ordered tests and then chaining them together in a specific order to test broader functionality.

Test Results and Tracking Bugs

Executing any kind of test generates some results that testers will use to determine whether a defect exists or if a Quality of Service requirement wasn't met. These situations will require action. All test results for recently run tests are available through the Test Results window. Figure 7-17 shows the Test Results window with results from running a variety of the tests mentioned in the last section. You can quickly identify which tests have run, are in progress, and are awaiting execution. You can also easily identify which tests have passed and those that have failed.

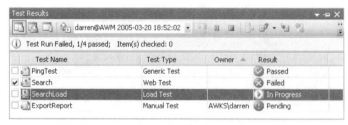

Figure 7-17 The Test Results window displaying execution status and results for all test types

Double-clicking a test displays either the results for that test if it has completed or the appropriate runner if the test is in progress. From a failed test, a tester can easily create a bug work item and assign it to a developer. The developer can query for this work item or, if properly configured, he or she will receive a notification (such as an e-mail) indicating that a new work item has been assigned. The developer can then easily retrieve the recorded test results. After the developer fixes the bug and marks the work item as completed, he or she could generate a new task work item asking the tester to rerun the test.

Bug work items can also be tracked by managers through the many queries and reports provided on the project portal Web site. Achieving this level of collaboration is what Visual Studio 2005 Team System is all about. This type of communication and workflow can really help maintain or increase the predictability of a project's success.

Microsoft will include many reports related specifically to testing:

- Test run results in general

- Tests that passed (but that have associated bugs that are still showing as active)

- Tests that failed (but that have associated bugs that are currently closed)

- Test effectiveness (showing a combined list of test results and the resulting code coverage numbers)

Test Run Configuration

Test run configurations affect how your tests run. When you define a test run configuration, you determine, for example, the way test runs are named, where the tests are executed, and whether unit tests generate code-coverage information. Figure 7-18 shows a Test Run Configuration file being edited and a remote server being specified as the location where the tests will be run remotely.

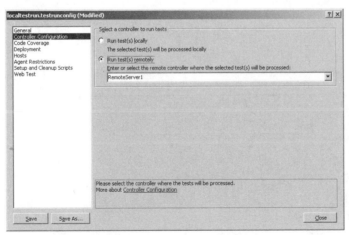

Figure 7-18   A Test Run Configuration file being edited

Run configuration settings are saved to disk in files with the .testrunconfig extension. You can create and save multiple run configurations, and then make a specific run configuration active, which is the run configuration that is used when tests are run. Only one run configuration can be active at a time. Your choice of an active run configuration is maintained from one user session to the next.

If your project is missing its test run configuration, you can add a new one to the solution (not to the test project!). Simply right-click on the solution in Solution Explorer, add the new item, and select Test Run Configuration as the template. This happens more commonly when you configure a Unit Test project for Code Coverage. In other words, if you choose Edit Test Run Configurations under the Test menu, you might see the "No Test Run Configurations Available" message.

Summary

Visual Studio 2005 Team Edition for Testers provides extensive testing tools for Quality Assurance testers that require no understanding of code. This suite of tools allows developers and testers to use a single environment for all their automated and manual testing. This level of integration ensures that all defects are recorded and available to team members through Visual Studio and the project portal Web site. This integration and visibility ensures that you can work together with developers and managers to drive quality into your applications.

You can use manual tests to address scenarios that require manual execution of test scripts. Generic tests allow you to execute any application with a command-line interface as a test. This is often the preferred way to reuse any existing test assets that cannot or will not be converted to new tests. Web tests enable the automated testing of Web interfaces, and they can be incorporated into load tests to ensure that a Web site meets its performance-related operational requirements.

Part III
Methodologies and Extensibility

In this part:

Chapter 8: Microsoft Solutions Framework..175

Chapter 9: Customizing and Extending Team System 211

Chapter 10: Wrapping It Up: The Endgame and Deployment.......247

This part of the book offers some good reference and wrap-up chapters. By now, you've been introduced to Microsoft Visual Studio 2005 Team System and seen its capabilities and features by each team member role. I will expose you to a few more topics before I can expect you to achieve a high level of Team System productivity.

Regardless of the methodology you choose, you should be familiar with the Software Development Life Cycle (SDLC). SDLC is a generally accepted workflow for constructing software. If you've ever been part of a software development effort, you'll probably recognize many of its tenets. It is interesting to see how the Microsoft Solutions Framework (MSF) 4.0 methodologies support SDLC.

As I've said before, the customization and extensibility of Team System will be critical to its success in the marketplace; therefore, I'll expose you to some key extensibility points, such as Team Foundation Server, Visual Studio tools, and methodology templates. Finally, you should know how to wrap up a project (or at least an iteration) and know about Team Build, deployment, closing down an iteration, running reports, and continuing to track and report bugs throughout the application's lifespan.

Chapter 8
Microsoft Solutions Framework

In this chapter:

What's New in MSF 4.0. 177

MSF for Agile Software Development 186

MSF for CMMI Process Improvement 193

Implementing MSF 4.0 with Team System 208

Summary. 210

Up until now, this book has focused on the *tools* that Microsoft® Visual Studio® 2005 Team System offers for managing the software development process. Let's step back now and take a closer look at the process itself. Regardless of team or project, every software development effort goes through a sequence of activities to produce a product. This sequence of activities is commonly referred to as the software development life cycle (SDLC).

Visual Studio 2005 Team System acts as a powerful engine for managing your SDLC. This extremely flexible tool can be configured to support a variety of software development processes. This flexibility is essential, but it requires you to make important choices about how you want to configure and use Team System. If Team System were a jet aircraft, the question would be, "How do I fly this thing?" This is where the Microsoft Solutions Framework (MSF) comes in. It's a flight manual. More accurately, MSF helps you solve a common problem: "How do I build and deliver my product within schedule and budget?"

The Microsoft Solutions Framework (MSF) version 4.0 is a metamodel for describing an SDLC. This framework can be instantiated into one or more prescriptive methodologies (or processes) that reflect the specific needs of your organization. We'll explore what this means in a moment. But first let's give it some historical perspective.

MSF is the product of an evolutionary process. First introduced in 1994 as a collection of best practices from Microsoft product-development efforts and Microsoft Consulting Services engagements, MSF has evolved based on lessons learned from successful, real-world experiences of Microsoft product groups, Microsoft Services, the Microsoft internal Operations and Technology Group (OTG), Microsoft partners, and customers.

Now a robust and mature framework, MSF is managed and developed by a dedicated product team within Microsoft, with guidance and review from an international advisory council of subject matter experts. MSF continues to draw upon current Microsoft experience. Teams within various Microsoft lines of business regularly create, find, and share best practices and tools internally. The knowledge gained from these internal project efforts are consolidated and distributed outside of Microsoft through MSF.

MSF and Team System

Software development teams often perceive software development methodologies as an impediment to productivity. Usually this perception occurs because the team must deal with poorly integrated tools that were never meant to support the methodology. As a result, the developers struggle with the methodology and come to view the additional effort as an unproductive waste of time. Visual Studio Team System addresses these realities with a set of integrated process tools that can be easily configured to match the methodology.

With the introduction of Visual Studio Team System, Microsoft provides your development team with a powerful set of tools for managing the entire software development life cycle, from initial planning to deployment. Visual Studio Team System extends the Visual Studio integrated development environment (IDE) with a set of tools for workflow management, architectural design, software testing, version control of source files, data collection, and metrics reporting.

Although MSF offered many useful best practices for the software development process, it became clear that the true value could not be realized without proper integration of the tools required to enact the process. Now that you have this powerful new suite of tools, how does your development team make the best use of it? This is where the MSF comes in.

Each MSF process template for Visual Studio Team System includes work item tracking, security settings, process guidance, process reports, source check-in policies, document templates, and a Microsoft Windows® SharePoint® Services (WSS) site template configured to support the MSF processes.

Visual Studio Team System comes with two MSF process templates: MSF for Agile Software Development and MSF for CMMI Process Improvement. MSF for Agile Software Development is geared toward an adaptive process for smaller teams that don't require a great deal of ceremony. MSF for CMMI Process Improvement, however, is geared toward a refinement process for larger teams that require a more structured approach. Both versions of MSF are based on a highly iterative, adaptive, agile software development process. The main difference is that MSF for CMMI Process Improvement meets the requirements for the Software Engineering Institute's (SEI) Capability Maturity Model Integration (CMMI) Level 3 and provides a smooth transition all the way to Level 5.

Agile development methods have proven the test of time. Agile methods delivers superior results in less time through short development cycles, pervasive unit testing, continuous integration, and most importantly, a strong focus on the customer. MSF 4.0 builds on proven agile development techniques by being the first agile methodology that covers the entire software development life cycle and all the team roles. Also, MSF 4.0 is the first methodology to implement CMMI by combining agility with formal quality assurance.

Choosing a Process Template

If your organization does not have an established software development methodology, your best bet is to use one of the pre-built Visual Studio Team System process templates. Although Visual Studio Team System includes the MSF process templates in the box, you can choose from a variety of other process templates developed by Microsoft partners. Third-party templates include the following:

- Avenade Connected Methods—dAvanade Inc.
- Feature Driven Design—Cognizant Technology Solutions
- Scrum—Conchango

Note   Remember, too, that you can also modify an existing template or create your own.

Perhaps your organization has invested in developing its own methodology. Visual Studio Team System protects that investment by enabling you to create a custom process template that expresses your organization's methodology. Be sure to read Chapter 9 for more information.

Whether you start with a prebuilt template or a custom template, Visual Studio 2005 Team System builds on your investment by enabling your organization to update the process template, at the end of the project, based on lessons learned. At project conclusion you can roll all of the important changes back into the original template. You can then use this new, altered template on future projects.

Note   On longer projects, the development team might decide to make midcourse corrections to the methodology. If this is required, and depending upon the level of change required, you may need to start a new team project, after having altered the methodology template. Branching from the old project's source code might be an option in this case.

What's New in MSF 4.0

MSF 4.0 is a descriptive framework. In fact, the MSF 4.0 framework is similar to MSF 3.0 in many respects, but here's the big difference: MSF 4.0 also includes the aforementioned prescriptive methodologies: Agile and CMMI Process Improvement. One way of looking at it is to consider these methodologies as instances of the framework. These prescriptive methodologies are implemented in Visual Studio 2005 Team System.

Descriptive vs. Prescriptive

A descriptive SDLC model documents the process passively, from the point of view of an observer. Descriptive models are useful as the basis for understanding and improving software development processes. A prescriptive SDLC model, on the other hand, describes the process in terms of the players involved, the sequence of activities, and the end products. If software development is like baking a cake, the descriptive model is a narrative that contains useful guidelines for baking cakes in general, while the prescriptive model is the recipe for baking a particular cake, say, German chocolate (my favorite). Put yet another way, a descriptive model can be translated into one or more prescriptive models, and each prescriptive model can be translated into action.

The MSF 3.0 framework and the MSF 4.0 metamodel are structurally similar. They both contain foundational principles, a team model, a process model, and disciplines. As you might expect, MSF 4.0 makes changes to these components based on the current state of the art, but these changes are incremental in nature. Because the notion of incremental improvement is built into MSF, it makes sense to apply that philosophy to MSF itself. We'll briefly review the changes to each of the MSF components before examining the MSF 4.0 metamodel in detail.

> **Note**   The MSF 4.0 framework is often referred to as the MSF 4.0 metamodel. The terms *framework* and *metamodel* are interchangeable, although Microsoft appears to prefer the term *metamodel* in MSF 4.0. We'll use the term *metamodel* from here on.

MSF 3.0 contains eight foundational principles:

- Foster open communications.
- Work toward a shared vision.
- Empower team members.
- Establish clear accountability and shared responsibility.
- Focus on delivering business value.
- Stay agile, and expect change.
- Invest in quality.
- Learn from all experiences.

MSF 4.0 includes all the foundational principles in MSF 3.0 and adds two more:

- Partner with customers.
- Always create shippable products.

The Team Models for both MSF 3.0 and MSF 4.0 describe a team of peers with shared responsibility, clear accountability, and open communications.

MSF 3.0 describes team member roles in terms of the following Role Clusters:

- Product Management
- Program Management
- Development
- Test
- User Experience
- Release Management

MSF 4.0 replaces the term *Role Cluster* with *Advocacy Groups*, where each Advocacy Group has a Constituency with representation on the team. The MSF 4.0 Advocacy Groups are identical to the MSF 3.0 Role Clusters except that MSF 4.0 adds another Advocacy Group: Architecture. (See Figure 8-1.)

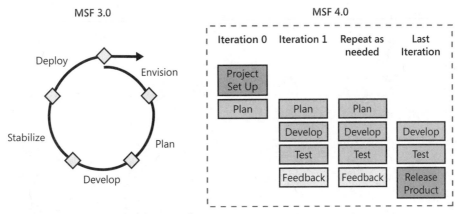

Figure 8-1   Process Model comparison

The MSF 4.0 Process Model builds on MSF 3.0. It includes the same iterative development process, including a setup iteration at the beginning and a release iteration at the end of the project cycle. The MSF 4.0 Process Model is definitely an improvement because it more accurately reflects the complete life cycle of a development project.

MSF 3.0 includes three disciplines: Project Management, Risk Management, and Readiness Management. Disciplines tend to be prescriptive in nature, and they can vary significantly from one methodology to the next. For this reason, the MSF designers chose to remove disciplines from the metamodel altogether and add them to the methodology process guidance instead. You can find the MSF 3.0 disciplines more or less intact in the process guidance for MSF for Agile Software Development, but the disciplines in the process guidance for MSF for CMMI Process Improvement will more closely reflect the Capability Maturity Model (CMM) Key Practice Areas for a Level 3 organization.

CMMI, CMM, and Key Practice Areas will be covered later in the chapter.

MSF 4.0 Key Concepts

MSF 4.0 was built on a foundation of key concepts that inform the methodology. These concepts fall into four major groups: principles and mindsets, the team model, cycles and iterations, and governance. Let's examine each group in more detail.

Principles and Mindsets

MSF 4.0 principles describe the behavior of highly effective software development teams. These principles are divided into core ideas and mindsets. The core ideas embody an overall philosophy, whereas the mindsets suggest a way of thinking that motivates the actions of individual team members.

Principle: Partner with Customers   Customer validation is often the difference between real and fictional business value. Understanding the value proposition of your solution and communicating it effectively are key success factors.

Principle: Foster Open Communications   To maximize members' individual effectiveness and optimize efficiencies in the project, information has to be readily available and actively shared.

Principle: Work Toward a Shared Vision   Having a generally long-term and unbounded vision inspires the team to rise above its fear of uncertainty and preoccupation with the current state of things and to reach for what could be.

Principle: Quality First   Quality requires both bug prevention and solution verification. Utilize practices such as code analysis and buddy reviews to prevent bugs as well as to maximize the testing to find bugs. All roles are responsible for the prevention and verification of bugs.

Principle: Stay Agile, Adapt to Change   The more an organization seeks to maximize the business impact of a technology investment, the more it ventures into new territories that are inherently uncertain and subject to change. This uncertainty requires the team to stay responsive to changing conditions and unanticipated situations.

Principle: Always Create Shippable Products   The team should be committed to creating the highest-quality product while making changes. Each change should be done in the context of the belief that the product should be ready to ship at any time.

Principle: Flow of Value   Plan, execute, and measure progress and velocity based on the delivery of increasing value to the customer and rising return on investment. Minimize those activities that do not add customer value because they are wasteful. Use iterations to maintain the cadence of work products that your customer can evaluate. Make the handoffs of work from one team member to another as efficient as possible.

Mindset: Quality Is Defined By Customers   Satisfied customers are priority number one for any great team. This satisfaction includes both internal and external customers.

A customer focus throughout development means having a commitment from the team to understand and solve the customer's business problem.

Mindset: Pride of Workmanship   Taking pride in contributing to a solution is an important part of creating a quality product. Motivation and a sense of responsibility result from this pride.

Mindset: Team of Peers   The "team of peers" mindset places equal value on each constituency. This mindset requires unrestricted communication between the roles, transparency, and a single visible backlog. The result is increased team accountability and effective communication.

Mindset: Frequent Delivery   Nothing establishes credibility like frequent delivery. It's more than having a nearly shippable product every day; it's about responding to the needs of your customers with small, quality deliverables that show progress. Through frequent delivery, process and infrastructure are proven and improved. Risks, bugs, and missing requirements are detected early. Feedback can be provided when it can make a difference.

Mindset: Willingness to Learn   Because each development project, environment, and team is unique, each project and iteration within the project creates a learning opportunity. However, there can be no learning without honest feedback and reflection. Unless there is a supportive environment that fosters courage and personal safety, feedback will be limited and not placed in a light of improvement. After these factors are in place, individuals and teams can focus on ongoing self-improvement, gathering a sharing of knowledge, and beneficial lessons learned. Additionally, there will be opportunities to implement proven practices of others and to commit time in the schedule for learning.

Mindset: Get Specific Early   Too many projects lose time because of people procrastinating about the "big" picture instead of tackling solvable problems. This mindset stresses taking one step at a time and learning from specifics rather than the abstract. Defining the project in everyday terms is a key to effectively building working code, passing tests, and creating deployable bits.

Mindset: Qualities of Service   A quality of service (QoS) mindset looks at the solution and develops plans based on every aspect of the customer experience. The idea is that qualities of service such as performance and security should not be considered late in the project but throughout it.

MSF 4.0 Structure

MSF 4.0 contains both descriptive and prescriptive components. (See Figure 8-2.) The descriptive component is called the *MSF 4.0 metamodel*, which is a conceptual description of SDLC best practices. The metamodel is not tied to any specific methodology—it can be implemented in various ways.

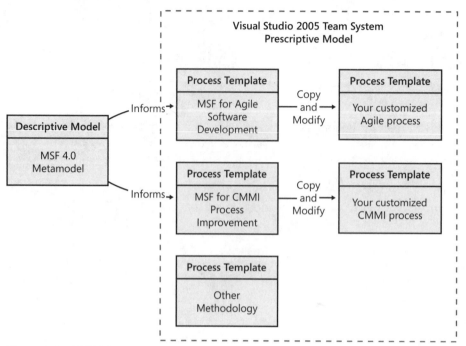

Figure 8-2   MSF 4.0 structure

MSF 4.0 implements the metamodel as prescriptive methodologies that provide specific process guidance. Team System comes with two MSF 4.0 methodologies: MSF for Agile Software Development and MSF for CMMI Process Improvement. You'll see how Team System implements these methodologies later in this chapter. But first, let's take a closer look at the MSF 4.0 metamodel and the two MSF 4.0 methodologies. Figure 8-3 shows the MSF 4.0 metamodel.

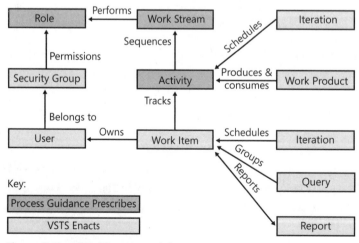

Figure 8-3   MSF 4.0 metamodel

The MSF 4.0 Team Model

The MSF 4.0 Team Model consists of peers who represent all the constituencies involved in the production, use, and maintenance of the product. There is no hierarchy involved—no team member is more important than another. There is, however, a reporting structure, but it is not that important in the context of the Team Model. This approach reduces risk by producing a system of checks and balances that guides the team toward the right solution.

Each team member acts as an advocate on behalf of the constituency that he or she represents. There are seven constituencies in the MSF 4.0 Team Model:

Product Management

Advocates for the Customer Business. Product management is responsible for project success from the standpoint of the customer requesting the solution.

Program Management

Advocates for Solution Delivery. Program management is responsible for delivering the solution within project constraints.

Architecture

Advocates for Systems in the Large. Architecture is responsible for ensuring that the solution is correct in terms of its place in the business or product family road map, its ability to interoperate with other services, and its compatibility with the infrastructure in which it will be deployed.

Development

Advocates for the Technical Solution. Development is responsible for designing and building the solution, including unit tests and providing estimates as needed to program management.

Test

Advocates for Solution Quality from the Customer Perspective. Test is responsible for identifying and reporting any issues that diminish the solution quality in the eyes of the users or customers.

User Experience

Advocates for the Most Effective Solution in the Eyes of the Intended Users. User experience is responsible for understanding the user's context as a whole and ensuring that the rest of the team keep the user experience in mind.

Release/Operations

Advocates for the Smooth Delivery and Deployment of the Solution into the Appropriate Infrastructure. This group is responsible for the timely readiness and compatibility of the infrastructure for the solution.

The MSF 4.0 Team Model, which you can see in Figure 8-4, can be scaled to fit various projects. For small projects, each team member might represent multiple constituencies. Larger projects can be organized into a team of smaller MSF teams.

Figure 8-4   MSF 4.0 Team Model

> **Note**   Working in a team of peers is not always easy. There's an art to making a team of peers work well. It requires a great deal of collaboration, negotiation, and effective communications, as well as clear ground rules that all the team members buy into. For really useful information about creating an effective team, I recommend *The Team Handbook, Third Edition* by Barbara J. Streibel (Joiner/Oriel Inc., 2003).

MSF 4.0 Cycles and Iterations

The MSF 4.0 Cycles and Iterations describe a process model consisting of a series of short development cycles. Small iterations support continuous learning and refinement, reduce the margin of error in estimates, and enable incremental testing and delivery of the product.

The first iteration deals with the startup activities associated with a new project—typically project planning and setting up the development and test environments. Each subsequent iteration focuses on implementing specific features of the system, resulting in a stable, functional version of the product. Each incremental version of the product might be an unreleased alpha test version, released to the user community as a beta test version or released as a functional incremental version that can begin delivering value immediately. Each iteration often includes testing deployment procedures as well. The final iteration involves the transition of the product from development to production. This transition includes final acceptance testing and deployment. Figure 8-5 shows you the MSF 4.0 Cycles and Iterations.

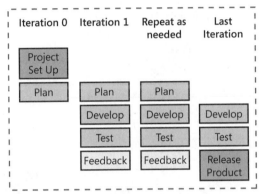

Figure 8-5   MSF 4.0 Cycles and Iterations

MSF 4.0 Governance

Governance refers to the executive decision-making process that allocates software development resources based on the flow of value. MSF 4.0 defines five tracks that roughly correspond to phases in the project. Each track concludes with a governance checkpoint, a go/no-go decision point that provides an opportunity to authorize continued work on the project or to cancel or suspend the project.

Do not confuse tracks with the Cycles and Iterations described earlier—they deal with the operational aspects of the project (the day-to-day activities). Tracks, on the other hand, deal with organizational governance—the allocation of resources. Another way to think of it is that Cycles and Iterations produce tangible work products, whereas Governance tracks produce decisions.

It's interesting to note, though, that tracks and iterations are related. Looking at Figure 8-6, you can see that each iteration involves one or more tracks, and the tracks involved give each iteration its focus.

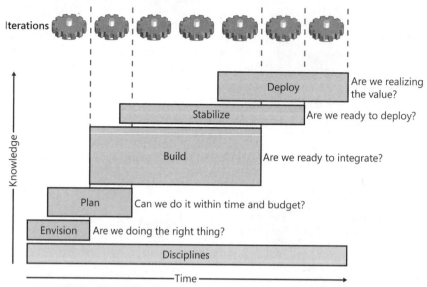

Figure 8-6   MSF Governance

MSF for Agile Software Development

MSF for Agile Software Development is a prescriptive implementation of the MSF 4.0 metamodel designed for rapid development using adaptive techniques. This methodology uses best practices from the emerging agile development movement.

Roles

MSF for Agile Software Development implements the Team Model by prescribing a team of peers that represent all the constituencies involved in the project. Each team member assumes one or more of the following roles:

- **Business Analyst**   Defines the business opportunity and recommends the solution to realize the opportunity. The business analyst works with the customers and other stakeholders to understand their needs and goals and translates those into *persona*—fictitious characters that represent the cross-section of typical users, described in terms that are relevant to the project.

- **Project Manager**   Delivers business value within the agreed schedule and budget. The project manager is charged with planning and scheduling duties, including developing project and iteration plans, monitoring and reporting status, and identifying and mitigating risk. The project manager is also expected to consult with business analysts to plan scenarios and QoS requirements for an iteration, consult with architects and developers to estimate work, consult with testers to plan testing, and facilitate communication within the team.

- **Architect**   Ensures success of the project by designing the foundations of the application. This includes defining both the organizational structure of the application and the physical structure of its deployment. In these endeavors, the architect's goal is to reduce complexity by dividing the system into clean and simple partitions. The resulting architecture is extremely important because it not only dictates how the system will be built going forward, but it also establishes whether the application will exhibit the many traits that are essential for a successful project. These include its usability, whether it is reliable and maintainable, whether it meets performance and security standards, and whether it can be evolved easily in the face of changing requirements.

- **Developer**   Implements the application as specified within the planned time frame. The developer is also expected to help specify the features of physical design, estimate the time and effort to complete each feature, build or supervise implementation of features, prepare the product for deployment, and provide technology subject-matter expertise to the team.

- **Tester**   Discovers and communicates problems with the product that could adversely affect its value. The tester must understand the context for the project and help others to make informed decisions based on this context. A key goal for the tester is to find and report the significant bugs in the product by testing the product. Once a bug is found, it is also the tester's job to accurately communicate its impact and describe any workaround solutions that could lessen its impact. The tester makes bug descriptions and the steps for re-creating the bugs easy to understand and follow. The tester participates with the entire team in setting the quality standards for the product. The purpose of testing is to prove that known functions work correctly and to discover new product issues.

- **Release Manager**   Manages the rollout of the product. The release manager coordinates the release with those constituents who are responsible for operations or media control. The release manager also creates a rollout plan and certifies release candidates for shipment or deployment.

> **Note**   On smaller teams, it might be necessary for team members to assume multiple roles.

Work Item Types

A work item is a database record that Visual Studio 2005 Team Foundation uses to track the assignment and state of work. Each work item is assigned to a work item type. MSF for Agile Software Development includes the following items:

- **Scenario**   This item records a single path of user interaction through the system. As team members attempt to reach a goal, the scenario records the specific steps that they will take. Some scenarios will record a successful path; others will record an unsuccessful one. When writing scenarios, be specific. Because an infinite number of possible scenarios exist for all but the most trivial systems, you must be discerning when deciding which scenarios to write.

- **Quality of Service (QoS) Requirement**   This item documents the required characteristics of the system, such as performance, load, availability, stress, accessibility, serviceability, and maintainability. These requirements usually take the form of constraints on how the system should operate.

- **Task**   This process template item communicates the need to do some work. Each role has its own requirements for a task. For example, a developer uses development tasks to assign work derived from scenarios or QoS requirements to component owners. The tester uses test tasks to assign the job of writing and running test cases. A task can also be used to signal regressions or to suggest that exploratory testing be performed. Finally, a task can be used generically to assign work within the project. On the work item form, certain fields are used only in cases when a task relates to a particular role.

- **Bug**   This item communicates that a potential problem exists or has existed in the system. The goal of opening a bug is to accurately report bugs in a way that allows the reader to understand the full impact of the problem. The descriptions in the bug report should make it easy to trace through the steps used when the bug was encountered, thus allowing the bug to be easily reproduced. The test results should clearly show the problem. The clarity and understandability of this description often affects the probability that the bug will be fixed.

- **Risk**   This item documents and tracks the technical or organizational risks of a project. When concrete action is required, these risks might translate into tasks to be performed to mitigate the risk. For example, a technical risk can set off an architectural prototyping effort. The team should always regard risk identification in a positive way to ensure contribution of as much information as possible about the risks it faces. The environment should be such that individuals identifying risks can do so without fear of retribution for honest expression of tentative or controversial views. Teams creating a positive risk management environment will be more successful at identifying and addressing risks earlier than those teams operating in a negative risk environment.

Work Streams

Each work stream is characterized by entry criteria, activities, and exit criteria. MSF for Agile Software Development defines the following work streams by role:

Business Analyst

- **Capture project vision**   Getting a project started requires the clear establishment of the project vision. Capturing and communicating this central vision is the most important element to keeping a project focused. During the project, this vision might change as a result of the business or project climate. If change occurs, you'll have to realign the project to the new vision. From the vision, you begin to understand who the users will be. Usage patterns and goals of these users will be captured using personas. You'll also understand whether the project is driven by date or by content. The vision and its related activities create the solid foundation on which a project can be built.

- **Create a scenario**   Scenarios capture the functional goals of the system. To find these goals, examine the unique needs for each persona of the system. These goals can be initially listed and later written as scenarios. For each of these goals, also consider the scenarios that might result from unsuccessful or nonoptimal attempts to reach the goal. Scenarios are created through brainstorming, lifestyle snapshots, or exploratory testing, and they are added to the scenario list. Scenarios are prioritized and written when they are scheduled for an upcoming iteration. Scenario creation is complete when all the scenarios scheduled for delivery in an iteration or architectural prototype are written.

- **Create a QoS requirement**   Quality of Service requirements are used to capture nonfunctional requirements or constraints on the functionality of the system. QoS requirements must be precise and not subjective in their definition. The requirements are identified, prioritized, and if scheduled for the current iteration, written.

Project Manager

- **Plan an iteration**   To plan an iteration, determine the right balance of scenarios, QoS requirements, and bug allotments for the upcoming iteration. The amount of work that can be done in an iteration is limited. The scenarios and QoS requirements with the biggest business value are prioritized for inclusion in the current iteration. An initial iteration plan is created using the estimated scenarios and QoS requirements. After the scenarios and QoS requirements are part of the iteration plan, they are written up by the business analyst as scenarios. Developers and testers then divide the scenarios into tasks and create more detailed estimates. The new detailed estimates are used to load balance the tasks assigned to developers. The iteration planning meeting brings together the appropriate business analysts, project managers, and developers to finalize the iteration plan.

- **Guide project**   To guide a project, progress must be constantly monitored and reported. Changes should be made as necessary to keep the project on track. The progress being made within an individual iteration as well as the overall project progress should be tracked. Bugs and risks need to be identified and assigned a priority.

- **Guide iteration**   Similar to guiding a project, but just for a particular iteration. Within the iteration, the project manager must monitor the progress of those tasks relating to the scenarios and QoS requirements of that iteration.

Architect

- **Create solution architecture**   A good architecture has a clean and simple internal structure for the major elements of the application. A simple structure reduces the complexity of the application. The architecture can define structural elements that enable the application to better handle changing requirements and allow areas of the application to develop independently. Good architecture also takes advantage of layering to increase structural reliability and decrease time to market. When technology risks pose a threat, prototyping can be used to mitigate those risks and provide greater insight. Finally, security and performance are architectural concerns for which work must be done over the entire system.

Developer

- **Implement a development task**   A development task is a small piece of development work that stems from a QoS requirement or scenario. Implementing a development task involves adding the appropriate new functionality to the architectural form of the system. After the development task has been completed, it must be unit-tested, reviewed, code-analyzed, integrated, and checked in to the existing code base. The scenario or QoS requirement is then passed on to test.

- **Fix a bug**   A bug indicates a potential need for corrective work on already implemented work product—typically source code. Fixing a bug might result in no action beyond a change of state of the bug, or it might result in changes to code. To prevent bug fixes from disrupting working code, the bug-fixing process must be systematic and controlled. After a bug fix has been completed, the changed code must be checked against the design and coding guidelines, unit tested, reviewed, integrated, and checked in. The bug owner follows all code requirements that pertain to the affected code, as well as the design concepts and guidelines that drove the implementation. Failing to do so can cause the "fix" to be worse than the original problem.

- **Build a product**   A build compiles all new changesets and existing code into a single product. However, when a new set of changes is checked in to the build, it must be acceptable. The changeset must compile and pass build verification tests. Ensuring that the changesets added to the build do not cause problems is part of accepting a build. Each build contains a set of build notes that outlines all the new changes.

Tester

- **Test a scenario**   A scenario is divided into test tasks as well as development tasks. These tasks are assigned to testers to develop and run test cases. The assignment of a scenario to test indicates that the functionality has been integrated into a build and is ready to be tested. Validating that a build reflects the functionality envisioned in the scenario requires an understanding of the scenario and its boundary conditions. Validation tests must be written to cover the complete functionality and the boundary conditions of the scenario. Validation tests are run until none is blocked. Bugs are created to report any bugs that were found.

- **Test a QoS requirement**   The assignment of a QoS requirement to test indicates that the build reflects the constraint and is ready to be tested. Validating that a build reflects the constraints envisioned in a QoS requirement requires knowledge beyond the constraint. In many cases, scenarios are attached to the requirement to show the areas to be constrained. Testing a QoS requirement demands that performance, security, stress, and load tests be completed and that none be found to be blocked. Based on the test results, bug reports are created to document the issues discovered.

- **Close a bug**   A bug can be closed for several reasons. Once closed, no more work is done on the bug during the current iteration. Valid reasons for closing a bug include that it is fixed, deferred to another release, demonstrated invalid, not reproducible, or a duplicate of the bug already logged. Closing bugs usually occurs during triage or to verify a fix.

Release Manager

- **Release a product**   Releasing a product marks the end of an iteration of application development. If the project is date driven, allow time to "finish" the product. A rollout plan for the release is created. The release process and corresponding rollout plan differ depending on the type of product and whether it is for internal or external consumption. For externally released software products, marketing effort and sales collateral are often included. Internal systems require training and operations support. Each of these cases requires a different rollout plan.

Disciplines

Disciplines are non-technical areas of expertise that span the entire project and concern all members of the team. MSF 4.0 includes two disciplines: project management and risk management.

- **Project management**   A project is a venture of finite duration—it has a clearly defined beginning and end. *Project management* refers to the set of skills required to plan and control a project. These skills include planning, scheduling, managing scope, and managing cost. Although the Project Manager role assumes primary responsibility for project management, all the team members are expected to participate.

- **Risk management**   The MSF *risk management* discipline emphasizes taking a proactive approach to dealing with uncertainty, assessing risks continuously, and using risks to influence decision-making throughout the life cycle. The discipline describes principles, concepts, and guidance together with a five-step process for successful, ongoing risk management: identify risks, analyze risks, plan contingency and mitigation strategies, control the status of risks, and learn from the outcomes.

Qualities of Service

Quality as it relates to software takes many forms. MSF 4.0 organizes software quality into three categories: security, performance, and user experience. Everyone on the team should be conscious of the QoS requirements for the project and use these requirements to inform design, implementation, testing, and deployment.

- **Security**   This QoS becomes ever more important as software evolves into a distributed architecture. Security starts with threat modeling, which then drives the requirements for authentication, authorization, validation, and other security measures.

- **Performance**   This QoS relates to several aspects of performance. The most obvious performance considerations involve responsiveness, performance under stress, and availability. Performance can also include other aspects, such as serviceability and maintainability.

- **User experience**   This QoS relates to the quality of the application from the user's point of view. The user experience starts with overall ease of use, or usability. The user experience is also affected by the quality of the user documentation, training, and support.

Governance and Tracks

Governance involves the control of time and money relative to the flow of value for a project. MSF defines five governance checkpoints, each of which focuses on a specific question to answer. The activities and work streams leading to the checkpoints are called *tracks*. It's important to note that these tracks are not the same as the cycles within the MSF 4.0 Process Model shown in Figure 8-5. Rather, tracks group the activities that lead to governance checkpoints. Each track can span multiple iterations. Tracks also overlap and interact as continuous feedback occurs among activities in different tracks.

The MSF for Agile Software Development tracks are defined as follows:

- **Envision**   The envision track addresses one of the most fundamental requirements for project success—unification of the project team behind a common vision. The team must have a clear vision of what it wants to accomplish for the customer and be able to state it in terms that will motivate the entire team and the customer. Envisioning, by creating a high-level view of the project's goals and constraints, can serve as an early form of planning. As such, it typically occurs during the setup iteration.

- **Plan**   The plan track is where the bulk of the planning for the project is completed. Within this track the team prepares the functional specification, works through the design process, and prepares work plans, cost estimates, and schedules for the various deliverables. Each iteration also includes a planning cycle, where the team revisits the plan, makes adjustments as needed, and performs the planning specific to the iteration.

- **Build**   The build track is where the team accomplishes most of the construction of solution components (documentation as well as code). However, some additional development work might occur in the stabilization track in response to testing. The build track involves more than code development and software developers. The infrastructure is also developed during this track, and all roles are active in building and testing deliverables.

■ **Stabilize** The stabilizing track is where the team conducts testing on a solution whose features are complete. Testing during this phase emphasizes usage and operation under realistic environmental conditions. The team focuses on resolving and triaging (prioritizing) bugs and preparing the solution for release.

■ **Deploy** The deploy track is where the team deploys the core technology and site components, stabilizes the deployment, transitions the project to operations and support, and obtains final customer approval of the project. After the deployment, the team conducts a project review and a customer satisfaction survey.

■ **Continuous** These other five tracks are analogous to phases of a software development project. Continuous involves work streams and activities that occur throughout the duration of the project. These work streams and activities can occur in any iteration, from startup to release.

> **Note** Although these tracks may look a lot like the concept of phases from MSF 3.0, they have been completely reworked and are similar only in name.

MSF for CMMI Process Improvement

MSF for CMMI Process Improvement (MSF CMMI) is a lightweight, agile approach to CMMI. It's designed for organizations looking to achieve and maintain a CMMI Level 3 status, as defined by the Capability Maturity Model (CMM) developed by the SEI (an organization we will discuss shortly). Actually it's a stretched version of MSF for Agile Software Development, modified to include the process areas required by a CMMI Level 3 appraisal. Future versions of MSF for CMMI Process Improvement will be stretched all the way to CMMI Level 5.

Although MSF CMMI does not include a number of the traditional project management techniques—such as estimating and tracking, earned value, and critical path method (CPM)—it does offer guidance on incorporating these techniques by using the Microsoft Office Project interface to Team System.

The Capability Maturity Model Integration (CMMI) is not an SDLC model per se, but rather a process improvement framework. It was developed by the Software Engineering Institute (SEI), a federally funded research and development center sponsored by the U.S. Department of Defense. The foundation of the CMMI is the Capability Maturity Model (CMM), originally developed by SEI in the mid-1980s. The CMM was developed primarily as a tool for evaluating the software development capabilities of defense contractors, with the goal of avoiding the spectacular and costly failures that were all too common in those days. Using the CMM, the Department of Defense could objectively assess the "maturity" of a software development organization.

> **Note**   The SEI was founded by the United States Department of Defense in 1984 to formu-
> late methods and guidelines that help organizations efficiently create high-quality software
> that's delivered on time, completed within budget, and performs reliably. The SEI is operated
> by Carnegie Mellon University in Pittsburgh under contract to the Department of Defense.
> Although the SEI's primary customers are defense contractors, any organization is welcome
> to take advantage of the many resources available on their Web site: *http://www.sei.cmu.
> edu/cmmi*.

The CMM rates an organization's maturity on a five-tier scale. The various tiers are defined
as follows:

- **Level 1–Initial**   There are few stable software processes in evidence, and
  performance can be predicted only on the capability of individuals rather than
  organizational capability.

- **Level 2–Repeatable**   Planning and tracking of software projects is stable and earlier
  successes can be repeated.

- **Level 3–Defined**   The organization uses a defined software process, and software
  quality is tracked.

- **Level 4–Managed**   The software development process is measured and operates
  within measurable limits.

- **Level 5–Optimizing**   The entire organization is focused on continuous process
  improvement.

Each maturity level is composed of a set of key project areas (KPA). Each KPA is a
group of related activities that achieve a set of goals deemed important for establishing
process capability at that maturity level. For instance, the Level 2 KPAs are Requirements
Management, Project Planning, Project Tracking, Configuration Management, and Quality
Assurance. Get those right, and you're a Level 2 shop.

As it turns out, the CMM proved to be an excellent process improvement tool for large
software engineering organizations. Once an organization knew its current maturity level,
the CMM told it exactly which KPAs to work on to get to the next maturity level. In this way,
the CMM provided prescriptive guidance for process improvement.

As experience with the CMM grew, the SEI found that it needed to specialize the CMM
for various disciplines such as systems engineering, software engineering, software
acquisition, workforce management and development, and integrated product and process
development. So it developed a CMM for each of these disciplines. That solved one problem
but created another. Many organizations wanted to focus their improvement efforts across
the disciplines. However, the differences among these discipline-specific models made this a
difficult and costly proposition.

This is where the CMMI comes in. Its purpose is to combine several source models into a single improvement framework for use by organizations pursuing enterprise-wide process improvement. In the process of merging the models, the CMMI Product Team built a framework that accommodates multiple disciplines. MSF for CMMI Process Improvement offers a proven sequence of improvements, beginning with basic management practices and progressing through a predefined and proven path of successive levels.

Principles

Microsoft Solutions Framework for CMMI Process Improvement encapsulates a lightweight approach to formal software development and continuous process improvement. The method, which is rooted in the teaching of Edwards Deming and others, asks the team to focus on the difference between special cause variation and common cause variation in its software engineering practices. The method seeks to eliminate special cause variation through the use of frequent, high-bandwidth communication, aggressive issue management, and progressive risk management. Common cause variation is reduced, and productivity on valuable working software is increased by implementing improvement suggestions under controlled circumstances, and monitored and assessed using a standard set of metrics provided in the tooling. Like many agile methods, MSF for CMMI Process Improvement is focused on the flow of value to the customer in short cycles using small batches of requirements, but unlike agile methods, it introduces an extra dimension of variation reduction and elimination. The net result is a lightweight, agile, adaptive process for highly productive software engineering that provides a significant accelerator to achieving a CMMI Level 3 assessment and lays the groundwork for achievement of Levels 4 and 5 in future.

Following are the core ideas of MSF for CMMI Process Improvement:

Partner with Customers

The customer is the consumer at the end of the value chain. To maximize customer value, everyone in the value chain must partner by seeking to better understand customer value and share that information back up the value chain.

Foster Open Communications

To maximize individual effectiveness, encourage improvement suggestions, facilitate root cause analysis, and help eliminate special cause variations. Open, direct, high-bandwidth communication and information sharing must be a core to the culture to the team.

Work Toward a Shared Vision

Shared vision aligns the interests and work focus of all team members throughout the value chain. Collaboration is improved. A shared vision provides a framework against which decisions can be assessed and made by consensus.

Quality Is Everyone's Business, Every Day

Quality is everyone's business, every day. Quality encapsulates the ideas of pride of workmanship, right first time, and continuous improvement. Everyone on the team should understand variation and specifically understand how to measure and interpret the variation in their inputs, their rate of input, their working method, their lead time, and their rate of output. Eliminating special cause and reducing common cause variations should be everyone's business, every day. Suggestions for improvement could come from anyone, any time, and be implemented by a local consensus. Continuous improvement in productivity, on-time delivery, with agreed functionality, and within bug tolerance levels is more easily achieved when everyone on the team is contributing.

Stay Agile, Adapt to Change

Profits come from differentiation, and differentiation requires innovation. By its very nature, innovation is new and unknown, and innovative projects contain uncertainty. Uncertainty adds variation and change. Because change is a fact of life in innovative software development, the engineering method must be designed to cope gracefully with it.

Make Deployment a Habit

"Teams that learn to ship, ship!" is a saying commonly used in Microsoft product groups. It is important for risk management, eliminating special cause variation, and facilitating the flow of value to knock the kinks out of the delivery and deployment processes. By making deployment a habit and by practicing and testing deployment procedures, even with early life-cycle prototypes, the whole team learns how to make deployments run smoothly and predictably.

Flow of Value

Flow of value separates out the notion of a functional resource with a capacity from the flow of customer-valued functionality. A project is a collection of value scheduled for realization, whereas a functional resource has a capacity to create working software of value at a known pace or velocity. Focusing on flow of value means scheduling cohesive small batches of customer value for deployment at regular intervals and facilitating that flow by eliminating special cause variation. Meanwhile, functional managers responsible for capacity can focus on reduction of common cause variation in the method of software engineering and increasing capacity through continuous improvement of productivity measured as velocity.

Mindsets

A mindset is a framework for thought (also known as a paradigm). A mindset is defined by a collection of principles, which are abstract concepts used to guide and constrain concrete activities. When a team member is deciding how to act and is forced with a complex decision, principles provide a guiding set of constraints—a framework—within which to decide the correct course of action. Mindsets and principles of MSF should become ingrained in the mind of every team member. They should be referred to daily as team members make decisions to guide and steer the project, prioritize work, and interact with stakeholders.

Following are the mindsets of MSF for CMMI Process Improvement:

Quality Is Defined By Customer

Satisfied customers are priority number one for any team. The customer in this case is the end consumer of the product or service. There is only one customer in the value chain: the consumer at the end of the chain. Everyone on the team should be aware of the consumers for the product and be focused on delivering something that they need, want, and will derive value from. In MSF, consumers are defined using personas. A persona focus throughout development means having a commitment from the team to understand and solve the persona's problems. Once understood, real consumer involvement must be maximized to the degree possible to ensure that consumer expectations are aligned with the product features committed to for the project. Techniques that support setting and managing consumer expectations include reporting on the backlog, building small batch sizes (or highly iterative delivery), and high quality in terms of functioning without errors, but more so in terms of correct interpretation of the needs and wants of the persona and the consumers that the persona represents.

Pride of Workmanship

Pride of workmanship is core to any craft or profession. In software development, pride of workmanship is the notion that every team member involved in a product takes a deep, heartfelt care and passion in the quality of the finished product. Division of labor and 20th century mass-production thinking tended to weaken pride of workmanship. It was too common to simply throw the work to the next person in the chain and wait for the quality control department to reject the defects. Much of this thinking crept into software engineering with the idea that specialized analysts pass work to specialized designers, who pass it to coders, who pass it to testers, and so forth. Pride of workmanship in the quality of the end product was lost. MSF asks all team members to take pride in the quality of the end product and to do their best to ensure that Quality Assurance is embedded at every step in the life cycle.

Team of Peers

A team of peers implies that equal value is given to each constituency in the Team Model. Although different roles have different foci within different tracks, all constituencies are equally important to the risk management of the project and successful delivery of a quality product. A team of peers calls for team accountability and shared responsibility for effectiveness and project success.

Frequent Delivery

Early and frequent delivery builds trust among the team and externally with sponsors, business owners, and product consumers. Trust is the grease that lubricates a highly productive software engineering organization. Trust enables agility and reduces the need for verification, documentation, and checkpoints. The frequency of delivery should be tuned to the cadence of the business domain. In some domains, delivery every day makes sense, whereas in others it will be quarterly, biannually, or annually. There is a transaction cost to delivering a shippable product, and that cost must be understood and factored against the desire to make the frequency of delivery as short as possible. Frequent delivery reduces the batch size for an iteration or release, so the iteration or release cycle is shorter. Small batch sizes are good for risk management and also facilitate flow of value and quality. It is easier to keep a small batch moving; the number of issues and risks to monitor and resolve will be smaller. Quality is higher with small batches because each individual function receives better focus and attention from the team. Through frequent delivery, process and infrastructure are proven and improved. Risks, bugs, and missing requirements are detected early. Feedback can be provided when it can make a difference. Some keys to frequent delivery are keeping batch sizes small, working on deliverables in a "just-in-time" manner, and keeping options open by postponing decisions until the last responsible moment. This is embodied in the late planning techniques, which lock only fine-grained commitments at the start of each iteration. Frequent delivery enables quality, continuous improvement, trust, better flow, increased productivity, and overall better economic performance from the organization.

Willingness to Learn

Because each development project, environment, and team is unique, each project and iteration within the project creates a learning opportunity. However, there can be no learning without honest feedback and reflection. Unless there is a supportive, risk-tolerant environment that fosters personal safety, feedback will be limited and cannot facilitate continuous improvement. After a framework is in place to facilitate learning, individuals and teams can focus on continuous improvement, gathering and sharing of knowledge, and root-cause analysis of special cause (or chaotic) events that disrupt plans, schedules, and commitments. Proven best practices from external sources can be introduced under controlled, objective conditions and monitored for their effects. Learning opportunities include peer reviews, iteration retrospectives, operations reviews, and process- and guideline-tailoring activities.

Get Specific Early

Abstract thinking is a useful tool. However, abstractions by their very nature lack definition and detail. Using abstract techniques often leads to a diversity of thought across a team. By getting specific early and developing concrete examples using personas and scenarios, a team can better align its thinking and come to a shared vision and consensus on the work to be undertaken. Being abstract too long adds risk to a project and undermines team effectiveness. Too many projects lose time because of people procrastinating about the "big" picture instead of tackling solvable problems. Take one small step at a time, get specific, use concrete examples, and build concrete working code. Learn from these specific examples rather than debate abstract vaporware. Techniques supporting this mindset include personas, scenarios, design for deployment, and test cases.

Qualities of Service

A QoS mindset looks at the solution and develops plans based on every aspect of customer experience. The idea is that qualities of service such as performance and security should not be considered late in the project, but throughout the entire project. When ignored, these qualities of service are ultimately consumer dissatisfiers. The consumer is dissatisfied because the QoS is implicitly assumed. In the spirit of getting specific early, MSF turns implicit assumptions into explicit QoS requirements. Techniques supporting this mindset include using specialist expertise where you need it and discovering risks as early as possible.

Citizenship

Be a good project and software engineering organization citizen. Team members are encouraged to treat others as they would want to be treated and to treat project and organization assets as if they were their own. A good citizen is a steward of corporate, project, and computing resources. Members seek to reuse resources and to provide resources that can be reused. They clean up their own messes. Citizens keep their home and its precincts tidy. Citizens share resources and do not hog valuable assets for their own use. They share knowledge and recognize that the whole takes precedence over the individual. Citizens act for the greater good. Citizens think holistically about the system of software engineering. Citizens value every contribution toward the achievement of the product vision and delivery of successful projects.

Roles

In MSF for CMMI Process Improvement, a team of peers advocates for the seven constituencies in the MSF Team Model. The Team Model was created to model all the views of a project that must be represented and monitored to reduce risk and increase the likelihood of a successful project. Experience with earlier versions of MSF has shown that failure to have all the constituencies in the Team Model represented leads to the increased likelihood of project failure or disappointment. The Team Model constituencies represent the full project life cycle including vision, production, use, and maintenance. Each team member plays at least one of the roles and is accountable for advocating on behalf of a given constituency within the Team Model. No constituency is more important than any other, so no specific role is more important than any other. MSF for CMMI Process Improvement is a consensus lead process definition that requires facilitated agreement among role players. Together, the Team Model and the consensus-oriented nature of role-playing in MSF for

CMMI Process Improvement provide the necessary checks and balances to ensure overall quality and satisfied customers within a framework of good governance.

The team of peers breaks down into seven advocacy groups. Here is a list of these groups with the roles they contain:

- Product Management–product manager, business analyst
- Program Management–project manager, sponsor
- Architecture–architect, subject matter expert
- Development–developer, developer manager, build engineer
- Test–tester, test manager, auditor, QoS specialist
- Release/Operations–release manager, integrated program management (IPM) officer
- User Experience–user experience architect, user education specialist

Here are the roles as defined by MSF for CMMI Process Improvement:

- **Product Manager**   The product manager is the main advocate for the product management constituency in the MSF Team Model. The product manager is the proxy for the end consumer of the product and has overall product mix responsibility for the requirements. The product manager must ensure that the product vision is met through the requirements and that the acceptance tests are developed to validate the product. The product manager must show that the product aligns with the organization's strategic planning and fits the market segment(s) intended in the original vision statement. The product manager will ensure that the project stays within budget and that the business case is realized. The product manager's work is used as the primary source for the track checkpoints in the MSF Governance Model.

   Work streams and activities: capture the product vision and release a product.

- **Business Analyst**   The business analyst's main goal is to advocate for the product management constituency in the MSF Team Model. This goal is achieved by working with sponsors, subject matter experts, product managers, and user experience architects to analyze and define the business opportunity and the product outlined in the vision statement for the project. The business analyst will work on defining personas, writing scenarios, and acting as a proxy for the users and customers by interfacing directly with developers, testers, and other roles active in the later project life cycle.

   Work streams and activities: analyze, create a QoS requirement, create a scenario, create product requirements, establish project process, issue management, manage change requests, plan an iteration, release a product, risk management, test a scenario, test a QoS requirement, verify a functional requirement, and verify an operational requirement.

- **Project Manager**   The project manager advocates for program management constituency in the MSF Team Model. The project manager is responsible for the flow of knowledge creation and ultimately the realization of value, which comes from delivery of the product outlined in the vision statement. The project manager owns the life cycle of the project from end to end. The main goal is to deliver business value within the agreed-upon schedule and budget. The project manager is charged with planning and scheduling duties, including developing project and iteration plans, monitoring and reporting status, and identifying and mitigating risk. The project manager is also expected to consult with business analysts to plan the backlog for the project and its iterations; and consult with architects, developers, testers, user education specialists, and user experience architects to estimate work and facilitate communication within the team.

  Work streams and activities: capture product vision, create product requirements, develop documentation, establish project processes, issue management, plan an iteration, plan a project, risk management, test a scenario, test a QoS requirement, verify a functional requirement, and verify an operational requirement.

- **Sponsor**   A project should not be undertaken without a sponsor. A sponsor advocates for the product management constituency in the MSF Team Model. A sponsor is responsible for providing the business case and finances for the project. The sponsor's input controls the governance of the project. The sponsor holds the business case and product vision against which the project governance is measured. Without a sponsor, there can be no governance.

  Work streams and activities: capture the product vision, create product requirements, and release a product.

- **Architect**   The architect role is to advocate for the architecture constituency in the MSF Team Model. The architect is responsible for maintaining the architectural integrity of the product and for ensuring the success of the project by designing the foundations on which all the value can be realized. This role includes defining both the organizational structure of the application and the physical structure of its deployment. In these endeavors, the architect's goal is to reduce complexity, decrease coupling and regression effects, and increase the cohesiveness of components by partitioning the system into parts that can be built and tested independently. The resulting architecture is extremely important because it not only dictates how the system will be built going forward but also establishes whether the application will exhibit the many traits that are essential for a successful project. These traits include its usability, whether it is reliable and maintainable, whether it meets performance and security standards, and whether it can be evolved easily in the face of changing requirements.

  Work streams and activities: analysis, create a QoS requirement, create product requirements, create solution architecture, establish environments, establish project process, test a scenario, test a QoS requirement, verify a functional requirement, and verify an operational requirement.

■ **Subject Matter Expert**   A subject matter expert is someone who advocates for the product management constituency in the MSF Team Model. A subject matter expert can be anyone who happens to have the knowledge of an area of the business or product vision or technical solution. A subject matter expert is responsible for communicating and transferring their knowledge into other members of the team, so that the appropriate area of the product vision can be realized.

Work streams and activities: analysis, create a QoS requirement, create product requirements, test a scenario, test a QoS requirement, verify a functional requirement, and verify an operational requirement.

■ **Developer**   The developer advocates for the development constituency in the MSF Team Model. The developer is responsible for the bulk of the work building the product. Other development roles, such as the lead developer and development manager, have additional communication and project management responsibilities. The developer should suffer a minimum of communication overhead allowing for a maximum effort on construction of code. In addition, during the early stages of a project, developers might be expected to help specify product requirements not included in the customer requirements and to work on analysis and architecture activities as part of a multi-disciplinary team. A lead developer's role is to lead and to communicate on behalf of other developers. A lead developer advocates for the development constituency in the MSF Team Model, lends experience and skill, and shows leadership by coaching fellow developers. Lead developers carry responsibility for code reviews, design, and unit testing coverage. Lead developers act as a conduit to the rest of the project for the developers. As an aid to productivity, lead developers funnel communications between the wider project team and external organizations, and shield developers from noise and random interference in their daily schedules. Because of this, lead developers can seldom dedicate themselves to development tasks. Typically, they will spend about
50 percent of their time on communication and split the remainder between leading and coaching the developers on their team, and actually writing code for development tasks.

Work streams and activities: analysis, create solution architecture, develop documentation, establish environments, establish project process, fix a bug, implement a development task, release a product, test a scenario, test a QoS requirement, verify a functional requirement, and verify an operational requirement.

■ **Developer Manager**   The development manager is the functional line manager for software development. Lead developers and developers will report in to a development manager. A development manager advocates the development constituency in the MSF Team Model. They are responsible for the capacity of the software development team as measured by metrics such as velocity, and for the variation in capacity and rate of productivity and quality as measured by metrics such as unplanned work, work remaining, quality indicators, and actual quality versus planned velocity. The development manager takes responsibility for the continuous improvement and learning in the software development team. The development manager does not have direct responsibility for the flow of a project and the value in the product solution, but instead works with the project manager to provide the resources to facilitate the smooth flow of the project through development.

Work streams and activities: create product requirements, establish environments, establish project process, and release a product.

- **Build Engineer**   A build engineer is a specialist who performs the function of facilitating the build or integration of the source code. The build engineer advocates for the development in the MSF Team Model. By specializing the build and integration skills in a single role, the developer is freed to focus on understanding the product vision and the creation of value. The build engineer will run the build and develop scripts for automation of the build and automated reporting mechanisms such as the build report. Within Visual Studio Team System, the build engineer owns the "Team Build" functionality.

Work streams and activities: build a product, establish environments, and establish project process.

- **Tester**   The tester advocates for the test constituency in the MSF Team Model. The tester's main goal is to discover and communicate problems with the product that could adversely affect its value. The tester must understand the context for the project and help others to make informed decisions based on this context. A key goal for the tester is to find and report the significant bugs in the product by testing the product. After a bug is found, it is also the tester's job to accurately communicate its impact and describe any workaround solutions that could lessen its impact. The tester makes bug descriptions and steps for re-creating the bugs easy to understand and follow. The tester participates with the entire team in setting the quality standards for the product. The purpose of testing is to prove that known functions work correctly and to discover new product issues.

Work streams and activities: analysis, close a bug, develop documentation, establish environments, establish project process, release a product, test a scenario, test a QoS requirement, verify a functional requirement, and verify an operational requirement.

- **Test Manager**   The test manager is responsible for the capacity and quality of the testing function. Testers report to the test manager. The test manager advocates for the test constituency in the MSF Team Model and takes responsibility for the continuous improvement and learning in the software test team. A test manager does not have direct responsibility for the flow of a project and the value in the product solution but instead works with the project manager to provide the resources to facilitate the smooth flow of the project through test.

Work streams and activities: create product requirements, establish environments, establish project process, release a product, test a scenario, test a QoS requirement, verify a functional requirement, and verify an operational requirement.

- **Auditor** An auditor is external to the project and offers an independent objective view of a project and its processes. An auditor effectively advocates for the product management constituency in the MSF Team Model by auditing the QA (quality assurance) in the project's product and its processes. The auditor is responsible for assessing the quality in the product as measured by quality control and the QA measured as conformance against process definition. An auditor reports variance from specification, variance from plan, and variance from process definition. An auditor's reports can be used to assess the likely quality of the product and whether or not the organization exhibits control in its operations.

  Work stream and activity: establish project process.

- **Quality of Service Specialist** A quality of service specialist is a developer with particularly specialized skills in one or more areas of technology that are needed to deliver qualities of service requirements such as performance, scalability, reliability, security, and so forth. A quality of service specialist advocates for the development constituency in the MSF Team Model. By specializing qualities of service knowledge into a single role, the regular developer is freed up to focus on the product vision, the customer requirements, and delivering customer value while a specialist can assist him or her to ensure that his or her code meets the exacting requirements of challenging qualities of service. A quality of service specialist can either rework code written by developers or develop prototypes and examples and publish these as patterns for use in code reviews. A quality of service specialist can coach other team members about how to develop code using the appropriate design patterns to deliver the required quality of service.

  Work stream and activity: establish project process.

- **Release Manager** The release manager advocates for the Release and Operations constituency in the MSF Team Model. This role's goal is to manage the rollout of the product. The release manager coordinates the release with operations or media control, creates a rollout plan, and certifies release candidates for shipment or deployment.

  Work streams and activities: baseline configuration management, create product requirements, establish project process, manage change requests, and release a product.

- **Integrated Program Management (IPM) Officer** The IPM officer is the executive responsible for the overall organizational scheduling, planning, and resource allocation. The integrated program management office (IPMO), which is run by the IPM officer, coordinates all projects in a portfolio and provides a means for project members to communicate schedule and resource information to each other. The IPM officer advocates for the program management constituency in the MSF Team Model. The IPM officer is responsible for the organization-level flow of projects in a portfolio, whereas a project manager is responsible for the flow of a single project. The IPM officer's main role is to hold coordinating meetings among project managers and to facilitate the negotiation of priorities, schedules, and resource allocation. This becomes particularly important when scarce specialist shared resources have conflicting demands from two or more projects in a portfolio. A good IMP officer is a diplomat, a negotiator, and a facilitator.

Work streams and activities: create product requirements, establish project process, issue management, plan an iteration, and release a product.

- **User Experience Architect**   A user experience architect advocates the user experience constituency in the MSF Team Model. A user experience architect is responsible for the product design; not the technical architecture of the technical solution, but the form and function of the user interface, its aesthetics, and the overall product usability. Within the field of user experience architects, there is room for specialization. In many organizations, this role is represented by a team of people with specialist job titles such as usability engineer, interaction designer, and graphic designer. In MSF, these disciplines are represented in a single role. A user experience architect gets involved at the very beginning of a project. He or she will seek to understand the goals of the consumer for the product and to envision a design that meets those goals. A user experience architect will develop the personas and usage scenarios for the customer requirements. He or she may also develop prototypes or storyboards and conduct usability testing at several stages in the project life cycle during the planning, build, stabilize, and deploy tracks in the MSF Governance Model.

Work streams and activities: analysis, capture product vision, create a scenario, create product requirements, establish project process, and release a product.

- **User Education Specialist**   The user education specialist is typically a technical writer who advocates for the user experience in the MSF Team Model. The user education specialist focuses on consumer-focused technical writing that reinforces or enhances product value and helps to realize the product vision. A user education specialist can work on product manuals, online help, operations manuals, maintenance manuals, training manuals, and any other documentation that can be used to enhance the usage and value delivered with the product. User experience architects typically work closely with user education specialists. A good user experience and product design typically leads to a lower workload for the technical writing team. Excessive documentation may be an indicator that the user experience is poor, and the writing is compensating for poor overall product design.

Work streams and activities: analysis, develop documentation, establish project process, and release a product.

Work Item Types

MSF for CMMI Process Improvement includes the following items:

- **Bug**   This item communicates that a potential problem exists or has existed in the system. The goal of opening a bug is to accurately report bugs in a way that allows the reader to understand the full impact of the problem. The descriptions in the bug report should make it easy to trace through the steps used when the bug was encountered, thus allowing the bug to be easily reproduced. The test results should clearly show the problem. The clarity and understandability of this description often affects the probability that the bug will be fixed.

- **Change Request**   A change request work item identifies a proposed change to some part of the product or baseline. Change requests must be created when a change is proposed to any work product that is in the configuration management system. The change request work item is used by the change control board to analyze, accept, and reject proposed changes. If a change request is accepted, it is used to generate tasks to implement the change. After changes are implemented, the change request is eventually closed.

- **Issue**   The issue work item documents an event or situation that may block work or is currently blocking work on the product. Issues differ from risks in that they are identified spontaneously, generally during daily team meetings. Issue work items are reviewed and analyzed to create tasks to resolve the issue. After corrective action is taken by completing the tasks, the issue is resolved. Finally, if the corrective action is deemed acceptable, the issue is closed.

- **Requirement**   Requirements capture and track what the product needs to do to solve the customer problem. There are several types of requirements: scenario, QoS, functional, operational, and interface. As requirements are identified, they begin in the Proposed state. When a requirement is accepted for the current iteration, it moves to the Active state and is analyzed to create tasks to implement it. When the tasks are complete and system tests are passed to show that the requirement is successfully implemented, it moves to the Resolved state. Finally, when the requirement is validated, it is moved to the Closed state.

- **Review**   The review work item documents the results of a design or code review. The review work item must include detailed information about how the design or code met standards in areas of name correctness, code relevance, extensibility, code complexity, algorithmic complexity, and code security. If the review found that the design or code needed no changes, the review work item can be closed. If minor changes or major changes are needed, the active review work item is assigned to a developer to resolve. If minor changes are needed, the developer can close the review work item directly. If major changes are needed, a second review is required, and the review work item is closed only if the second review passes successfully.

- **Risk**   This item documents and tracks the technical or organizational risks of a project. When concrete action is required, these risks might translate into tasks to be performed to mitigate the risk. For example, a technical risk can set off an architectural prototyping effort. The team should always regard risk identification in a positive way to ensure contribution of as much information as possible about the risks it faces. The environment should be such that individuals identifying risks can do so without fear of retribution for honest expression of tentative or controversial views. Teams creating a positive risk management environment will be more successful at identifying and addressing risks earlier than those teams operating in a negative risk environment.

- **Task**   This process template item communicates the need to do some work. Each role has its own requirements for a task. For example, a developer uses development tasks to assign work derived from scenarios or QoS requirements to component owners. The tester uses test tasks to assign the job of writing and running test cases. A task can also be used to signal regressions or to suggest that exploratory testing be performed. Finally, a task can be used generically to assign work within the project. On the work item form, certain fields are used only in cases when a task relates to a particular role.

Disciplines and Qualities of Service

MSF for CMMI Process Improvement defines the same disciplines as does MSF for Agile Software Development: project management and risk management. Qualities of service are the same as well: security, performance, and user experience.

Governance

Governance concerns utilization of resources through the control of time and money relative to the flow of value. MSF for CMMI Process Improvement defines five tracks for the project life cycle that encapsulate sets of work streams and activities. Each track concludes with governance checkpoints, and each checkpoint provides an opportunity to authorize continued work on the project or to cancel or suspend the project. The checkpoint for each track asks a different question or set of questions. The objective for the work within a track is to provide the answers to the governance questions and back those answers with transparent project data gathered through the day-to-day operations of the software engineering organization.

The MSF Governance Model is designed to be risk-tolerant and to facilitate the easy flow of a project. Tracks start when the required inputs are available; that is, tracks are event-driven. Work in several tracks can run in parallel. Governance checkpoints at the end of tracks provide the opportunity to shut a project down with the understanding that some work on subsequent tracks may already be under way. The risk of waste is balanced against the desire to keep the project moving and be both agile and productive within a formal governance framework.

MSF for CMMI Process Improvement seeks to separate out the operational management of the organization from the corporate governance of the organization. The first asks for a focus on "Are we good at software engineering?" whereas the second asks for a focus on "Are we making best use of our software engineering resources?" Operational management is about capacity, quality, and reliable low-variation engineering. Governance is about making best use of the shareholder's or taxpayer's funds through the optimal utilization of capacity.

The MSF for CMMI Process Improvement defines seven tracks: envision, plan, build, stabilize, deploy, operational management, and governance.

Implementing MSF 4.0 with Team System

Visual Studio 2005 Team System uses a mechanism called the process template that defines both the configuration and initial content of new team projects. In effect, the process template defines the methodology for a new project by rigging the project to facilitate the methodology.

Team System supports multiple methodologies by containing multiple process templates. When creating a new team project, the user selects a methodology from the list displayed by the New Team Project Wizard, and Team System uses the corresponding process template to set up the new project. This turns out to be a simple and elegant way to incorporate methodology at the project level.

> **Note**   Team System allows you to add, remove, and customize process templates as needed to reflect the software development processes of your team. This is performed at the Microsoft Visual Studio 2005 Team Foundation Server level and not at the team project level. Once a team project has been created with a given methodology, the process cannot be added or removed for that particular project. You'll learn how to manage process templates in Chapter 9.

Team System includes two process templates for MSF 4.0, one for each of the MSF implementations: MSF for Agile Software Development and MSF for CMMI Process Improvement. In this section, we'll walk through the structure of a Team System process template to see exactly how it implements a methodology.

The process template consists of the following components: project structure, groups and permissions, work items, project portal, version control, and reports. It's important to remember that the process template configures the initial settings for a new project. Once the project is created, most of these settings can be modified by an authorized user.

Let's take a closer look at each of the process template components:

- **Project structure**   Team System manages project structure using the Classification Structure System (CSS). The process template defines the classification structure of a project. The classification structure for MSF Agile includes project hierarchy and iterations.

Project classification also specifies the name of each iterative development cycle in the project. Examples of iteration names include Setup, Alpha, Beta 1, Beta 2, and Release.

Refer to Chapter 4 for more information on configuring the project structure.

- **Users, Groups, and Permissions**   Each Team System project has its own set of users, groups, and permissions. Visual Studio Team System uses the security infrastructure implemented by Active Directory® directory service to manage project security. Active Directory groups are created to represent process roles. These groups are then assigned permissions appropriate for the roles they represent. Finally, users are added to each group based on their roles in the project. When a new Team System project is created, the groups and permissions are automatically set up. These settings can be modified as needed by authorized users.

- **Work Items, Work Streams, and Work Products**   A work item is a database record that Visual Studio Team Foundation Server uses to track the assignment and state of work. Work streams are a sequence of related work items. Work products are the documents, spreadsheets, project plans, source code, and other tangible output from the work items or activities. The work item types, work streams, and work products for each product are configured based on the process template selected.

- **Project portal**   Team System uses WSS to create a Web portal for each new project. The process template specifies the initial content to be automatically added to the project portal.

  The project portal is commonly used to store project documentation, including the process guidance associated with the process template. In addition, the project portal displays key team reports generated by Microsoft SQL Server™ 2005 Reporting Services.

- **Version control**   Source plays an important role in the SDLC process. Visual Studio Team System includes a robust version control system that integrates with work item tracking and the build process to create a complete software configuration management system. Each Team System project includes version control settings that specify check-out settings, check-in policies, and check-in note requirements. When a new Team System project is created, these settings are configured based on the process template selected. Changes to the check-in policies must be made after the project is created.

- **Metrics and reporting**   Visual Studio Team System records metrics from all the Team System tools in a central data warehouse. For example, these metrics include information about work items, check-ins, build results, and test results. Because all the process metrics are in a single data repository, the project manager no longer has to spend time collecting and cross referencing metrics across tools. More data is available to the project stakeholders, and flexible reporting via Microsoft SQL Server 2005 Reporting Services provides an unprecedented degree of real-time visibility on project health. Standard reports for each Team System project are configured based on the process template selected.

Customization and Extensibility

Visual Studio Team System offers many ways to customize its tool set to match your development process. We'll discuss each briefly here.

Process Templates

Authorized team members can use the Process Template Manager in Visual Studio Team System to upload and download process templates. A team can customize an exported template without having to do any programming or use any proprietary tools. This enables the team to build their own processes into Team System and then continually refine Team System to reflect process improvements based on lessons learned.

Custom Reporting

Although Team System includes many useful reports out of the box, organizations can create their own custom reports using SQL Server 2005 Reporting Services. In addition, organizations can define, capture, and store custom metrics in Team System's central data warehouse, providing additional reporting capabilities.

The Team Foundation Server architecture allows teams to extend the capabilities of Team System by adding services to the Team Foundation Client API. This enables teams and software life cycle tool providers to add tools to the suite with the same rich integration found in the Team System tools. Read more about the customization and extensibility of Team System in Chapter 9.

Summary

Microsoft Solutions Framework version 4.0 is the latest in an evolving series of SDLC frameworks based on the best practices of Microsoft and its customers. MSF 4.0 offers both a descriptive metamodel of best practices and two prescriptive process templates that implement MSF 4.0 in Team System.

Taken together, MSF 4.0 and Team System are powerful tools for teams of all types. MSF provides process guidance that can be easily customized, and Team System provides an integrated, extensible tool set that seamlessly enacts the process.

Chapter 9
Customizing and Extending Team System

In this chapter:

Customizing Versus Extending 211

Extensibility Toolkit. 239

Partners. 239

Summary. 246

Extensibility is one of the key features of Microsoft® Visual Studio® 2005 Team System, and it's inevitable that developers, architects, testers, and project managers will want to customize the out-of-the-box features. In addition, Microsoft's partners are preparing tools that plug into Team System and complement the basic Team System offering. For this reason, Team System has been built from the ground up to ensure that its fundamental architecture supports customization and extension.

Microsoft knew that the success of Team System would not be based on how well it could anticipate the specific needs of all the development teams in the world. The built-in methodologies, work item types, policies, and reports support most of the development efforts in today's industry; however, the success of Team System lies in how well it can be adapted to work for specific teams, in specific environments, for specific projects.

Customizing Team System can include something as trivial as modifying a work item type to include an additional field or creating a new report. *Extending* Team System can include building new clients and/or Microsoft Visual Studio 2005 Team Foundation Server extensions to enable new tools, workflows, or policies. Before we move ahead, let's discuss the differences between *customizing* and *extending*.

Customizing Versus Extending

What's the difference between customizing and extending? Both terms mean "changing or altering" the existing software in some way. Customizing means using the mechanisms that exist out of the box to tweak Team System, whereas extending typically involves writing code and building and registering assemblies. Customizing, therefore, can be thought of as being a little easier to accomplish by an audience that is a little less focused on building tools, where extending requires more time, and effort, by an audience that is more comfortable with application programming interfaces (APIs) and software development kits (SDKs). These are just general guidelines, however.

Table 9-1 shows some of the other differences.

Table 9-1   Customizing versus Extending

	Customizing	Extending
What is it?	Tailoring Team System and/or Team Foundation Server to your environment	Adding new functionality to Team System and/or Team Foundation Server
Who performs it?	Team System users, project managers, developer leads	Internal IT/developer, ISV (independent software vendor) partners
Why is it performed?	To adjust basic capabilities to suit your team's needs	To deeply integrate complementary features
How is it performed?	Configuration through user interface (UI), authoring XML files, or possibly some light automation	Web service development, database development, Visual Studio Integrator Program (VSIP) integration, and so on

First, we'll take a close look at how you can customize Team System to match your own team's development processes. Then we'll take a quick look at how Team System can be extended to integrate custom tools from Microsoft partners.

Customizing Team System

Many areas can be customized. One could argue that by selecting a different methodology template when you create a new team project, you have customized the process. I will ignore those kinds of settings and properties and focus instead on some not-so-obvious areas that can be customized, specifically the following:

- **Process Guidance.**   Modify existing template or documentation (or build your own).
- **Work Item Types.**   Modify existing work item types to add new fields, ToolTips, or drop-down lists.
- **Version Control.**   Select version control policies.
- **Reporting.**   Modify existing reports or add your own.
- **Project Portal.**   Add new documents and lists, and change the layout.

Customizing Process Templates

Team System uses process templates to automate the configuration of new Team System projects. Simply put, a process template tells Team System step by step exactly how to set up a new project. In a very direct way, the process template defines the methodology for a project by specifying which process tools will be used and how those tools will be configured for the project. The process template even installs the project's process guidance documentation.

The truly marvelous thing about a process template is that a team can take an existing template and customize it without having to do any programming or use any proprietary tools. This flexibility enables the team to build its own processes into Team System and then improve those processes over time based on lessons learned.

Team System comes with two process templates: Microsoft Solutions Framework (MSF) for Agile Software Development and MSF for Capability Maturity Modeling Integration (CMMI) Process Improvement. These templates can be used as-is or customized as needed.

Let's explore the process template for MSF for Agile Software Development. If you launch Microsoft Visual Studio 2005, connect to your Team Foundation Server, and then bring up the Process Template Manager (shown in Figure 9-1), located in the Team menu under Team Foundation Server Settings, you see that you can import and export process templates. After they are exported, you can browse the directory containing the process template to see the structure. Typically, there are many folders, containing many files. These folders and files can be altered, and then the Process Template Manager can be used to import new or changed templates back into Team System.

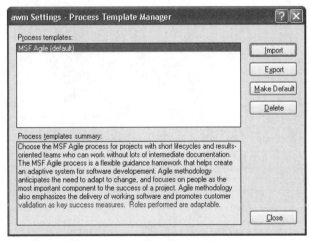

Figure 9-1   Process Template Manager

Figure 9-2 shows the structure of the process template for MSF for Agile Software Development. Notice that there are XML files throughout the template. These files are called Process Definition Files. These files tell Team System which Process Template Plug-Ins to use and also define the sequence of tasks the Process Template Plug-Ins should perform. Two important definition files are the MetaData.xml and MethodologyTemplate.xml files. If you want to create a new template, rather than just edit an existing one, you need to alter the contents of these two files, changing the names and descriptions. The subdirectories contain other tool-specific files, most of which have been omitted from the figure for clarity.

Figure 9-2   Process template—MSF for Agile Software Development

Process Template Plug-Ins are components that Team System uses to create a new team project. Each plug-in plays a specific part in the setup process. Microsoft provides six plug-ins with Visual Studio 2005 Team System, as shown in Table 9-2.

Table 9-2   Process Template Plug-Ins

Plug-In Name	Description
Classification Structure System (CSS)	Defines a team project's initial iterations, organization units, components, or feature areas
Group Security Service (GSS)	Defines a team project's initial security groups and their permissions
Microsoft Windows® SharePoint® Services (WSS)	Defines the project portal for the team based on a WSS site template; also defines template files and process guidance
Currituck	Defines a team project's initial work item types, queries, and work item instances
Rosetta	Defines a team project's initial reports
Source Code Control (SCC)	Defines a team project's initial version control security permissions and check-in notes

Let's take a behind-the-scenes tour of the process template in action. It all starts when a user, typically the team lead, launches the New Team Project Wizard in Visual Studio. The wizard asks for the project name and description. Then it asks the user to select a process template. Team System starts by examining the process definition file called MethodologyTemplate.xml in the root directory of the selected process template. This is the main process definition file, and it looks something like this:

```xml
<methodology>
  <metadata>
    <name>MSF for Agile Software Development</name>
    <description>Choose the MSF Agile process for projects
with short lifecycles...</description>
    <plugins>
      <plugin name="Microsoft.Pcw.Css" wizardPage="false"/>
      <plugin name="Microsoft.Pcw.Rosetta" wizardPage="false"/>
      <plugin name="Microsoft.Pcw.wss" wizardPage="true"/>
      <plugin name="Microsoft.Pcw.gss" wizardPage="false"/>
      <plugin name="Microsoft.Pcw.currituck" wizardPage="false"/>
      <plugin name="Microsoft.Pcw.scc" wizardPage="true"/>
    </plugins>
  </metadata>
  <groups>
    <group id="CSS"
      description="Structure definition for the project."
      completionMessage="Project Structure uploaded."
      failureMessage="Project Structure upload failed.">
      <dependencies>
      </dependencies>
      <taskList filename="Css\CssTasks.xml"/>
    </group>
    <group id="GSS"
      description="Create Groups and Permissions."
      completionMessage="Groups and Permissions created."
      failureMessage="Groups and Permissions failed.">
      <dependencies>
        <dependency groupId="CSS" />
      </dependencies>
      <taskList filename="Gss\GssTasks.xml" />
    </group>
    <group id="WSS"
      description="Creating project Site"
      completionMessage="Project site created."
      failureMessage="Project site creation failed.">
      <dependencies>
        <dependency groupId="CSS"/>
        <dependency groupId="Currituck"/>
        <dependency groupId="Scc" />
      </dependencies>
      <taskList filename="Wss\WssTasks.xml"/>
    </group>
    <group id="Rosetta"
    description="Project reports uploading."
    completionMessage="Project reports uploaded."
    failureMessage="Project reports upload failed.">
    <dependencies>
      <dependency groupId="CSS"/>
      <dependency groupId="WSS"/>
    </dependencies>
    <taskList filename="Reports\ReportsTasks.xml"/>
  </group>
```

```
    <group id="Currituck"
      description="Work item definitons uploading."
      completionMessage="Work item definitons uploaded."
      failureMessage="Work item definitons creation failed.">
      <dependencies>
        <dependency groupId="CSS"/>
        <dependency groupId="GSS"/>
      </dependencies>
      <taskList filename="Currituck\CurrituckTasks.xml"/>
    </group>
    <group id="Scc"
      description="Creating version control."
      completionMessage="Version control created."
      failureMessage="Version control creation failed.">
      <dependencies>
        <dependency groupId="CSS"/>
        <dependency groupId="Currituck" />
      </dependencies>
      <taskList filename="Scc\SccTasks.xml"/>
    </group>
    </groups>
</methodology>
```

The name and description sections are self-explanatory. The plug-in section lists the process template plug-ins that will be used to create the new team project. The groups section contains a list of task groups that must run. The group section for WSS (group id="WSS") is the task group for the WSS plug-in, which creates the Web portal for the new team project. Notice that the group section contains a description, completion message, and the failure message that the wizard uses when it runs the WSS task group. The dependencies list indicates that the CSS, Currituck, and SCC task groups must finish their tasks successfully before the WSS task group can start. Finally, the taskList section contains the name of the XML file containing the task list for the WSS task group.

Generally, there is one task group per plug-in, but Team System does not impose this limitation. It's possible to use multiple plug-ins within one task group, but that can get confusing and should be avoided if possible. Also, there need not be a task group for every plug-in. In fact, the CSS plug-in for Classification Structure Service is the only one required by the process template—all the other plug-ins are optional.

> **Note**   The file MetaData.xml in the process template's root directory is simply a copy of all the metadata elements (name, description, plug-ins) from the MethodologyTemplate.xml file. MethodologyTemplate.xml and all other folders are compressed into a single binary object and stored in the Team Foundation Server database. MetaData.xml is stored in a separate field so that the New Team Project Wizard and Process Template Manager can retrieve basic process template attributes without unzipping the binary object.

Back at the New Team Project Wizard, each plug-in listed in MethodologyTemplate.xml is given an opportunity to collect configuration settings from the user by displaying a data-entry screen in the wizard. When the user clicks the wizard's Finish button, Team System starts the process to create the new team project.

Team System processes the task groups one at a time. The order in which they are processed is based on the dependencies in the task group definitions. When a task group is invoked, Team System examines the task list file associated with the task group. Here is the task list for Currituck, the process template plug-in for work item tracking.

```xml
<tasks>
  <task
    id="WITs"
    name="WorkItemType Definitions"
    plugin="Microsoft.Pcw.Currituck"
    completionMessage="WorkItemTypes created"
    completionDescription = "Processing the WorkItemTypes used by Currituck">
    <taskXml>
      <WORKITEMTYPES>
        <WORKITEMTYPE fileName="Currituck\TypeDefinitions\Bug.xml"/>
        <WORKITEMTYPE fileName="Currituck\TypeDefinitions\Task.xml"/>
        <WORKITEMTYPE fileName="Currituck\TypeDefinitions\Qos.xml"/>
        <WORKITEMTYPE fileName="Currituck\TypeDefinitions\Scenario.xml"/>
      </WORKITEMTYPES>
    </taskXml>
  </task>
  <task
    id="WIs"
    name="WorkItems"
    plugin="Microsoft.Pcw.Currituck"
    completionMessage="WorkItems uploaded"
    completionDescription = "Processing the actual WorkItems used by Currituck">
    <dependencies>
      <dependency taskId="WITs" />
    </dependencies>
    <taskXml>
      <WORKITEMS>
        <WI type="Task">
          <FIELD name="Title" value="Setup: Set Permissions" />
          <FIELD name="ShortDescription" value="" />
          <FIELD name="Iteration Path" value="Iteration 0" />
          <FIELD name="State" value="Active" />
          <FIELD name="Reason" value="New" />
          <FIELD name="Issue2" value="No" />
          <FIELD name="Scheduled" value="No" />
          <FIELD name="Summary Task" value="No" />
          <FIELD name="Exit Criteria" value="Yes" />
        </WI>
        ...
        <WI type="Task">
          <FIELD name="Title" value="Create Project Checklist Items" />
          <FIELD name="ShortDescription" value="" />
          <FIELD name="Iteration Path" value="Iteration 1" />
          <FIELD name="State" value="Active" />
          <FIELD name="Reason" value="New" />
          <FIELD name="Issue2" value="No" />
```

```
                <FIELD name="Scheduled" value="No" />
                <FIELD name="Summary Task" value="No" />
                <FIELD name="Exit Criteria" value="Yes" />
            </WI>
          </WORKITEMS>
        </taskXml>
    </task>
    <task
      id="Queries"
      name="Stored Query Definitions"
      plugin="Microsoft.Pcw.Currituck"
      completionMessage="Queries uploaded"
      completionDescription = "Processing the stored queries used by Currituck">
      <dependencies>
        <dependency taskId="WIs" />
        <dependency taskId="WITs" />
      </dependencies>
      <taskXml>
        <QUERIES>
          <Query
            name="All Scenarios"
            fileName="AllScenarios.wiq" />
...
          <Query
            name="All My Team Project Work Items"
            fileName="MyWorkItemsAllTeamProjects.wiq" />
        </QUERIES>
      </taskXml>
    </task>
</tasks>
```

This task list file contains three tasks: Work Item Definitions, Work Items, and Stored Query Definitions. Note that each task section has an ID field, which uniquely identifies the task within the task group. It also has name, completionMessage, and completionDescription sections that are used by the wizard. Each task section also specifies the plug-in to use. All the tasks in this task list use the Currituck plug-in. The dependencies section for each task indicates the tasks that must complete before that task can be performed. Looking at the Stored Query Definitions task, you can see that the other two tasks must be completed first.

The structure of the taskXml section is "owned" by the plug-in, and it varies from task to task. For instance, the taskXml section for the Work Item Definitions task contains the list of work item definitions, while the taskXml section for the Stored Query Definitions task contains a list of query definitions.

By editing the MethodologyTemplate.xml file and the associated task list files, you can customize every aspect of the project-creation process. Follow these best practices when creating your own custom process template:

- Always start by exporting and editing an existing template. Creating a process template from scratch is very difficult.

- Make small incremental changes to the template, and then test it to make sure it is working properly.

- List your tasks in each XML process definition file in the same order as their dependencies. This will make it easier to eliminate any dependency problems, and it will be easier to read.

- Import your new process template into a test environment, and make sure it's working properly before importing it into your production environment.

Customizing Process Guidance Documentation

The MSF for Agile Software Development process template automatically creates a Windows SharePoint Services Web site containing, among other things, the process guidance documentation. You might want to edit this documentation to more accurately reflect your development process. The process guidance Web pages are generated from an XML file call ProcessGuidance.xml, which is transformed to HTML for display in a Web browser. You can edit this document with an XML editor like the one in Visual Studio, but there's an easier way. The tool of choice in this case is InfoPath®. (See Figure 9-3.) It presents the document as an intuitive data entry form that's easy to edit.

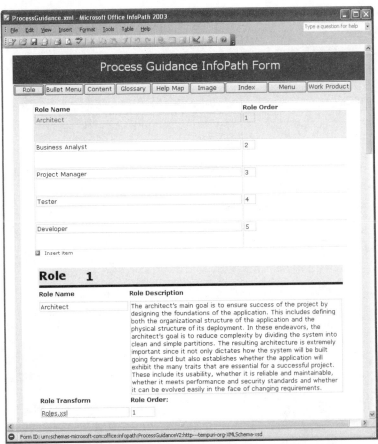

Figure 9-3   Editing the Process Guidance document using InfoPath

Back up the process guidance document, make your changes using InfoPath, and then open ProcessGuidance.htm to view your changes in the Web browser.

Customizing Work Item Types

Depending upon the methodology template you choose, your team project will be able to use various work item types. For example, MSF for Agile Software Development defines Scenarios, Quality of Service (QoS) Requirements, Bugs, and Tasks. The schema or available fields are also predefined by Microsoft. This is also an area that can be customized, especially for shops that want to create new work item types or alter existing work items to ask additional questions. For example, a company might want to customize the schema of a task, to prompt for the *Security Classification* of the task. In addition, it might not want the users to enter free-form text, but instead keep them constrained to a predefined list of *Unclassified*, *Confidential*, and *Secret*. By using some export and import tools provided by Microsoft, customization can be easily accomplished.

The Team System Partner Extensibility Kit provides four command-line utilities:

■ **witexport.exe.**   Exports an existing work item type from a team project as XML.

■ **witimport.exe.**   Imports an XML work item type definition to a team project or validates a definition before import.

■ **glexport.exe.**   Exports global lists defined on the Team Foundation Server as XML.

■ **glimport.exe.**   Imports global lists defined in XML to a Team Foundation Server.

Here are the steps to export an existing work item type, add a new field, and then import the type back into Team Foundation Server:

1. Open a command prompt and type the following command to export the standard task work item type to another file:

   ```
   witexport /f SampleTask.xml /t TFSSer_ver /p TeamProjectName /n "Task"
   ```

2. Open a command prompt and type the following command to export any global lists currently in Team Foundation Server:

   ```
   glexport /f GlobalLists.xml /t TFSServer
   ```

3. Open the GlobalLists.xml file and add the following list to the *<GLOBALLISTS>* element:

   ```
   <GLOBALLIST name="SecurityClassifications">
     <LISTITEM value="Unclassified"/>
     <LISTITEM value="Confidential"/>
     <LISTITEM value="Secret"/>
     <LISTITEM value="Top Secret"/>
   </GLOBALLIST>
   ```

4. Open the SampleTask.xml file and add the following field to the other fields in the file:

   ```
   <FIELD name="Security" refname="Sample.Security" type="String">
     <HELPTEXT>The security classification of this task</HELPTEXT>
     <ALLOWEDVALUES expanditems="true" filteritems="excludegroups">
   ```

```
<GLOBALLIST name="SecurityClassifications"/>
</ALLOWEDVALUES></FIELD>
```

5. Specify where you want the new Security field to be displayed on the UI by adding the following after the Iteration control down in the FORM section of SampleTask.xml:

```
<Control Type="FieldControl" FieldName="Sample.Security"
Label="Security Classification" LabelPosition="Left" />
```

6. Open a command prompt and type the following to import the new global list:

```
glimport /f GlobalLists.xml /t TFSServer
```

7. Open a command prompt and type the following to import the updated task work item type:

```
witimport /f SampleTask.xml /t TFSServer /p TeamProjectName
```

8. Launch Visual Studio. Open Microsoft Visual Studio 2005 Team Explorer and create a new task work item for your team project. You should see a new field with a drop-down list containing the valid choices, as shown in Figure 9-4.

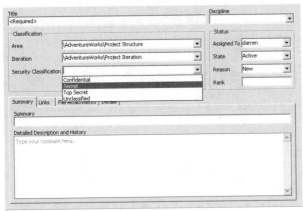

Figure 9-4   Updated task work item containing the new Security Classification field

When defining new fields, there are several properties you can associate with the field. In the preceding example, I associated only some help text (ToolTip) and a constrained list of valid answers. There are more properties and constraints you can associate with a field, for example:

■ **<REQUIRED/>**.   The field is required to be nonempty.

■ **<READONLY/>**.   The field cannot be modified.

■ **<EMPTY/>**.   The field value will be cleared on commit, and the user cannot enter any value. Used primarily during state transitions.

■ **<FROZEN/>**.   After a field has a value after a commit, it can no longer be modified. It can, however, be cleared using an *<EMPTY/>* constraint and filled in again later. Used primarily during state transitions.

- **<CANNOTLOSEVALUE/>**   After a field has a value, it cannot be cleared or made empty.

- **<NOTSAMEAS field="Example"/>.**   The field value cannot have the same value as the value in the field *"Example"*. For example, two fields cannot be empty at the same time, or the *"Code Reviewer"* field value cannot be the same as the *"Assigned To"* field value. Should be used for fields of like type. It is not supported for PlainText or HTML fields.

- **<VALIDUSER/>.**   The field value must be a valid user who is a member of Team Foundation Server Everyone. Note: If the *<REQUIRED/>* rule is not specified, this field will accept an empty value. Used for String field types.

- **<VALIDDATE mustbe="after now"/>.**   Validates a date field. The *mustbe* value can be either *"after now"* or *"not after now"*. *"after now"* is after the current time; *"not after now"* requires the field value to be the current time or before. Used for DateTime field types.

- **<ALLOWEXISTINGVALUE/>.**   Allows a field to retain an existing value, even if that value is no longer allowed. The alternative and default behavior is to force the user at edit time to conform to the latest allowed values for that field. This element has a modifying effect only on the elements in the same block. It cannot accept *"for"* or *"not"* attributes.

- **<MATCH pattern="<pattern>"/>.**   Enforces basic pattern matching for strings only. *"<pattern>"* should be replaced with the string pattern you want to match. Valid values are *"A"*, *"N"*, and *"X"*. All other values are taken as literals. *"A"* represents an alphabetical character; *"N"* represents a numeric character; *"X"* represents any alphanumeric character. Supported only for String field types. You can specify multiple *<MATCH>* elements. If just one element succeeds, the field has a legal value.

- **<ALLOWEDVALUES>.**   An enumerated list of values that is presented to the user as a drop-down list. Users must pick one of the values on this list. I used it in my example.

- **<SUGGESTEDVALUES>.**   An enumerated list of values that is presented to the user as a drop-down list. Users can select any one of the values or enter their own value, which is not one of the suggestions.

- **<PROHIBITEDVALUES>.**   Users cannot save a work item if the field contains any prohibited values. Prohibited values are typically used when a value was previously allowed but is no longer valid.

- **<DEFAULT>.**   When a user creates a new work item or edits a work item, the *<DEFAULT>* element fills in a field value if that field is empty. If a field already has a value, the default rule is ignored.

- **<COPY>.**   When a user creates a new work item or edits a work item, the *<COPY>* element fills in a field value regardless of any exiting value already in the field.

- **<SERVERDEFAULT>.**   Unlike *<DEFAULT>* and *<COPY>*, which fill in values at the beginning of editing, the *<SERVERDEFAULT>* rule fills in a value when the work item is committed to the database. This happens at Save time and the user cannot override the value. Fields appear read-only on the form. This rule is used for fields such as *"Last Changed By"* and *"Last Changed On"* to support secure audit trails.

You can set many other characteristics of work items. One of the more interesting is workflow—you can define the valid states, legal transitions, and legal reasons for those transitions. A common example is to consider the *status* field of a work item. Once a status is given, the transitions to another status, along with associated reasons, must be considered. For example, take a work item type with three status states: *Active, Unapproved,* and *Closed.* The Unapproved state precedes the Active state, and that Active state precedes the Closed state. Reasons identify why the user is changing from one state to another.

Customizing Version Control

Project managers or team leads can configure a team project's version control to include one or more check-in policies, such as clean build, associate with work item, or running one or more tests on the code. Additional policies can be created and registered (as I will discuss later in this chapter).

One way to customize version control is to add additional file types that can be handled by Team System. By default, only certain file types are supported. Some image files, such as .bmp and .tif files, for example, are not supported by default. By right-clicking the Team Foundation Server in the Team Explorer window, you can configure the file types that are supported, even specifying which ones support multiple check-outs. (See Figure 9-5.)

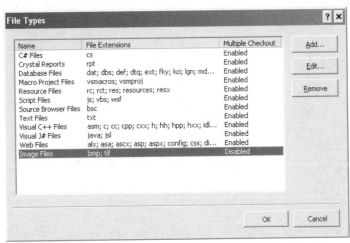

Figure 9-5   Configuring version control to handle additional file types such as images

Customizing Reporting

Remember that the reports found in Team System are simply Microsoft SQL Server™ 2005 Reporting Services reports. These are Report Definition Language (.rdl) files that have been created by Microsoft and uploaded to Reporting Services and made available through the project portal. There are a number of ways to customize these reports:

- **Create new reports.**   By using SQL Server Business Intelligence Developer Studio®, you can create new reports.

- **Edit existing reports.**   By editing the .rdl files provided by Microsoft, you can customize the existing reports with your company heading, formats, or additional fields.

- **Use Report Builder.**   By creating one or more report models, you can further empower your team to build its own custom Team System reports on their own.

> **Tip**   Remember, once you create some new reports, you can make them part of any future team projects by exporting the respective methodology template, adding the .rdl files to the appropriate folder, and then importing the template.

Customizing Project Portal

Portals are great. They are a quick way to build a clean Web site, with much of the basic framework (security, menus, lists, configuration, and themes) already built in. Team System uses the project portal as the one place to go for all documents, reports, and lists. Any member of the core team, as well as extended members who may not have Visual Studio, Microsoft Office Excel®, or Microsoft Office Project, can visit the portal for periodic status reports.

In the Beta edition of Team System, the project portal is hosted on WSS 2.0, running on Microsoft Windows Server™ 2003. This platform offers many customization options. Anybody with a few days' training in WSS can easily alter the look and feel of the portal in many ways:

- Add new documents

- Add new lists of documents

- Add new users or change existing users' capabilities

- Alter the WSS site template, changing the look and feel

Extending Team System

This section focuses on the more complex tasks of altering Team System in creative ways to offer new functionality that didn't exist before. This will be of interest to internal IT teams, who want to tweak Team System, as well as independent software vendors (ISVs) who may want to create and sell add-ons and plug-ins to Team System. Whatever your motivation, Microsoft has the support for you.

Each tool offered in Team Foundation Server is highly extensible and can be automated. Work item tracking, version control policies, build scripts, and programmability interfaces all enable customers to tailor Team System and Team Foundation Server to their specific needs. In addition, at the core of Team Foundation Server is a set of mechanisms intended to enable partner- and customer-written tools to integrate into the Team Foundation Server environment as first-class citizens.

Team System can be extended on any of its three tiers:

- **Database Tier.** SQL Server 2005 offers many extensibility and integration options.

- **Application Tier.** ASMX Web services and a robust Microsoft .NET object model offer many options.

- **Client.** Visual Studio Integration Partners (VSIP) have long been successful at adding new functionality to the client; many APIs support it.

There are object models and extensibility options for each of these tiers, as seen in Figure 9-6. There is plenty of support outside of Team System for modifying SQL Server 2005 and Microsoft ASP.NET Web services, for example, so the possibilities are limitless.

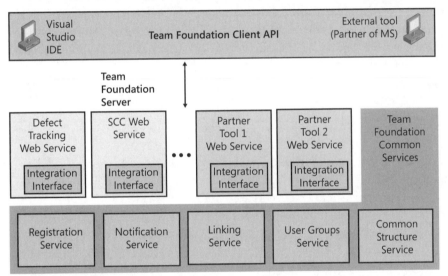

Figure 9-6   Extensibility architecture found in Team Foundation Services

We'll look at a more distinct set of ways that Team System can be extended:

- **Core Services.** Build new tools to support new artifacts/types, extend the databases, add new Web services, or link to other tools' artifacts, raise and subscribe to events, integrate with Team Explorer, or add pages to Project Creation Wizard.

- **Work Item Tracking.** Respond to events, spawn work items, link to other work items, integrate with other client applications, or build new client applications (that is, Web applications).

- **Version Control.** Respond to events, add (diff/merge) support for new file types, participate in integrated check-in, or define new policies.

- **Reporting.** Extend the database or data warehouse with other domain- or tool-specific data; perform data mining.

- **Team Build.**   Add new build tasks; track other build systems' data in the Team Foundation Server database.

- **Project Portal.**   Add new Web parts, such as queries or Reporting Services reports.

Extending the Core Services

Not only do the work item, version control, and build services have full integration interfaces, but Microsoft has created an extensive, pluggable array of services by which you can extend Team System.

Team Foundation Server's shared services are detailed in the following sections.

Linking Service   The linking service enables tools to establish loosely coupled relationships ("links") between data elements they hold. For example, in Team Foundation Server, the relationship between a defect (bug) work item and the source code that was changed to fix the defect is held as this sort of link. To participate, a tool must implement methods that expose their data as Team Foundation Server "artifacts," and it must respond to queries against them. Using this facility, a tool can participate in a relationship that it wasn't initially designed to recognize.

Security Service   The security service implements groups of Microsoft Windows identities within Team Foundation Server. These groups, local to a Team Foundation Server, are used to assign permissions to Team Foundation Server artifacts and services. The groups can be administered without the help of the IT department. When a new tool is introduced to Team Foundation Server, it should respect these groups by using the group security service API. The security service also provides authorization services. Tools that do not offer their own authorization mechanism have the option to use the security service to secure objects and establish permissions.

Eventing Service   The eventing service is a Web service–based publication and subscription mechanism. As you'd expect, tools can raise events to the eventing service. Subscribers can register to receive notification when an event matches their subscription criteria. A notification recipient can either be a Web service or an e-mail address. When it's a Web service, the subscription includes the URL of a Web service to be called when a notification is to be delivered. When it's an e-mail address, a notification can be delivered through e-mail via an SMTP server.

Visual Studio Team System includes a flexible, extensible mechanism for subscription and notification. The most common user notification mechanism is e-mail, although other mechanisms will be supported in future versions. The most common service notification mechanism is Web services. The Team Foundation Notification Service is a reliable, asynchronous publish/subscribe event notification system supporting the distributed Visual Studio Team System environment. Users and other services can subscribe to those events. When the source tool raises an event, the event is matched against subscriptions, and notifications are generated. For example, Figure 9-7 shows the notification alerts implemented directly inside the Visual Studio 2005 integrated development environment (IDE).

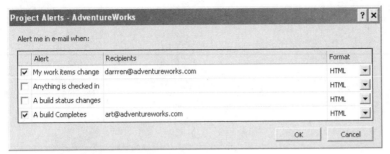

Figure 9-7   Configuring Visual Studio 2005 to send alerts when certain events occur

Classification Service   The classification service works in coordination with the linking service to allow classification of Team Foundation Server artifacts according to predefined taxonomies. This enables tools whose artifacts do not share a common "natural" taxonomy to organize their data in such a way that cross-tool reporting along common axes is possible. For instance, if work items are naturally organized by team and tests are naturally organized by component, tests can additionally be organized by team to enable them to be reported alongside work items.

Registration Service   When a new tool is introduced to Team Foundation Server, its artifact types, link types, event schemas, and service interfaces are registered via the registration service. Clients of the new tool discover its location by asking the registration service. Client configuration is easier because the client only needs to know how to find the registration service. This also makes it easier to move services from one Host to another because the registration service will redirect clients as needed.

Extending Work Item Tracking

Team Foundation Server includes a robust API from which you can build many custom applications that manipulate work items. Although this can be done directly with the ASMX Web Services, it is best to use the provided .NET object model because it simplifies the complexities of the Web Service API. By referencing the Team Foundation Client and Work Item Tracking assemblies, you can connect to a Team Foundation Server and manipulate its work items.

This extensibility creates many opportunities, from building your own client tools (Web-based, for example) to building your own Web services, tied into the eventing system previously mentioned, to spawn work items. Consider a scenario in which you want to "hook" into Team Foundation Server, and whenever a new scenario or bug work item is created, you want to "spawn" several related task work items. This would almost be like a macro, in which a few keystrokes spawned many more. Productivity like this is important because using Team Explorer to add work items can be tedious. Any automation that you can provide to your team can really speed up your process.

Here's some sample code for automating the creation of work items:

```
using System;
using Microsoft.VisualStudio.TeamFoundation.Client;
using Microsoft.VisualStudio.Currituck.Client;

namespace AdventureWorks
{
  class Program
  {
    private static void AddWorkItem(string AssignedBy,string Pwd,
      string type,string title, string state, string assignedTo,
      DateTime createdDate, string disciplineOrType,
      string areaPath, string iterationPath)
    {
      // Connect to TFS
      TeamFoundationServer tfs = new TeamFoundationServer("TFS1",
        new System.Net.NetworkCredential(AssignedBy, Pwd, "AW"));

      // Access the Work Item Store
      WorkItemStore store =
        (WorkItemStore)tfs.GetService(typeof(WorkItemStore));

      // Add Work Item
      WorkItemType taskType =
        store.Projects["AdventureWorks"].WorkItemTypes[type];
      WorkItem item = new WorkItem(store, taskType);
      item.Title = title;
      item.State = state;
      item.Fields["Assigned To"].Value = assignedTo;
      item.Fields["Created Date"].Value = createdDate.ToShortDateString();
      item.Fields["Discipline"].Value = disciplineOrType;
      item.Fields["Area Path"].Value = areaPath;
      item.Fields["Iteration Path"].Value = iterationPath;

      // Save
      item.Save();
    }
    static void Main(string[] args)
    {
      AddWorkItem("PM", "P@ssw0rd", "Task", "Design a Blog App",
        "Active", "Architect", DateTime.Today, "Development",
        @"\Development", @"\Alpha");
    }
  }
}
```

Note   The preceding code uses the Extensibility Toolkit. After installing the toolkit, you need to reference two assemblies: *Microsoft.VisualStudio.Currituck.Client.dll* and *Microsoft. VisualStudio.TeamFoundation.Client.dll*. Both are installed into the C:\Program Files\Microsoft Visual Studio 8\Common7\IDE\PrivateAssemblies folder.

Extending Version Control

Team System's version control can be fully automated using APIs, much like the previous work item section. By referencing the appropriate .NET assemblies, you can automate the check-in, check-out, and other administrative functions. With this kind of capability, you can build your own add-ins or plug-ins for other environments, much like what SourceGear has done with its Allerton product (which you will read about later in this chapter).

Here's some sample code that automates version control:

```
using System;
using System.IO;
using Microsoft.VisualStudio.Hatteras.Client;
using Microsoft.VisualStudio.TeamFoundation.Client;

namespace AdventureWorks
{
  class Program
  {
    static void Main(string[] args)
    {
      // Connect to TFS using the TeamFoundationServerFactory
      TeamFoundationServer tfs =
        TeamFoundationServerFactory.GetServer("TFFS1");

      // Reference the Version Control service
      VersionControl versionControl =
        (SourceControl)tfs.GetService(typeof(VersionControl));

      // Create a workspace
      Workspace workspace = versionControl.CreateWorkspace("VCExample",
        sourceControl.AuthenticatedUser);

      // Create a mapping to associate a path on the server with local disk
      workspace.CreateMapping("$/", @"c:\VCExample");

      // Get the files from the repository
      workspace.Get();

      // Create a directory and a test file
      String topDir = Path.Combine(workspace.Folders[0].LocalItem, "sub");
      Directory.CreateDirectory(topDir);
      String fileName = Path.Combine(topDir, "basic.cs");
      using (StreamWriter sw = new StreamWriter(fileName))
      {
        sw.WriteLine("revision 1 of basic.cs");
      }

      // Add the directory and file to version control
      workspace.PendAdd(topDir, true);

      // Display pending changes
      PendingChange[] pendingChanges = workspace.GetPendingChanges();
      Console.WriteLine("Your current pending changes:");
```

```
   foreach (PendingChange pendingChange in pendingChanges)
   {
     Console.WriteLine("  path: " + pendingChange.LocalItem +
       ", change: " +
       PendingChange.ChangeTypeToString(pendingChange.ChangeType));
   }

   // Checkin the items we added (will create a new changeset)
   int changesetNumber =
     workspace.CheckIn(pendingChanges, "Sample changes");
   Console.WriteLine("Checked in changeset " +
     changesetNumber.ToString());

   // Checkout and modify the file
   workspace.PendEdit(fileName);
   using (StreamWriter sw = new StreamWriter(fileName))
   {
     sw.WriteLine("revision 2 of basic.cs");
   }

   // Get the pending change and check in the new revision
   pendingChanges = workspace.GetPendingChanges();
   changesetNumber = workspace.CheckIn(pendingChanges, "Modified basic.cs");
   Console.WriteLine("Checked in changeset " + changesetNumber.ToString());
    }
  }
}
```

Another interesting way to extend Team System's version control is by creating your own custom check-in policies. Remember that Team System includes only a few policies out of the box. Your team or company might want to create and deploy something more interesting. For example, ensure that your domain-specific business rules are not violated, such as Sarbanes-Oxley (SOX) Requirements.

A custom check-in policy needs to implement two interfaces: *IPolicyDefinition* and *IPolicyEvaluation*. The *IPolicyDefinition* interface assists the user in identifying and enabling the policy, and the *IPolicyEvaluation* interface performs the actual policy validation and messaging during a check-in.

Here's some sample code that implements a simple check-in policy:

```
using System;
using System.Windows.Forms;
using Microsoft.VisualStudio.Hatteras.Client;

namespace AdventureWorks
{
  [Serializable]
  public class SimplePolicy : IPolicyDefinition, IPolicyEvaluation
  {
    [NonSerialized]
    public static readonly PolicyFailure[] m_noFailures =
      new PolicyFailure[0];
```

```csharp
private IPendingCheckin m_pendingCheckin = null;

// IPolicyDefinition Members

// Description displayed in the UI.
public string Description
{
  get { return "Prompt user to decide if they are in compliance."; }
}

// Method invoked by policy framework when checkin policy created
public bool Edit(System.Windows.Forms.IWin32Window parent,
  IServiceProvider serviceProvider)
{
  if (MessageBox.Show(parent,
    "Do you want to turn on the Prompt Policy?", "Prompt Policy",
    MessageBoxButtons.YesNo) == DialogResult.Yes)
  {
    return true;
  }
  return false;
}

// Instructions stored with the definition on the VC server
public string InstallationInstructions
{
  get { return "To install this policy, follow the instructions!"; }
}

// Policy type, displayed in a list of all installed policy types
public string Type
{
  get { return "Prompt Policy"; }
}

// Policy type description, displayed when the policy type is selected
public string TypeDescription
{
  get { return "This policy prompts the user checkin or not."; }
}

// IPolicyEvaluation Members

// Method to perform the actual evaluation, called by the policy framework
public PolicyFailure[] Evaluate()
{
  if (MessageBox.Show("Should we let you checkin?",
    "Evaluate", MessageBoxButtons.YesNo) == DialogResult.Yes)
    return m_noFailures;
  else
  {
    PolicyFailure[] toReturn = new PolicyFailure[1];
    toReturn[0] = new PolicyFailure(
      "You told us not to let you checkin.", this);
    return toReturn;
```

```
      }
   }

   // Method instantiating policy (accesses the pendingCheckin object)
   public void Initialize(IPendingCheckin pendingCheckin)
   {
     m_pendingCheckin = pendingCheckin;
     m_pendingCheckin.PendingChanges.CheckedPendingChangesChanged +=
       new EventHandler(PendingChanges_CheckedPendingChangesChanged);
   }

   // Method to dispose the policy object
   public void Dispose()
   {
     m_pendingCheckin.PendingChanges.CheckedPendingChangesChanged -=
       new EventHandler(PendingChanges_CheckedPendingChangesChanged);
     m_pendingCheckin = null;
   }

   // Event handler for changes in the checked-in source files
   private void PendingChanges_CheckedPendingChangesChanged(
     Object sender, EventArgs e)
   {
     OnPolicyStateChanged(Evaluate());
   }

   // Event subscribed-to by the policy framework
   public event PolicyStateChangedHandler PolicyStateChanged;

   // Method to notify the policy framework that policy compliance has changed
   private void OnPolicyStateChanged(PolicyFailure[] failures)
   {
     PolicyStateChangedHandler temp = PolicyStateChanged;
     if (temp != null)
     {
       temp(this, new PolicyStateChangedEventArgs(failures, this));
     }
   }

   // Method called if the user double-clicks on a policy failure in the UI
   public void Activate(PolicyFailure failure)
   {
     MessageBox.Show("The next time you are prompted, try clicking \"Yes.\"",
       "How to fix your policy failure");
   }

   // Method called when user presses F1 with an active policy failure
   public void DisplayHelp(PolicyFailure failure)
   {
     MessageBox.Show("This policy lets you decide if you are in compliance.",
       "Prompt Policy Help");
   }
  }
}
```

Extending Reporting

Initially, as you begin adopting Team System, your team probably won't begin using 100 percent of its capabilities. The odds are that you already have (and will continue to use, at least for awhile) some other work item, bug-tracking, version control, or build systems. These might be popular third-party products or home-grown solutions. Either way, you are or will be storing a lot of other data outside of Team System.

One way to extend reporting is by combining the data from your other systems with data inside of Team System. For example, if you are using a third-party build utility, you might want to report on that data to the Team System users.

Remember that Team System includes a data warehouse in which data from work item tracking, version control, builds, and testing tools are stored. This data warehouse includes both relational and online analytical processing (OLAP) databases. The OLAP data warehouse consists of several relational star schema databases that are implemented as a number of SQL Server 2005 analysis services cubes. At the center of the star schemas are several types of facts. Each type of fact has a primary relational table and a cube in the OLAP database that draws from that table. Each fact is composed of dimensions, measures, and details.

Cubes are the main objects in OLAP, a technology that provides fast access to data in a data warehouse. A cube is a set of data that is usually constructed from a subset of a data warehouse and is organized and summarized into a multidimensional structure defined by a set of dimensions and measures.

Dimensions are properties that are used to slice the data in a report. For example, the Work Item facts include Type and State dimensions. Dimensions are realized in the relational database as tables, with foreign key references to the dimension tables from the primary fact table.

Measures are properties that are aggregated (counted, added, and so forth) to provide the quantitative values in reports. For example, the version control's CodeChurn cube includes LinesAdded, LinesRemoved, and LinesChanged measures. Measures are columns in the primary fact table.

Details are columns that appear in the relational database only. They are generally longer text strings such as work item titles that are used primarily in list reports that can be drawn as efficiently from a relational database as it can from an OLAP database. Details are columns in the primary fact table that do not appear in the OLAP cube.

Understanding the data warehouse is important because Team System also includes a service that manages the updates to the warehouse. It allows custom or third-party tools to participate in the warehouse by describing their schema extensions and by providing an adapter to pull data from its operational store and place it in the warehouse. The schema is described in XML. The adapter is a managed assembly that implements an *IWarehouseAdapter* interface and uses the warehouse object model to interact with the warehouse.

If you will build your own adapter, you need to also implement the *IWarehouseAdapter* interface, and specifically the following methods:

- **void Initialize(IDataStore ds).**   Initializes your adapter.

- **InitRunResult InitRun().**   Provides the means by which an adapter can indicate that it will change schema on this run.

- **void Run( ).**   Performs the primary work by pulling data from the data store and writing it to the warehouse.

- **void RequestStop( ).**   Stops your adapter in an orderly fashion if the service is taken down.

Extending Team Build

Team Build includes many common tasks to support actions such as running tests and getting sources from version control. Your build process, however, might require other tasks to be run as part of the process. For example, a build administrator might want to have output assemblies deployed to a specified location after the compilation is complete but before testing begins, or a company might require a specific build numbering system, thereby overriding one of the default numbering schemes included in Team Build.

Team Build uses MSBuild for building applications and supports custom tasks to extend the build process. This topic discusses concepts for creating a custom Team Build task. Team Build can be extended so that a custom task can be executed at any phase of the build process. These tasks are simply .NET classes that inherit from *Task*. This class is found in the *Microsoft.Build.Utilities* namespace. The class derived from the *Task* class must implement the *Execute* method, which is invoked by MSBuild.

The first step is to code your custom task (a custom *BuildNumberGenerator* in this example). This task generates a unique build number based on current time in milliseconds. Take note of the *Output* attribute, which identifies the *BuildNumber* property as being an output of the *Task*.

```
using System;
using Microsoft.Build.Utilities;
using Microsoft.Build.Framework;
namespace AdventureWorks
{
  public class BuildNumberGenerator : Task
  {
    private string buildNumber;
    public override bool Execute()
    {
      buildNumber = DateTime.UtcNow.Ticks.ToString();
      return true;
    }
    [Output]
    public string BuildNumber
    {
```

```
    get { return buildNumber; }
  }
 }
}
```

After coding, you need to define the *build type* of this custom task by using the Team
Build client. The build type consists of TeamBuild.proj, VCOverrides.props, and
WorkspaceMapping.xml files. Every build type is represented by a folder that contains these
files. After creating the build type, you need to customize the definition by referencing your
custom task. For this example, you need to check out the TeamBuild.proj file and add the
following code to the file:

```
<!-- Add UsingTask line just after import statement - - >
<UsingTask
  TaskName="BuildNumberGenerator.BuildNumberGenerator"
  AssemblyFile="BuildNumberGenerator.dll"/>
<! -- Override the Target near the end of proj file - - >
<Target Name = "BuildNumberOverrideTarget" >
  <BuildNumberGenerator>
    <Output TaskParameter="BuildNumber" PropertyName="BuildNumber"/>
  </BuildNumberGenerator>
</BuildNumberOverrideTarget>
```

After coding and configuring the task, you need to add your task assembly to the same
location as TeamBuild.proj by using the appropriate command-line utility.

Extending Project Portal

The project portal can be extended by adding new Web parts or by building custom ones.
These new Web parts can expose specific reports, custom queries, or other functionality.
For example, SQL Server 2005 Reporting Services allows any reports to be called directly via
a URL. By following these steps, you can add a Page Viewer control to your portal site and
point it toward a report:

1. Modify the project portal and choose Design this Page.

2. Add a Page Viewer Web part (you may have to search or import).

3. Specify the link (URL) to the report. For example:
    *http://server/reports/pages/report.aspx?ItemPath=%2fAW%2fWork+Item+List_*

4. Specify any appearance and layout settings.

What you end up with is a Web part that executes the report when the portal is refreshed.
(See Figure 9-8.) This way, you can have your important reports executed and the results
available right on the main page, without requiring a user to click anything.

Creating your own custom Web parts is the true definition of project portal extensibility.
Rather than just use one of the built-in Web parts, such as the Page Viewer, the WSS
architecture allows developers to build their own Web parts, deploy them to WSS, and
install them so they can be used on various pages.

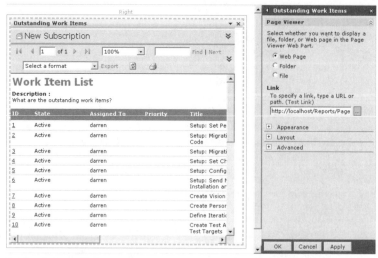

Figure 9-8   Adding a Page Viewer Web part to the project portal

The Microsoft Windows SharePoint Products and Technologies 2003 SDK contains conceptual overviews, programming tasks, samples, and references to guide you in developing solutions based on SharePoint products and technologies.

From Visual Studio, you can create a new Web Part Library project in your favorite language. This project needs to reference the WSS assembly and should specify a good version number and a strong name.

Here's some sample code that implements a simple Web part:

```
using System;
using System.ComponentModel;
using System.Runtime.InteropServices;
using System.Web.UI;
using System.Web.UI.WebControls;
using System.Xml.Serialization;
using Microsoft.SharePoint;
using Microsoft.SharePoint.WebPartPages;
using Microsoft.SharePoint.Utilities;
using System.Web.UI.HtmlControls;

namespace MyWebParts
{
  [XmlRoot(Namespace="MyWebParts")]
  public class SimpleWebPart : WebPart
  {
    private const string defaultText = "Team System";
    private string text=defaultText;
    HtmlButton _mybutton;
    HtmlInputText _mytextbox;

    // Event handler for button control to set Title property
    public void _mybutton_click (object sender, EventArgs e)
```

```
  {
    this.Title = _mytextbox.Value;
    try
    {
      this.SaveProperties=true;
    }
    catch
    {
      Caption = "Error... Could not save property.";
    }
  }

  // Override to create the objects for the Web Part's controls
  protected override void CreateChildControls ()
  {
    // Create _mytextbox control.
   _mytextbox = new HtmlInputText();
   _mytextbox.Value="";
    Controls.Add(_mytextbox);

    // Create _mybutton control and wire its event handler.
   _mybutton = new HtmlButton();
   _mybutton.InnerText = "Set Web Part Title";
   _mybutton.ServerClick += new EventHandler (_mybutton_click);
    Controls.Add (_mybutton);
  }

  [Browsable(true),Category("Miscellaneous"),
    DefaultValue(defaultText),WebPartStorage(Storage.Personal),
    FriendlyName("Text"),Description("Text Property")]
  public string Text
  {
    get { return text; }
    set { text = value; }
  }

  protected override void RenderWebPart(HtmlTextWriter output)
  {
    RenderChildren(output);
    output.Write("<BR>Text Property: " + SPEncode.HtmlEncode(Text));
  }
 }
}
```

You can take this basic structure and scale it out to almost any functionality. Web parts are essentially ASP.NET server controls that render the appropriate HTML back to the portal when asked to do so. You could add code to create work items or manage version control and start building a Team System Web client (something that's missing from the current offering from Microsoft).

 Note   To develop custom Web parts, you need to download the SharePoint Services SDK from *http://www.microsoft.com.*

Visual Studio 2005 Tool Integration

In addition to exploiting these shared services, you can also take advantage of a variety of additional plug-ins to fully integrate a tool into Team System. Figure 9-9 shows the various places where you can plug in your tools, services, and data.

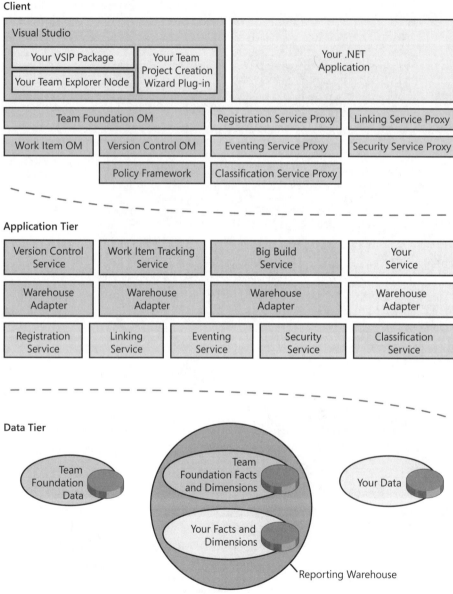

Figure 9-9   Using plug-ins within Team System

If you're planning on integrating tools with Team System, you should use the Visual Studio Integration Partner program SDK. Using the SDK will result in a consistent client experience, integrating your UI into the Visual Studio 2005 IDE. Alternatively, you can build a standalone .NET application that accesses the application tier by using the intelligent proxy layer.

Here are some specific areas of integration that are possible with Team System:

- Add creation of your tool's artifacts to the Team Project Creation Wizard (and, by implication, the process template that drives it).

- Make your tool and its data visible as nodes on Visual Studio 2005 Team Explorer.

- Use the warehouse dynamic schema modification facilities to extend the warehouse with your tool's data, and then build a warehouse adapter to pull your tool's operational data into the warehouse structures.

Extensibility Toolkit

The best way to get started extending is to explore the SDK. The kit consists of information and tools for customizing, extending, and integrating with Visual Studio Team System. Its intended audience includes partners, early adopters, and evaluators who want to explore the extensibility and integration characteristics of various components of the Visual Studio Team System suite.

Much like this chapter, the features in the Extensibility Toolkit are categorized into two groups: customer extensibility and partner extensibility. Customer extensibility includes features, tools, and documentation needed by users to customize Team Foundation Servers and Team Projects. These features are intrinsic to Team System. Partner extensibility includes features, tools, and documentation required by partners to build add-ins and integration components that add value and round out Team System.

 Note   The Extensibility Toolkit may end up becoming the Team System SDK.

Partners

What better way to demonstrate the extensibility of Team System than to list some partners who are doing exactly that? The following sections list a few of the various partners who are planning products. Keep in mind that this list is not complete and is based on information available at the time of this writing.

Borland

Borland's *CaliberRM* product provides requirements management for Team System. Users will be able to leverage requirements management capabilities critical to successful software delivery throughout the entire life cycle.

CaliberRM is designed to work within Team Foundation Server's infrastructure, linking life-cycle artifacts with requirements throughout the application life cycle and providing end-to-end, requirements-to-test traceability. This integration allows users to manage and track requirements from directly within the Team System environment. Users can also generate reports that formalize requirements data, the state of product tests, and requirements, as well as generate custom reports. In addition, organizations will be able to automate ALM metrics and reporting with dashboard views of data. Requirements information will be loaded into the data warehouse with the capability to then link from CaliberRM to other objects within the environment.

CaliberRM will support Microsoft's process model guidance in Visual Studio Team System, including those established via both the MSF Agile and CMMI process models. Users will set up templates based on their process of choice. For example, analysts, developers, testers, and project managers can access guidance extensions to the MSF Formal process, helping organizations make the most of the CaliberRM integration into Team System with minimal effort and apply requirements engineering best practices.

Microsoft initially approached Borland to partner on this initiative, which shows just how imperative requirements management is to the software delivery process. It is making a statement about how important requirements are to its platform and overall software development. You can access more information at *http://www.borland.com*.

SourceGear

Allerton is the code name for a suite of client applications being developed by SourceGear to provide access to Team Foundation Server from outside the Visual Studio environment. Using one of three offered client interfaces, developers will be able to use the version control and work item tracking features of Visual Studio Team System from other platforms, including Mac OS and Linux.

The Allerton clients are Java applications and will run on any platform that supports the Java runtime, including Mac OS, Linux, and Windows. All GUI development is being done in SWT to give each user a native interface on his or her platform.

The first Allerton client is an Eclipse Plugin, which is a team provider plug-in for Eclipse 3.0. It will allow developers to perform version control operations from within the Eclipse IDE. The Eclipse Plugin will also be fully supported in IBM's suite of WebSphere Software, including WebSphere Studio and Rational Application Developer.

The second Allerton client is a standalone GUI application, which is an Eclipse RCP application providing users with a native GUI client with an Explorer-style interface. Allerton also consists of a third client, which is a command-line client supporting the same operations and syntax as the one being provided by Microsoft with Team System.

Allerton will support all the version control features of Team System, from basic operations such as Add, Get, Check Out, Check In, and Undo, to more advanced features such as

Branch, Merge, and Shelve. Users will also be able to update work items when performing version control operations such as Check In. The Allerton clients communicate directly with the Team Foundation Server using HTTP and Web services. Security is provided through the use of SSL.

Allerton is the codename for the product. The actual product name has not yet been made public. SourceGear plans to release version 1.0 of the product in the same time frame as the final 1.0 release of Team Foundation Server. You can access more information about SourceGear at *http://www.sourcegear.com*.

AutomatedQA

AutomatedQA has several developer-related and quality assurance tools. Some of these overlap in functionality, and others offer solutions for missing functionality in Team System. AutomatedQA plans to integrate its *TestComplete*, *AQTime*, and *Automated Build Studio*. With each of these products, managers can browse the results from the various tests. Since the data is saved directly in Team System, the eventing services can automatically receive e-mail or instant message alerts when tests fail.

TestComplete offers functional GUI testing to developers. Whereas Team System offers basic test types for unit, manual, and Web load testing, TestComplete extends Team System with automated GUI testing. Together, TestComplete and Team System provide developers with a complete and well-integrated testing solution. Because UIs commonly undergo rapid changes during the development life cycle, TestComplete's object-aware architecture enables testers to create flexible tests that are easy to update and maintain. TestComplete integrates with and extends Team System and adds support for testing Microsoft Visual Basic® 6, Microsoft Visual C++® MFC/ATL, Microsoft ASP.NET, WinForms, Java, and Borland VCL applications.

AQtime brings in-depth memory usage analysis and more detailed performance-profiling features. With AQtime, developers can find memory leaks and performance bottlenecks from inside Visual Studio Team System. AQtime does line-level performance profiling to pinpoint the source of performance problems.

Automated Build Studio provides release management features for Team System, such as a graphical script builder, integrated testing, and continuous integration. It can prevent bad releases by automatically running TestComplete tests as part of the build validation process, and it can automatically create Team System tasks when tests fail. You can access more information at *http://www.automatedqa.com*.

Identify

AppSight, from Identify Software, enhances Visual Studio Team System by automating and accelerating the tasks of application problem resolution—one of the most time-consuming and costly processes of life-cycle application management. *AppSight* is integrated with Visual

Studio 2005 Team System, through the addition of embedded user interfaces and new work flows, for all members of the application life cycle, including architects, developers, and testers. By enabling collaboration on problem triage and resolution among all members of a software team—architects, developers, testers, and operations managers—AppSight can significantly reduce the complexity of the life-cycle management processes required to design, develop, deploy, and support applications.

While testers execute manual and automated tests through Visual Studio Team Test, *AppSight's* problem resolution system leverages black box technology to transparently capture a complete execution record. This saves the tester the time-consuming tasks of problem replication and documentation. The *AppSight* black box log files, linked to Work Items, are automatically saved in the Team Foundation Server. Developers use *AppSight's* analysis views to analyze the logs to determine the root cause of any application problem—hangs, crashes, incorrect logic, slowdowns, interoperability issues, misconfiguration, and more. Identify's *AppSight* accelerates application testing and delivery, enhances software quality, and helps development teams deliver on time and within budget.

As a complete life-cycle solution, the AppSight problem resolution system extends into the next phase, as applications are deployed in production, providing automated problem capture capabilities with communication back to development teams. By transferring all required data from production into the hands of the development team, AppSight minimizes finger-pointing and accelerates problem resolution cycles, enabling developers to focus on development rather than spend cycles on problem solving. More information is at *http:// www.identify.com.*

Compuware

Compuware TestPartner is an automated testing tool that accelerates functional testing of complex applications developed with Microsoft, Java, and Web technologies. TestPartner bridges the gap between development and testing teams while fostering a cooperative environment for problem resolution early in the development cycle. You can visit the Compuware Web site at *http://www.compuware.com.*

Integration between *Compuware TestPartner* and Visual Studio Team System gives development access to the same testing assets as testers allowing them to resolve errors more quickly, improve communication and collaboration and improve application quality in a cost-effective way. By building test assets early on, Quality Assurance (QA) teams find more time for thorough testing to deploy applications confidently. *Compuware QACenter* extends Visual Studio Team System testing capabilities with comprehensive environment support (including Web, ERP/CRM, Java, packaged application, mainframe, and distributed client/ server technologies) allowing Visual Studio customers to ensure quality across application environments. Specific integration points include:

- Drag-and-drop assets from *TestPartner* into your Visual Studio Team System projects.

- Execute *TestPartner* functional tests directly within their IDE along with other Visual Studio Team System testing assets or monitoring capabilities.

- All test results are logged back into Visual Studio Team System so testers and developers have access to pass/fail details directly from the IDE.

- Seamless integration between Visual Studio Team System and *TestPartner* allows IDE users to launch TestPartner to edit scripts or drill into failed runs for further analysis.

AVIcode

AVIcode is a software development company that produces application fault management software. AVIcode's products are designed to protect software investments by simplifying application maintenance and troubleshooting. This dramatically reduces defect resolution time. AVIcode's flagship product, *Intercept Studio*, detects crashes and performance degradations of production applications running on the .NET platform.

Intercept Studio contains a management infrastructure that enables operations personnel to monitor application health within datacenter management consoles. Visual Studio integration enables developers to design application health models and to build Microsoft Operations Manager (MOM) management packs. *Intercept Studio* correlates various root cause diagnostic information with related application code and System Definition models (SDM) that streamlines application support and provides a foundation for effective incident management process.

Intercept Studio integrates with Team Foundation Server, enabling IT operations teams to reduce the cost associated with application maintenance and support by quickly identifying the root cause of operational problems. This is performed through the automatic creation of new work items for issues detected in the production environment. Architects can use tools to customize and prioritize application health information. These tools are integrated into Microsoft Visual Studio 2005 Team Edition for Software Architects. Please visit *http://www.avicode.com* for more information.

Mercury Interactive Corporation

Mercury Interactive Corporation has long supported the entire application quality ecosystem from product design and development to application delivery and management. It plans to integrate with Team System by sharing testing assets such as unit tests and functional and load tests in both development and quality assurance through integration with *Mercury Quality Center*™ and *Mercury Performance Center*™.

Mercury Diagnostics™ will integrate with regard to collaboration on the diagnosis and resolution of application defects, performance bottlenecks, and scalability problems across the entire application life cycle. Full visibility of the application testing process will be delivered through the *Mercury Application Delivery Dashboard*™. You can access more information about Mercury Interactive Corporation at *http://www.mercury.com*.

Serena

Serena Software is a company focused on managing change in the IT environment. Serena's products and services automate process and control change for teams managing development, Web content, and IT infrastructure. Its *ProcessView Composer* product will integrate with Team System by enabling business users to rapidly visualize their application requirements while collaborating more effectively with IT architects, developers, and testers. You can access the Web site for Serena Software at *http://www.serena.com*.

Conchango

Conchango has developed a *Scrum* methodology template for Team System. The plug-in, which will be available as a free download from *www.scrum-master.com*, will provide development teams with deep support for the use of Scrum, a popular Agile Alliance methodology, when using Visual Studio Team System. The software life-cycle development product will recognize the best practices that are defined by Scrum and build them into any work and processes conducted by the development team.

As a leading proponent of Agile product delivery and an active user of the Scrum methodology, Conchango will use the tool within its own projects as well as offer it as an aid to other organizations adopting Scrum.

Some key benefits of the Scrum plug-in include the following:

- Being able to align the terminology, artifacts, and processes of the tools with those of Scrum, ensuring that projects flow more smoothly

- Providing "scaffolding" to help teams or individuals who are new to Scrum project delivery by providing contextual Scrum guidance

- Supporting those in Scrum roles carrying out their responsibilities

- Making the product simple and flexible so that it is not onerous to use or overly prescriptive

Ken Schwaber, who founded the Agile Alliance in 2001, concluded, "The very best productivity and quality has come from teams that know how to do their work, and how to use the best tools to do their work. The steps that Conchango is taking with the Scrum community and Microsoft to make a Scrum version of Visual Studio Team System will make these productivity improvements more scalable and understandable." Go to *http://www.conchango.com* to learn more.

Osellus

Software development organizations that are planning to implement Microsoft Visual Studio 2005 Team System as the standard platform for enacting their life-cycle processes use *IRIS Process Author* to tailor the underlying process models in accordance to their specific enterprise environments. *IRIS* generates process templates for Visual Studio Team System as well as templates for Microsoft Project from the tailored processes.

IRIS Process Author is used to tailor the two process types of Microsoft Solutions Framework (MSF) that are shipped with Visual Studio Team System, or to assemble entirely new processes. Visual Studio Team System instantiates the resulting process models across multiple development projects. The combination of *IRIS* as an authoring environment and Visual Studio Team System as an enactment platform constitutes a leading process automation solution for the enterprise. The IRIS visual modeling environment can be used to model your software development processes, irrespective of your choice of methodology (MSF, proprietary, or RUP). The resulting process models are fully compliant with Visual Studio Team System and can be enacted across multiple Visual Studio Team System projects.

IRIS Process Author is also available as a hosted offering under *IRIS-on-Demand* service, as seen in Figure 9-10. The product is fully Web based, and its entire functionality is available through a simple Web browser. You pay for the service on a per-user, per-month basis. The elimination of a large up-front investment and the pay-per-use pricing model ensures an immediate positive Return on Investment (ROI) in large or small MSF tailoring initiatives. To give you a head start, *IRIS-on-Demand* includes the full contents of the MSF for Agile Software Development or MSF for CMMI Process Improvement. You can obtain more information at *http://www.osellus.com*.

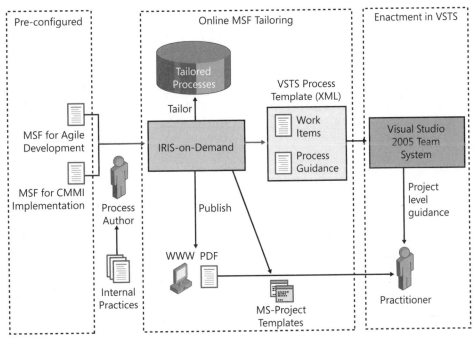

Figure 9-10   IRIS-on-Demand and Team System

Summary

Team System is built on a core set of services that offer unlimited customization and extensibility. Process templates enable teams to customize the configuration of new projects and to customize process guidance documentation without writing any code or HTML. Team System also offers a software development kit that Visual Studio Integration Partners can use to tightly integrate their process tools into Team System, thereby extending Team System's capabilities. In this way, Team System will not only meet your needs now, but also change as your needs change in the future.

Chapter 10
Wrapping It Up: The Endgame and Deployment

In this chapter:
Team Build 247
Deploying the Application. 248
Closing Down the Current Iteration 248
Summary. 258

Endgame. Just like in the game of chess, this small but key segment can make or break you, and it must be played carefully. In the application-development-process endgame, players are the operations team that will deploy and maintain the completed system. Microsoft® Visual Studio® 2005 Team System will define these engineers' areas of responsibility through the assignment of tasks, the deployment of reports and checklists, the creation of setup files, and the continued tracking and reporting of defects. This chapter, which addresses the culmination of the software construction project, will round out the remaining features of Team System.

Testing often occurs after development, most often in the traditional waterfall development model. There have been many studies on software development efficiencies and they all have the same message: As the project progresses, the cost of fixing bugs becomes much more costly. Not only is finding and fixing bugs that evade daily development practices expensive, but it's also difficult to keep test and development environments in sync and diagnose run-time errors. Throughout this book, we looked at how Team System assists in helping different members of the project team solve these and other challenges, thus increasing the predictability of project success.

Team Build

As discussed in Chapter 6, one of the most difficult tasks throughout this process is to get a good public "team build" because all source code in the team project must be built—including changes by the entire development team—on a separate build machine. Although this process is normally very tedious, Team Build provides a straightforward way to assist with this build process—a simple wizard that generates a build script.

This build script automates the entire out-of-the-box Team Build process, and it can be edited if the process needs to be further customized or extended. To fully support this crucial part of the application development process, Team Build integrates seamlessly with other Team System tools such as Team Foundation Version Control, Work Item Tracking, and various testing utilities available to developers and testers.

At the completion of the build process, a full report is generated with information about the build result as well as the general health of the build. This report shows relevant information about the state of the build, including the following items:

- The associated number of errors and warnings for each build configuration with log file links

- Test run and code coverage results

- A complete list of changesets that includes the build and who checked it in

- Work items associated with a build

The bottom line is that Team Build might very well become your new best friend because it can give you final, stable .MSI files that are ready to deploy.

Deploying the Application

Although deployment has minimal support in the initial release of Team System, there are options to assist with the various deployment-related tasks. Integration with Team Build and the creation of .MSI files are key for helping the development team deploy the solution. Another is the deployment report that is generated after you test-deploy an application against a datacenter. This report, similar to a bill of materials, allows you to inventory which files are included for deployment. These tools will assist in planning and implementing your next deployment.

Closing Down the Current Iteration

As each iteration ends, certain tasks must be accomplished. Part of the "fit and finish" of software development is to determine which work items are left and whether they can be completed within the current iteration. If any of the remaining work items cannot be finished, they must be moved into the next (or later) iteration, as determined by the project priorities. You must also make sure that the files in source control are properly labeled so that you can locate them as needed. Another consideration for future iterations is the need to possibly branch code as an option if the next iteration forks or takes a weird turn.

Continuing to Track Bugs and Defects

Even after a successful development iteration, build, and deployment, work item tracking might start tracking user-encountered bugs and defects. During development, primarily the testers and developers were logging in bugs. Keep in mind that even if an iteration is closed out for development, work items can still be logged in. Visual Studio 2005 Team System assists the team in continuing to stabilize the application long after the initial release.

Reporting

When Visual Studio 2005 Team System is used during your project, data is automatically captured in the data warehouse and used in reports that provide additional insight into trends and activity within your project. For example, when project tasks are performed, the data warehouse automatically collects data that enables reports such as the following:

Remaining Work Report

The Remaining Work Report (in a cumulative flow diagram form) shows work remaining measured as scenarios and Quality of Service (QoS) requirements being resolved and closed in the iteration.

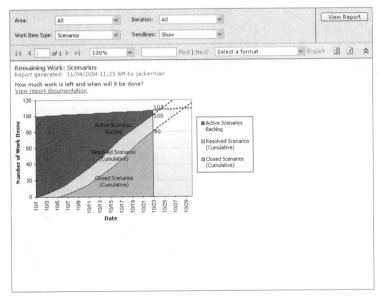

Figure 10-1   Remaining Work Report

The following table explains the various sections of the Remaining Work Report example in Figure 10-1.

Data Series	Line Description
Work Item States	Each color band represents the number of work items that have reached the corresponding state as of the given date.
Chart Height	The total height is the total amount of work to be done in the iteration. If the top line increases, the total work is increasing. Typically, the reason is that unpla nned work is adding to the total required. That may be expected if you've scheduled a buffer for unplanned work, such as bug fixing. (See "Unplanned Work Report," later in this section.) If the top line decreases, it means that total work is decreasing, probably because work is being cut out of the iteration.

Data Series	Line Description
Work in Progress	Current status is measured by height on a particular date. The remaining backlog is measured by the current height of the leftmost area, Active in this case. The current completions are shown by the current height of the rightmost area, Closed. The height of the band in between indicates the work in progress—in this case, items Resolved but not Closed.
Resolved	An expansion in the middle bands can reveal a bottleneck—for example, if too many items are waiting to be tested and testing resources are inadequate. Alternatively, a significant narrowing of the band can indicate spare capacity (a rare discovery!).
End Date	Although it can be easy to extrapolate an end completion inventory or end date for the backlog from a cumulative flow diagram like this, a small caution applies. Many projects observe an S-curve pattern, in which progress is steepest in the middle. The commonsense explanations for the slower starting and ending rates are that startup is always a little difficult, and tough problems tend to get handled at the end of a cycle.

Velocity Report

The Velocity Report, one of the key elements for estimation, shows how quickly the team is actually completing planned work and how much the rate varies from day to day or iteration to iteration. Use this data to plan the next iteration in conjunction with the quality measures. Similar to the Remaining Work Report, this report is most useful when looking at days within an iteration or iterations within a project.

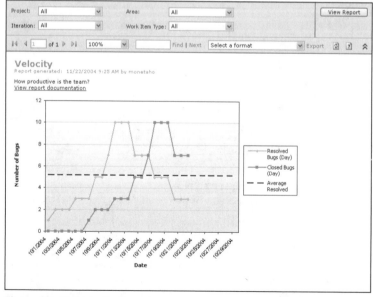

Figure 10-2   Velocity Report

The following table explains the various sections of the Velocity Report example in Figure 10-2.

Data Series	Line Description
Resolved Work Items	This line shows the count of work items resolved on each day.
Closed Work Items	This line shows the count of work items closed on each day.
Bugs Found per Scenarios Resolved	This line divides the sums of bugs found by scenarios resolved. This quality indicator should stay low. If it goes up, more time is needed to find and fix bugs.

Unplanned Work Report

This report distinguishes the total work from the Remaining Work Report into the planned and unplanned. Very few teams know all the work to be done ahead of time, even within the iteration.

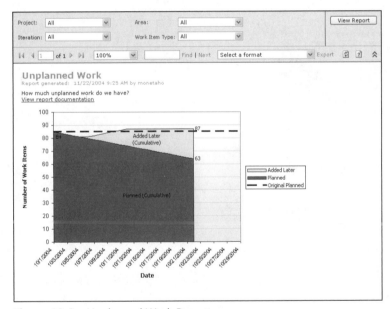

Figure 10-3 Unplanned Work Report

The following table explains the various sections of the Unplanned Work Report example in Figure 10-3.

Data Series	Line Description
Chart Height	The top line of this graph matches the top line of the Remaining Work Report. The total height is the total amount of work to be done in the iteration.

Data Series	Line Description
Added Later	The areas then divide the work into the planned and unplanned segments ("unplanned" means unscheduled as of the beginning of the iteration).
Interpretation	For monitoring, use this graph to determine the extent to which unplanned work is forcing you to cut into planned work. For estimation, use this to determine the amount of schedule buffer to allow for unplanned work in future iterations.

Quality Indicators Report

This report combines the test results, code coverage from testing, code churn, and bugs to help you see many perspectives at once.

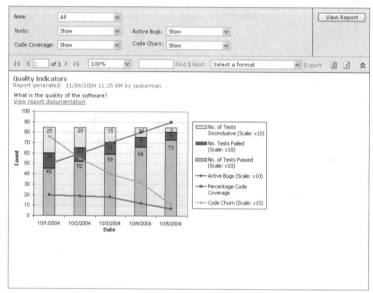

Figure 10-4   Quality Indicators Report

The following table explains the various sections of the Quality Indicators Report example in Figure 10-4.

Data Series	Line Description
Bars	The height of the bar shows you how many tests have been run and, of those run, how many have returned Pass, Fail, and Inconclusive results.
Code Coverage	The first series of points is the Code Coverage attained by those tests (specifically, the ones run with code coverage enabled). Ordinarily, as more tests are run, more code should be covered. On the other hand, if test execution and test pass rates rise without a corresponding increase in code coverage, it might indicate that the incremental tests are redundant.

Data Series	Line Description
Code Churn	The second series of points is Code Churn (in other words, the number of lines added and modified in the code under test). High churn obviously indicates a large amount of change and the corresponding risk that bugs will be introduced as the side effect of the changes. In a perfectly refactored project, you can see code churn with no change in code coverage or test pass rates. Otherwise, high code churn might indicate falling coverage and the need to rewrite tests.
Active Bugs	The third series is the active bug count. Clearly, there should be a correlation between the number of active bugs and the number of test failures. If the active bug count is rising and your tests are not showing corresponding failures, your tests are probably not testing the same functionality that the bugs are reporting. Similarly, if active bug count is falling and test pass rates are not increasing, you might be at risk for a rising reactivation rate.

Bug Rates Report

Bug rates are best interpreted with your knowledge of all of the current project activities and the other metrics on the Quality Indicators graph. For example, a high find rate can be a sign of sloppy code (a bad thing), newly integrated code (an expected thing), effective testing (a good thing), or exceptional events such as a bug bash (an infrequent thing). In contrast, a low find rate can mean high-quality product or ineffective testing. Use code coverage, code churn, and test rates to help you assess the meaning.

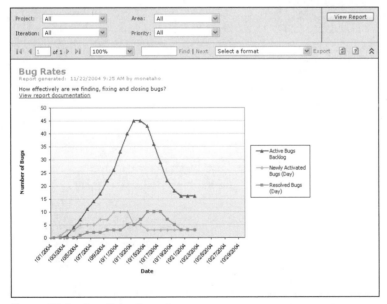

Figure 10-5   Bug Rates Report

The following table explains the various sections of the Bug Rates Report example in Figure 10-5.

Data Series	Line Description
Newly Active Bugs	The number of new bugs found on the date
Resolved Bugs	The number of bugs resolved on the date

Reactivations Report

Reactivations are the case of work items that have been resolved or closed prematurely. A small amount of noise (for example, < 5%) might be acceptable, but a high or rising rate of reactivation should warn the project manager to diagnose the root cause and fix it.

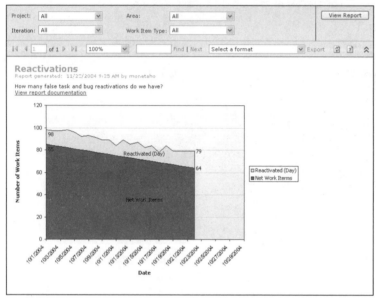

Figure 10-6   Reactivations Report

The following table explains the various sections of the Reactivations Report example in Figure 10-6.

Data Series	Line Description
Chart Height	The top line of this graph shows the total work items of the selected types (for example, bugs) resolved in the build.
Reactivated	The height of top area is the number of reactivations (for example, work items) previously resolved or closed that are now active again.
Net Work Items	The height of the lower area is the difference between the total work items resolved and the reactivated work items.

Bugs By Priority Report

This report type assesses the effectiveness of two things: bug hunting and triage. Bugs happen and finding them is a good thing. Often, however, the easy-to-find bugs aren't the ones that will annoy customers the most. If the high-priority bugs are not being found, and a disproportionate number of low-priority bugs ones are, redirect the testing efforts to look for the bugs that matter. In triage, it is easy to overprioritize bugs beyond the capacity to resolve them or underprioritize them to the point where customers are highly dissatisfied.

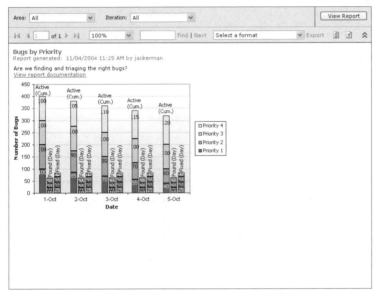

Figure 10-7   Bugs By Priority Report

The following table explains the various sections of the Bugs By Priority Report example in Figure 10-7.

Data Series	Line Description
Side By Side	The series includes total active bugs at the time of the build, number found in build, and number resolved in build. These are the same three series of bars that represent similar data in the Bug Rates Report.
Stacking	Each series is further broken into priority, so each bar stacks from highest to lowest priority, with the lowest on top.
Interpretation	If there are many high-priority bugs active, be sure that the capacity exists to address them. On the other hand, a significant debt of low-priority bugs might also lead to customer dissatisfaction.

Actual Quality Versus Planned Velocity Report

How fast can we go before quality suffers? As much as teams believe that "haste makes waste," there is usually a business incentive to go faster. A project manager's goal ought to be to balance the two by finding the maximum rate of progress that does not make quality suffer. This graph presents the relationship, for each iteration, of estimated size to overall quality.

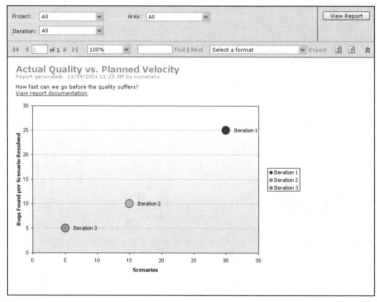

Figure 10-8   Actual Quality Versus Planned Velocity Report

The following table explains the various sections of the Actual Quality Versus Planned Velocity Report example in Figure 10-8.

Data Series	Line Description
Scenarios	The x-axis is the number of scenarios actually closed (completed) in the iteration. Each bubble is labeled according to its iteration.
Bugs Found per Scenarios Resolved	The y-axis is the total number of bugs found divided by the scenarios closed (in other words, the average number of bugs per scenario).
Total Estimated Work	The area of each bubble is the amount of work estimated in the iteration, computed as the sum of ROM estimates on the scenarios.
Efficiency	Stoplight colors go from green for the lowest bugs per iteration to red for the highest. If haste is in fact making waste, larger bubbles (larger iterations) will be higher in the northeast, and smaller ones will be lower in the southwest. If you are working at a comfortable pace and have not seen quality drop with planned iteration size, all iterations will be at roughly the same height on the y-axis.

Other Reports

You can also create reports that are more complex because of the tight integration between these tools. The relationships are maintained in both the tools and the underlying data warehouse. This integration also enables you to create other reports that can provide an overview by showing test results, code coverage, and code churn, among other trends and metrics.

Each Visual Studio 2005 Team System process template uses its own set of unique reports. The reporting functionality is fully customizable using Microsoft SQL Server™ Reporting Services so that it can meet the individual tastes and needs of each development team.

The following is a list of all the reports available in Visual Studio 2005 Team System:

- Backlog
- Blocked Inventory
- Buffer Usage
- Bug List
- Bug Rates
- Build Details Report
- Build Report
- Build Summary of Tests
- Builds
- Code Complete
- Code Coverage Details
- Cumulative Flow
- Dev/QA Bug Counts
- Dev/QA Work
- Exit Criteria Status
- Generic Charting
- Issues
- Load Test Comparison
- Load Test Selection Report
- Load Test Summary Report
- My Bugs
- Number of Bugs by Priority
- Quality
- Regressions
- Scenario Stability
- Team Productivity
- Test Effectiveness
- Test Effectiveness
- Test Failures without Active Bugs
- Test Result Details
- Tests Passing with Active Bugs
- Unit Test Effectiveness
- Velocity
- Work Item List
- Work Progress

Project Integration

As we wrap up, the last area I want to discuss is that of Microsoft Project integration. How does Visual Studio Team System integrate with Microsoft Project? As I mentioned in Chapter 3, the integration between Project and Visual Studio Team System allows customers to be productive with the tools they are comfortable with. Customers who are comfortable with tracking all their project data in Project can still do so. Visual Studio Team System gives them the additional choice to synchronize aspects of their Project—most likely, the subset of project data that translates to developer tasks—with their development teams. Microsoft will release a solution starter to show how Visual Studio Team System can also integrate with Project Server to deliver even greater benefits of central planning.

The integration between Visual Studio Team System and Project is designed to be an added level of productivity and is meant to complement the advanced management that Project is capable of.

Summary

Throughout our journey through these pages, we've seen that no matter what role we play on the application development team, Visual Studio 2005 Team System can assist us in creating better software and increasing the predictability of its success. During software development, having the ability to follow a process that is supported by the right toolset is crucial. Visual Studio 2005 Team System enables all team members to accomplish the tasks set before them in a collaborative environment while providing the information to ensure that the project meets its milestones every step of the way.

Part IV
Appendixes

In this part:

Appendix A: A Day in the Life of Team System 261
Appendix B: Distributed System Designer Reference......................275
Appendix C: Codenames 287

Appendix A
A Day in the Life of Team System

In this chapter:

The Adventure Works Scenario. 261

The Adventure Works Team. 262

Using MSF for Agile Software Development 264

Probably the best way to learn about a new methodology and how to use a tool is to see them in practice. In this appendix, you will see a three-month walk-through demonstration using Microsoft® Visual Studio® 2005 Team System in presenting a fictitious scenario using a fictitious team. There are many scenarios for which Team System can be of assistance.

Here are a few of the more interesting scenarios, with some potential time spans:

- **Design, develop, test, deploy**   A fairly straight path and typical software development life cycle (SDLC) with planned work (1–6 months)

- **Maintain existing code**   Ad hoc, unplanned, operations-driven crisis work (3–5 days)

- **My first day**   For a new hire or other initial practitioner experience (1 day)

- **Our second project**   Administration of teamwork (1–10 days)

- **Oops—someone else touched it, too**   Parallel development and configuration management (2–3 days)

- **The sun never sets**   Multisite, globally distributed work (2–3 days)

The Adventure Works Scenario

Adventure Works is about to embark on a three-month development project to design, develop, test, and deploy a Weblog (*blog*) application to be used by both internal and external staff. Management has decided to use Visual Studio 2005 Team System to support the development process. All software is purchased and is properly installed.

This scenario will take a broad (but not too deep) end-to-end storyboard approach. Here are some key points about this scenario:

- The tracks don't overlap in my scenario. In other words, for my date examples, one track ends before the next begins. This was done for clarity.

- This scenario is based on the Microsoft Solutions Framework (MSF) for Agile Software Development methodology, although it doesn't implement every work stream and activity.

The Adventure Works Team

The Adventure Works team is a small one, with a total of 12 employees involved at least peripherally. All 12 employees will *touch* Team System, but only 8 of them will be using Visual Studio 2005 to do so. In addition to each of their roles and responsibilities, you will know what software they will be using in relation to this scenario.

The team consists of the following roles and individuals:

Stakeholder—*Tamara*

Tamara is the owner of Adventure Works and wants to improve its public image. She has complete trust in Jay (see the next entry) to ensure that any new marketing product will be a success. Tamara herself is not very technical, but she still wants to be apprised of the progress of any project that Jay launches.

Software used: *Microsoft Internet Explorer*

Business Sponsor—*Jay*

Jay runs the marketing department at Adventure Works and will be paying for the development of the company's blog software. Because he is paying for it, he is considered "the customer." Jay believes that having a blog, in which the public can read and subscribe to the daily happenings at Adventure Works, will improve the company's perception and image. Jay feels that this will help drive new business, as long as it is secure, performs well, and has a pleasant user interface. Jay has managed several IS projects of various sizes and therefore knows a thing or two about project management, so he plans to follow the progress of the project.

Software used: *Internet Explorer*

Business Analyst—*Robert*

Robert is the subject matter expert (SME) of the blog application. After much research, his main goal is to define the opportunities and determine how to capitalize on them. Robert will work with the potential users, such as employees of the company, a focus group of external customers, and other stakeholders to understand their needs and goals. Robert will then translate all this information into persona definitions, scenarios, and Quality of Service (QoS) requirements that the development team will use to build the application.

Software used: *Microsoft Office Excel®, Microsoft Internet Explorer*

Project Manager—*Glenn*

Glenn must deliver the blog application, and all its promised business value, within the agreed-upon schedule and budget. The length of the project has been initially set to three months. Glenn is charged with planning and scheduling duties, which include developing project and iteration plans, monitoring and reporting status, and identifying and mitigating risk. Glenn must consult with Robert to plan the scenarios and quality of service requirements for each iteration, consult with Martin and Amy to estimate work, and consult with Hugh to plan testing. Glenn is eager to use Visual Studio 2005 Team System to facilitate communication with his team.

Software used: *Microsoft Excel, Microsoft Office Project, Team Explorer (standalone), Internet Explorer*

Architect—*Martin*

Martin's responsibility is to ensure success of the blog project by designing a solid application foundation. This foundation includes both the organizational structure of the application and the physical structure of its deployment. Being the champion of the solution, Martin must ensure that the blog application's architecture is sound and that it will successfully deploy to the Adventure Works' datacenter.

Software used: *Microsoft Visual Studio 2005 Team Edition for Software Architects*

Lead Developer—*Jeff*

Jeff has worked with Martin for many years and is very experienced in leading software development efforts. Jeff will act on Martin's guidance to help design and drive the implementation of the blog application's various services and subsystems. Jeff is an expert in Microsoft .NET and Microsoft ASP.NET development. He will serve as the primary technical resource for the project.

Software used: *Microsoft Visual Studio 2005 Team Suite*

Developers—*Amy, Joe,* and *Donovan*

The developers' responsibility is to implement the blog application, which must be accomplished by following Jeff's guidance and Martin's designs. Each developer has been adequately trained in .NET and ASP.NET, and each has at least two years of experience.

Although each developer has worked on various projects at Adventure Works over the years, this will be the first project that they will work on together. Per Jeff's recommendation, this will also be the first project to use a strict Test-Driven Development (TDD) methodology.

Software used: *Microsoft Visual Studio 2005 Team Edition for Software Developers*

Testers—*Hubert* and *Mandy*

Hubert and Mandy will be required to discover and communicate existing problems or potential problems with the blog application to the rest of team. Hubert has .NET experience and can directly assist in unit testing the code and correcting minor flaws in the code. Mandy has more experience in testing Web applications and services, both for accuracy and performance. Both Hubert and Mandy will be involved in deep testing of the application and logging any bugs into Team System, including the steps to reproduce their impact and any workarounds. In addition, Mandy has training experience and familiarity working with users, so she will focus on the user experience activities.

Software used: *Microsoft Visual Studio 2005 Team Edition for Software Testers*

Operations Manager—*Tim*

As operations manager, it is Tim's environment into which the blog application will get deployment. Tim is responsible for the security and reliability of the datacenter and, as such, has already worked with Martin to help him create an accurate diagram using Microsoft Visio® Professional. Tim has agreed to manage the rollout of the blog application, but wants to be kept in the loop on the project's status. He wants to have access to any deployment reports as early as possible for planning. Tim will coordinate the release with other operations staff and create an appropriate rollout plan.

Software used: *Internet Explorer, Team Explorer (standalone)*

Using MSF for Agile Software Development

Given the nature of the team, the project, and the shortened time frame (three months), Glenn has chosen to follow the MSF for Agile Software Development methodology. Its smooth integration with Team System supports a rapid, iterative development environment. Small iterations will allow the team to reduce the margin of error in their estimates. They also provide quicker feedback about the accuracy of the project plans.

In MSF 4.0, a team of peers advocates for the seven constituencies in the MSF Team Model. The Team Model was created to model all the views of a project, which must be represented and monitored to reduce risk and increase the likelihood of a successful project. Here is how this development team maps to the MSF Team Model.

MSF Team Model	Team Member
Program Management Advocates for Solution Delivery The focus of program management is to meet the goal of delivering the solution within project constraints. This group ensures that the right solution is delivered at the right time and that all stakeholders' expectations are understood, managed, and met throughout the project.	Tamara (Stakeholder) Jay (Sponsor)
Product Management Advocates for the Customer Business Product management has to understand, communicate, and ensure success from the standpoint of the economic customer requesting the solution.	Robert (Business Analyst) Glenn (Project Manager)
Architecture Advocates for the Solution Architecture includes the services, technologies, and standards with which the solution will interoperate; the infrastructure in which it will be deployed, its place in the business or product family; and its roadmap of future versions. The architecture group has to ensure that the deployed solution will meet all qualities of service as well as the business objectives and be viable in the long term.	Martin (Architect)
Development Advocates for the Technical Solution In addition to being the primary solution builders, development is responsible for thoughtful technical decisions, clean design, good bottom-up estimates, high-quality maintainable code, and unit tests.	Jeff (Lead Developer) Amy, Joe, Donovan (Developers)
Test Advocates for Solution Quality from the Customer Perspective Test anticipates, looks for, and reports on any issues that diminish the solution quality in the eyes of the users or customers.	Hubert (Tester—Code) Mandy (Tester—Web applications and Web services)
Release/Operations Advocates for the Smooth Delivery and Deployment of the Solution into the Appropriate Infrastructure This group ensures timely readiness and compatibility of the infrastructure for the solution.	Tim (Operations Manager)
User Experience Advocates for the Most Effective Solution in the Eyes of the Intended Users User experience must understand the users' context as a whole, appreciate any subtleties of their needs, and ensure that the whole team is conscious of usability from their eyes.	Mandy (Tester—Web applications and Web services)

Project Timeline

This small project will take three months to complete. In that time frame, several iterations and development tracks will be accomplished, as you can see in Figure A-1. Iteration 0 is composed of setup and planning and will take three weeks. Development will span Iteration 1 and 2 and take six weeks. Stabilization, final test, and release will take the remaining three weeks.

Month	Week	Iteration	Sun	Mon	Tue	Wed	Thu	Fri	Sat
March	1	0		1	2	3	4	5	6
	2	0	7	8	9	10	11	12	13
	3	0	14	15	16	17	18	19	20
	4	1	21	22	23	24	25	26	27
April	5	1	28	29	30	31	1	2	3
	6	1	4	5	6	7	8	9	10
	7	2	11	12	13	14	15	16	17
	8	2	18	19	20	21	22	23	24
May	9	2	25	26	27	28	29	30	1
	10	3	2	3	4	5	6	7	8
	11	3	9	10	11	12	13	14	15
	12	3	16	17	18	19	20	21	22
			23	24	25	26	27	28	29
			30	31					

Figure A-1   Project timelines

Iteration 0: Project Setup and Planning (3 weeks)

Envisioning Track—March 1st to March 12th (2 weeks)

The envisioning track addresses one of the most fundamental requirements for project success, which is the unification of the project team behind a common vision. The team must have a clear vision of what it wants to accomplish for the customer and be able to state that in terms that will motivate both the entire team and the customer. By creating a high-level view of the project's goals and constraints, envisioning can serve as an early form of planning. It typically occurs during the setup iteration.

Storyboard

- **March 1st**—Tamara and Jay finalize the budget and time frame expectations.
- **March 2nd**—Jay approves plans and funding within his department.

- **March 3rd**—Jay meets with Robert to discuss specific needs and goals. A vision statement is created that summarizes the project background, explains the driving factors for the project, defines the application's key value, and identifies the application's users.

- **March 5th**—Robert and Jay begin defining the personas, which are the groups of users who will use the application; they then create a persona for each group. The two also start putting together a list of functional requirements using Excel.

- **March 12th**— Robert and Jay finalize the persona definitions and functional requirements.

Final Question

Are we doing the right thing?

Track Deliverables

- Vision statement and persona document

Plan Track—March 15th to 19th (1 week)

The plan track is where the bulk of the planning for the project is completed. Within this track, the team prepares the functional specification; works through the design process; and prepares work plans, cost estimates, and schedules for the various deliverables. Each iteration also includes a planning cycle, in which the team revisits the plan, makes adjustments as needed, and performs the planning specific to the iteration.

Storyboard

- **March 15th**—Glenn, Robert, and Jay meet to discuss the new project. They review the vision statement, functional requirements, and persona documents and start putting together a project plan. They discuss objectives, time frames, and resources and put the team together.

- **March 16th**—Using Team Explorer, Glenn creates the new Team Project, selecting *MSF for Agile Software Development* as the methodology. Version control is configured as well; Glenn provides Robert the URL to the project portal and Robert uploads his vision statement and persona documents. Martin then uploads the datacenter Visio diagram that he and Tim previously constructed, in both VSD and JPG formats for good measure. An e-mail is sent to the entire team, letting them know the URL to the project portal.

- **March 17th**—Glenn, Robert, Jay, Martin, and Jeff meet and define the list of scenarios using Excel and record a single path of user interaction through the proposed system. This meeting is part technical and part functional—Jay attends only the first part of the meeting to ensure that things are progressing.

- **March 18th**—Tim is invited to the meeting to help address specific QoS requirements and whether those requirements will be satisfied by the capabilities of his datacenter. A list of requirements is defined in Excel. Martin makes several architectural notes during the meeting.

- **March 19th**—Robert and Glenn finalize the project plan and the other lists, uploading them to the project portal.

Final Question

Can we do this within time and budget, and is the business case justified?

Track Deliverables

- Project plan, list of scenarios, and list of QoS requirements

Iteration 1: Release Candidate 1 (3 weeks)

Build Track—March 22nd to April 9th (3 weeks)

The build track is where the team accomplishes most of the construction of solution components (documentation as well as code). However, some additional development work might occur in the stabilization track in response to testing. The build track involves more than code development and software developers. The infrastructure is also developed during this track, and all roles are active in building and testing deliverables.

Storyboard

- **March 22nd**—Glenn uses Project to create a list of tasks. Initially only Martin, Jeff, and Tim are tasked to begin architecting the new blog application. Glenn publishes these tasks to Team System, as well as the personas and QoS requirements from the prior week that were entered into Excel. In addition, some risks that came up during the meetings are added. Glenn uses Team Explorer to verify and fine-tune all these work items. He then sends out an e-mail to the team, explaining that work items have been entered. In this e-mail, he requests the team to configure alerts within each of their Visual Studio 2005 environments, so he doesn't have to manually send out additional e-mails.

- **March 23rd**—Martin, Jeff, and Tim review their work items. Tim has been asked to review the datacenter.JPG diagram for completeness and to work with Martin to revise the model in Visual Studio. Martin is asked to begin creating the blog application diagram and update the logical datacenter diagram. Jeff is asked to begin researching the latest improvements to Web application and Web service security and performance.

- **March 24th**—Martin finishes his preliminary models and requests Tim's assistance in fine-tuning the datacenter diagram. Because there have been some recent Internet

Information Server (IIS) upgrades and new firewalls put in place, they sit down in front of the distributed system designers and ensure that the model is accurate. A couple of new risk work items are added to the project, and the diagrams are checked in version control for safekeeping.

- **March 25th**—Martin creates a system diagram that composes aspects of the blog application diagram into a security system, which will simplify deployment. Together, Tim and Martin perform a trial deployment and successfully validate the models that they created. A deployment report is printed for Tim to study. It is also saved as a Web archive (.mht) file and uploaded to the project portal. All the team members can now review it. All files are checked in.

- **March 26th**—Martin meets with Jeff to decide upon important technical requirements, such as language, namespaces, project templates, file locations, object-oriented techniques, and service orientation for the project. These notes are saved into a Microsoft Office Word document and uploaded to the project portal. The appropriate properties are then set in the application diagram and saved. Martin checks in all files to version control. Jeff returns to his desk and opens up the application diagram from version control and implements the various applications and services. Jeff checks in all files to version control.

- **March 29th**—Jeff opens and reviews the blog solution and related projects; all projects have been stubbed-out and are ready to be implemented. Jeff uses Class Designer to create some of the classes to be used in the project in the interest of time because the project has now exhausted one third of its hours. Jeff asks Martin to help him create the other classes that they discussed. As they work through the design, they create task work items for each of the developers—and some for Jeff, too.

- **March 31st**—After going back and forth on design and philosophy, the object-oriented design and application framework is finally complete. Martin and Jeff come to an understanding and have all the classes, interfaces, and inheritance designed correctly.

- **April 1st**—Jeff meets with his developers, Amy, Joe, and Donovan, to go over the designs, expectations, and tasks to be assigned to the team. Jeff splits up the scenarios and QoS requirements to the developers, based on their background and skill sets. Jeff explains TDD once again and expects the developers to abide by it. Meanwhile, Glenn configures the team project security and classifications for the development ahead. Because it has been one month, Jay and Robert want some updates, so Glenn tells them which reports to run from the project portal.

- **April 2nd**—Coding begins. Amy, Joe, and Donovan review their work items and begin construction of their respective classes, services, and applications. Jeff mentors the developers individually to make sure that they are using the features of Team System correctly and following the proper TDD process. Unit tests, for the most part, are being executed regularly, and the code coverage numbers are getting better every day. Bug work items are created by the developers—sometimes to themselves as a "to do" item, and sometimes to other developers whose code is responsible for the bug. All files are checked in regularly, associating the changesets with the appropriate work items.

- **April 8th**—Enough coding has been completed that meaningful builds can start taking place. Glenn, Jeff, and Tim meet to discuss the specifics of a build server and QA environment. Glenn configures Team Build while Jeff performs some test builds.

- **April 9th**—A release candidate version of the blog application is created and given to Tim for installation onto the QA server. Other copies are archived for safekeeping in Jay's office and Robert's office.

Iteration 2: Release Candidate 2 (3 weeks)

Build Track—April 12th to April 30th (3 weeks)

- **April 12th**—Glenn reviews the Quality Indicators, Velocity, and Bug reports to get a feel for the project's pulse. He stops by Robert's office and then Jay's office to help them bookmark these reports on the portal; Jay does the same for Tamara.

- **April 13th**—Jeff notices that some of Joe's checked-in projects compile with errors and this is causing the nightly builds to fail. An e-mail goes out to the development team about quality control, but to be safe, Jeff asks Glenn to enable the "clean build" check-in policy on the team project.

- **April 16th**—The blog application is starting to take shape; the nightly builds are occurring without error, and it's time to start functional testing. Glenn calls a meeting with Jeff, Hubert, and Mandy. Because Robert knows the functional requirements and expectations of the software, he is invited as well. Hubert is asked to work with the developers, writing additional unit tests and ensuring that all code is covered during those tests. Hubert is also asked to load test certain unit tests to ensure that the underlying data access layer and services are performing to their QoS requirements. Mandy is asked to start user interface testing of the blog Web application.

- **April 19th**—Mandy begins Web testing the blog application and finds a number of errors. She repeatedly right-clicks the various errors and creates bug work items. Glenn, seeing a spike in the number of bugs that day, visits the development team to find their source. It seems that it was caused by an oversight in the architecture. Later that day, Jay and Robert see the same reports and ask Glenn for an update.

- **April 20th**—Martin reopens the application diagram and splits a key Web service into two services for better interoperability and scalability. He revalidates the new diagram against the logical datacenter and generates a new deployment report, both for Tim and for the project portal. Everything looks good from the distributed system designers' points of view. Martin implements the new Web service and then works with Jeff to split the appropriate code between the services. Martin checks in all diagrams, associating the changes with the bug work items.

- **April 21st**—Jeff modifies the unit tests and then creates tasks for each of the developers to execute their unit tests. Amy, Joe, and Donovan rerun the tests and get green lights all the way down—they are learning to appreciate TDD more and more. All code is checked in, associating the changes with the bug work items. A clean build is generated that night.

- **April 22nd**—Mandy re-runs her tests, getting far fewer bugs this time. She closes out some open bug work items and generates a few new ones. Reports run later that day show a sharp drop in the number of bugs. Mandy and Hubert review what they've seen so far. Hubert makes some adjustments to the unit tests to accommodate Mandy's bugs. He checks in all code, associating the unit test changes with Mandy's bug work items.

- **April 23rd**—Glenn calls a meeting with Jay and Robert to discuss testing the blog application with some actual users. To this point, testing has been performed mostly through automation or using whatever spare time that the developers or testers could spare for functional testing. Ideally, Jay wants to have two groups of users: one internal and one external. Robert agrees that internal and external groups are needed so he starts organizing the beta testers. Glenn creates a few task work items for Hubert and Mandy to create manual tests and documentation, for Jeff to prepare another release candidate build, and for Tim to enable the QA environment for both internal and external testing.

- **April 26th**—Mandy and Hubert get alert e-mails from Team System; these alerts are generated by the tasks that Glenn sent out on Friday. They spend the day creating manual testing scripts and documentation and then uploading them to the portal. All files are checked in. Jeff's alert instructs him to create .MSI packages and share them with Tim, who will deploy them to the new QA server he is setting up.

- **April 29th**—Jay, Robert, and Glenn review the beta tester documentation and run through a few of the manual test cases together; some changes are made to the documentation on the project portal. Glenn submits a task to Mandy to update her manual tests as well.

- **April 30th**—Primary coding has completed and the blog application is feature complete. Unit tests, code coverage, load testing, and Web testing are all showing positive results. Amy and Donovan get pulled away to another project. Only Joe is left to do any final modifications.

Final Question

Have we built the scope envisioned in the business case and product vision statement?

Track Deliverables

Logical datacenter diagram, application diagram, system diagram, class diagram, code, changesets, builds, unit tests, load tests, Web tests, test results

Iteration 3: Stabilize and Deploy (3 weeks)

Stabilizing Track—May 3rd to May 21st (3 weeks)

The stabilizing track occurs when the team conducts testing on a solution whose features are complete. Testing during this phase emphasizes usage and operation under realistic environmental conditions. The team focuses on resolving and triaging (prioritizing) bugs and preparing the solution for release.

Storyboard

- **May 3rd**—The two testing groups meet at Adventure Works; one group is composed of various internal folks, and the other is a public group, friendly to the cause. All the testers are given user IDs and passwords to the testing environment. They also meet Mandy, who will be supporting the beta testing.

- **May 4th**—The two groups begin testing; they have many questions and begin finding bugs. Mandy enlists the help of Hubert and Joe to help classify the feedback as bugs, feature requests, or just lapses in the documentation. Joe makes any fixes that are warranted, checking in the code and associating the code with the appropriate work items. Regression testing is performed on any code changes—this process continues for the next two weeks.

- **May 18th**—The entire team, Jay, Robert, Glenn, Jeff, Joe, Hubert, Mandy, and Tim meet to discuss the progress of the beta testing. This triage session includes going through the feature requests from the users and deciding which are critical to this release, and which can be pushed back to "version 2." Only a few features are deemed critical, and Joe assures everyone that he can perform the coding by close of business tomorrow. They each agree that the product is stable enough to deliver and decide to shoot for its release this coming weekend. Jeff offers to come in over the weekend to help Tim deploy the application to the production datacenter. Glenn creates the appropriate work items for Joe's programming tasks and Jeff and Tim's deployment tasks.

Final Question

Is the product stable enough to release, or will it be stable enough in the foreseeable future?

Track Deliverables

- Bugs, code, changesets, test results

Deploy Track—May 22nd to 23rd (Weekend)

The deploy track occurs when the team deploys the core technology and site components, stabilizes the deployment, transitions the project to operations and support, and obtains final customer approval of the project. After the deployment, the team conducts a project review and a customer satisfaction survey.

Storyboard

- **May 22nd**—With the deployment report in hand, and the .MSI files on a public share, Jeff and Tim successfully install and configure the Adventure Works blog application on time, on budget, to specification, and to a high level of quality. Done by noon, they take the afternoon off and go golfing.

Appendix B
Distributed System Designer Reference

In this chapter:
Logical Datacenter Designer 275
Application Designer 279
Class Designer 284

This appendix serves as a reference to Microsoft® Visual Studio® 2005 Distributed System Designers and the Class Designer. In Chapter 5, we looked at the various tools that an architect would use to visually create logical datacenter diagrams and application diagrams. In Chapter 6, we looked at the various tools that a developer would use to implement the application's services. One of the most important tools is the Class Designer. This appendix complements both of those chapters by serving as a reference of all the Microsoft provided server prototypes, application prototypes, and Class Designer components that an architect or a developer might use.

Logical Datacenter Designer

Architects will use the Logical Datacenter Designer to define a logical representation of the target datacenter in which applications will be deployed. This tool allows architects to provide a description of the types of servers (known as *logical servers*) in the target environment and to record the configurations of the software packages loaded on those servers.

Here are the various Hosts that can be modeled using the Logical Datacenter Designer:

- Windows Client
- IIS Web Server
- Database Server
- Generic Server
- Zone

Windows Client

WindowsClient1
WindowsClient

Application Constraints

■ Application type allowed—Microsoft Windows® application, Microsoft Office, or generic

■ User defined

Logical Server Settings

■ Operating system type, version, and features

■ Directories for implementation

■ Common language runtime (CLR) version

■ Global assembly cache (GAC) information

■ Custom

Valid Endpoint Types

■ Generic Client Endpoint

■ Generic Server Endpoint

■ HTTP Client Endpoint

■ Database Client Endpoint

Applications

■ Windows application

■ Office application

■ Generic application

IIS Web Server

IISWebServer1
IISWebServer

Application Constraints

■ Application type allowed—Microsoft ASP.NET Web application, external Microsoft BizTalk® Web service, external Web service, or generic

■ ASP.NET application constraints—membership, security, session state

■ User defined

Logical Server Settings

- IIS Services—capabilities, connection, content, general, limits, logging, metabase, request, settings, version
- Application Pools—authentication, COM, general, limits, monitoring, multiple processors, orphan action, rapid fail, request, response, restart
- Web Sites—ASP classic, authentication, authorization, caching, CGI, COM, compression, connection, content, general, IIS5 reliability, logging, request, response, restart
- Operating system type, version, and features
- Directories for implementation
- Common language runtime (CLR) version
- Global assembly cache (GAC) information
- Custom

Valid Endpoint Types

- Generic Client Endpoint
- Generic Server Endpoint
- HTTP Client Endpoint
- Web Site Endpoint
- Database Client Endpoint

Applications

- ASP.NET Web application
- External BizTalk Web service
- External ASP.NET Web service
- Generic application

Database Server

Application Constraints

- Application type allowed—external database or generic

Logical Server Settings

- Custom

Valid Endpoint Types

- Generic Client Endpoint
- Generic Server Endpoint
- HTTP Client Endpoint

Applications

- External database
- Generic application

Generic Server

GenericServer1
GenericServer

Application Constraints

- Application type allowed—external Web service or generic

Logical Server Settings

- Custom

Valid Endpoint Types

- Generic Client Endpoint
- Generic Server Endpoint
- HTTP Client Endpoint
- Web Site Endpoint
- Database Client Endpoint

Applications

- External Web service
- Generic application

Zone

Zone Containment Constraints

- Logical server type allowed—database, generic, IIS Web Server, Windows client, Zone
- IIS Web Server constraints—CLR version, directory, IIS settings, operating system type and version
- Windows client constraints—CLR version, directory, operating system type and version
- User defined

Logical Server Settings

- Custom

Valid Endpoint Types

- Zone Endpoint—inbound or outbound, database client, database server, HTTP client, Web site, generic

Logical Servers

- Windows client
- IIS Web Server
- Database server
- Generic server
- Other Zones

Application Designer

Architects will use the Application Designer to define the applications that make up a distributed system. This tool allows architects to provide a description of the types of applications that compose the entire connected application and record the configurations of the software packages loaded on those servers.

Here are the various application prototypes that can be modeled using the Application Designer:

- Windows application
- ASP.NET Web service

- ASP.NET Web application
- Office application
- External Web service
- External database
- BizTalk Web service
- Generic application

Windows Application

Logical Server Constraints

- Logical server required—Windows client
- Windows client constraints—operating system type and version, CLR version, directory

Application Settings

- Directories for implementation
- Custom

Valid Endpoint Types

- Generic Endpoint

Logical Servers

- Windows client

ASP.NET Web Service

Logical Server Constraints

- Logical server required—IIS Web Server
- IIS Web Server constraints—operating system type and version, CLR version, directory, IIS settings

Application Settings

- Web Application—ASP classic, authentication, authorization, caching, CGI, COM, compression, content, general, IIS5 reliability, logging, request, response, restart, security, settings
- Custom

Valid Endpoint Types

- Generic Endpoint
- Web Content Endpoint
- Web Service Endpoint

Logical Servers

- IIS Web Server

ASP.NET Web Application

Logical Server Constraints

- Logical server required—IIS Web Server
- IIS Web Server constraints—operating system type and version, CLR version, directory, IIS settings

Application Settings

- Web application—ASP classic, authentication, authorization, caching, CGI, COM, compression, content, general, IIS5 reliability, logging, request, response, restart, security, settings
- Custom

Valid Endpoint Types

- Generic Endpoint
- Web Content Endpoint
- Web Service Endpoint

Logical Servers

- IIS Web Server

Office Application

Logical Server Constraints

- Logical server required—Windows client
- Windows client constraints—operating system type and version, CLR version, directory

Application Settings

- Directories for implementation
- Custom

Valid Endpoint Types

- Generic Endpoint

Logical Servers

- Windows client

External Web Service

Logical Server Constraints

- None

Application Settings

- Custom

Valid Endpoint Types

- Generic Endpoint

Logical Servers

- IIS Web Server

External Database

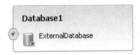

Logical Server Constraints

- Logical server required–Database server

Application Settings

- Custom

Valid Endpoint Types

- Generic Endpoint

Logical Servers

- Database Server

BizTalk Web Service

Logical Server Constraints

- None

Application Settings

- Custom

Valid Endpoint Types

- Generic Endpoint

Logical Servers

- IIS Web Server

Generic Application

Logical Server Constraints

- Logical server required—Database server, generic server, IIS Web Server, Windows client

- IIS Web Server constraints—operating system type and version, CLR version, directory, IIS settings

- Windows client constraints—operating system type and version, CLR version, directory

Application Settings

- Custom

Valid Endpoint Types

- Generic Endpoint

Logical Servers

- Database server

- Generic server

- IIS Web server

- Windows client

Class Designer

Although the Class Designer isn't technically a Microsoft Visual Studio 2005 Team System designer, I thought it was worth adding to this reference section. This designer is a fully functional, visual design environment for the common language runtime. It lets you visualize the structure of classes and other types, and edit their source code. Changes made to the class diagram are immediately reflected in code, and changes made to the code immediately affect the appearance of the designer.

Here are the various components that can be modeled using the Class Designer:

- Class

- Enum

- Interface
- Abstract Class
- Struct
- Delegate

Class

Member Types Allowed

- Method
- Property
- Field
- Event
- Constructor
- Destructor
- Constant

Enum

Member Types Allowed

- Field

Interface

Member Types Allowed

- Method
- Property
- Event

Abstract Class

Member Types Allowed

- Method
- Property
- Field
- Event
- Constructor
- Destructor
- Constant

Struct

Member Types Allowed

- Method
- Property
- Field
- Event
- Constructor
- Constant

Delegate

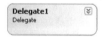

Member Types Allowed

- Parameter

Appendix C
Codenames

As Microsoft® Visual Studio® 2005 Team System was being developed, it was full of codenames. Most of these have since disappeared, so I have provided a list in this appendix. Microsoft employees and true geeks tend to refer to products by codename internally, up until the time the products are released to manufacturing. You might still see them from time to time, in magazine articles, Web sites, or blog postings.

- **Whidbey** The Microsoft .NET Framework 2.0, Visual Studio 2005, or both
- **Burton** The entire Visual Studio Team System suite of tools
- **Currituck** Team System's work-item tracking system; also a lighthouse in North Carolina
- **ELead** The work item
- **Hatteras** Team System's version control system; also a lighthouse in North Carolina
- **Ocracoke** Team System's Web testing system; also a lighthouse in North Carolina
- **F1** Team System's profiling system
- **Whitehorse** Team System's distributed system designers
- **BIS (Burton Integration Services)** Team Foundation Server's underlying extensibility model
- **FxCop** Static code analyzer for managed code
- **PREfast** Static code analyzer for C/C++ code
- **Rosetta** Microsoft SQL Server™ 2000 Reporting Services
- **Yukon** SQL Server 2005
- **Orcas** The Microsoft .NET Framework vNext, Microsoft Visual Studio vNext, or both

Index

A

AAs. *See* application architects (AAs)
abstract techniques, 198
abstractions, 46
Accepted risk, 90
access control list (ACL) security, 30
access rights, 34
ACT (Application Center Test), 164
active bugs, number of, 253
Active Bugs list, 88
Active Directory
  dual server requirement for, 20
  groups representing process roles, 209
  integrating Team System with, 76
  supported by TFS, 77
Active risk, 90
active run configuration, 171
Active state
  for a bug, 88
  for a quality of service requirement, 85
  for a requirement, 206
  for a scenario, 83
  for a task, 87
  for a work item type, 223
Active to Closed state transition
  for a risk, 90
  for a task, 87
Active to Resolved state transition
  for a bug, 88–89
  for a quality of service requirement, 86
  for a scenario, 84
activities in MSF Agile, 12
Actual Quality versus Planned Velocity Report, 256–257
.ad file, 47
ad hoc development process, 153
adapters, 47, 234
Add New Test Wizard, 159
Add Proxy Endpoint option, 118
Add Required button, 40
Add Tab feature, 107
Add to Toolbox feature, 106, 111
Add Web Reference dialog window, 57
add-ins, 7
.adprototype file, 111
Adventure Works scenario, 261–273
Advocacy Groups, 179
advocates. *See* project managers
agile, staying, 180, 196
Agile Alliance, 9

agile development
  methodology, 10
  methods, 176
  movement, 186
agile process, 9
agile process model, 9
agile software development life cycle, 10
Allerton suite, 240–241
ALLOWEDVALUES field, 222
ALLOWEXISTINGVALUE field, 222
ALM metrics, 240
Analysis Services cubes, 233
analysts. *See* project managers
APIs. *See* application programming interfaces (APIs)
Application Architect role, 16
Application Architect/Developer role, 16
application architects (AAs), 94, 95–96
  communicating to IT operations, 44
  defining an application's architecture, 107
  distinguished from infrastructure architects, 44
  settings and constraints in application diagrams, 56
  specifying properties prior to implementation, 113
  staying on Team System, 124
  Team edition for, 14
  visualizing service-oriented applications, 96
  working on the design ahead of time, 108–110
application architecture
  general understanding of, 95
  vetting against logical datacenter diagrams, 100, 108
Application Center Test (ACT), 164
application connection diagram, 127
Application Delivery Dashboard, 243
application design
  implementing as code, 109–110
  validating, 56
Application Designer, 55–58, 96, 107–115, 127
  advantages of, 55
  diagrams created with, 98
  modeling the structure of applications, 99
  setting implementation properties in, 114
  standard set of prototypes shipped with, 109
  toolbox, 109
Application Designer prototype file (.adprototype), 111
application diagrams, 45
  adding external Web Services to, 99
  adding to existing solutions, 108
  application and service types contained by, 55–56
  compared to system diagrams, 117
  connecting the shapes in, 57

application diagrams, *continued*
creating, 97, 108–110
defining element attributes, 116
in distributed system solutions, 47, 56
example, 111
as the foundation of system design, 117
listing all applications on, 119
SDM document copied from within, 114
solution-scoped, 108
testing against logical datacenter diagrams, 58
application endpoint types, 110
application fault management software, 243
application health models, 243
Application Hosting layer of SDM, 47
application Hosts, 96, 100, 101
application implementation, reusing, 112
Application layer of SDM, 47
application models, 48
application problem resolution, 241
application programming interfaces (APIs)
for building SDM Tools, 47
for the Team Foundation Server, 22
application prototypes. *See also* prototypes
in the Application Designer toolbox, 108, 109
creating reusable, 111–112
saving to the toolbox, 111
types of, 108
application requirements in SDM, 46
application specifications, propagating, 112
application systems, 60
application tier, 22–23
extending Team System on, 225
having all sites connect to, 29
applications
binding to a Host in Deployment Designer, 120
binding within a system to logical servers, 97
building, 145
communicating through endpoints, 110
composing into systems, 97
connecting to provider endpoints, 110
continuing to stabilize after the initial release, 248
defining in a distributed system solution, 47
defining the connected systems of, 95
deploying, 117, 248
designing, 108, 187
functional testing of complex, 242
identifying performance bottlenecks in, 136
saving as an Application Designer prototype file, 111
selecting exposing behavior of, 118
stressing, 145
approved branch, 34
AppSight, 241–242
AQtime, 241
Architect role, 16, 187, 201

architects, 94
on the Adventure Works team, 263
needs of, 44
roles of, 94
tools for, 44–61
using the implement feature, 112
work streams, 189
architectural diagrams, 127. *See also* Distributed
Application Diagrams (DAD)
architecture
advocates for the solution, 265
constituency advocate, 183
constructing with nested sub-systems, 118
layers of, 94
structure of, 189
support features, 94
Architecture advocacy group, 200
artifacts, 42, 226
As Designed bug, 88, 89
ASMX Web services, 22, 225
ASP.NET
newly implemented project, 114
security, 97
standard configuration for an application, 111
type of security, 53
type of session state, 53
Web applications, 57, 111, 114
ASP.NET Web services
automatically generating the code for, 127
BizTalk 2004 exposing orchestrations as, 100
combining into a system, 61
grouping into a Security system, 118
implementing, 63
implementing SOA architectures, 98
modeling, 108
modeling interaction with existing, 99–100
naming convention for, 57
wrapping existing code or code libraries up as, 99
ASP.NETWebApplication, 56
ASP.NETWebService, 55, 56
assemblies, custom, 99
assets, maintaining, 21
Associate, setting a Checkin Action to, 132
association relationship of classes, 129
asynchronous file opening in Visual SourceSafe, 35
audit trail support, provided by TFVC, 35
auditing, required for Sarbanes-Oxley, 34
Auditor role, 204
authorization services, provided by TFS security service,
226
AutoDiscovery feature in Visio 2002, 104
Automated Build Studio, 241
automated build system, 145
automated deployment, 123
AutomatedQA, 241

Avenade Connected Methods, 177
AVIcode, 243
Avoided risk, 90

B

base application types, 109
baseline performance statistics, 167
Baseline Security Analyzer test, 53
best practices. *See also* guidance, uploading to the
    project portal
    from the agile development movement, 186
    for creating custom process templates, 218
    for a development team, 5–7
    forcing developers to implement, 136
    restricting developers to follow, 153
    TDD (Test-Driven Development), 138, 141
binding, 59, 166
BIS (Burton Integration Services), 287
BizTalk applications, 100
BizTalkWebService, 56, 57
black box technology in AppSight, 242
blog, deploying, 261
Borland, 239–240
bottlenecks. *See* performance bottlenecks; scalability
    bottlenecks
boundaries, Zones representing, 101
branches, managing promotion levels using, 34
branching in TFVC, 29–30, 75
browser, interacting with Team System, 81
browser sessions, recording, 164
browser types, defining, 168
bug bash, 253
Bug List report, 151
Bug Rates report, 151, 253–254
bug report, 188, 206
bug work items
    creating, 87, 170
    in MSF Agile, 13
    tracking by managers, 171
bugs, 82. *See also* active bugs, number of; defects
    adding, 87–89
    closing, 88, 191
    continuing to track, 248
    cost of fixing, 247
    effectiveness of hunting, 255
    finding and reporting significant, 187, 203
    fixing, 135, 190
    found by scenarios resolved, 251
    goal of opening, 188, 206
    as an item type, 188, 206
    newly active, 254
    number of active, 253
    preventing and verifying, 180
    prioritizing, 255

querying existing, 88
reproducing, 89
resolved, 254
resolving, 88
state transitions of, 88–89
states of, 88
triaging, 193, 272
Bugs By Priority Report, 255–256
build and release management, 35–36
build automation, 36
Build Configuration dialog box, 150
build directory, 149
Build Engineer role, 203
build failure, result of, 88
build location, selecting, 149
build machine, 148
build management, 35
Build menu option, 35
build notes, 190
build process, 146
build reporting data, 147
build reports, 151
build results, 151
build script, 247
build track, 192, 268–271
build types, 147
    creating, 147–150
    for custom tasks, 235
    defining, 146
    executing specified, 148
    naming, 147
Build Type structure, 146
Build Verification Test (BVT), 150
builds, 35, 190
    executing, 146, 150
    maintaining multiple, 29
    validation tests for, 190
Builds report, 152
built-in constraints. *See* implicit constraints
built-in global groups, 76
built-in processes, 27
built-in project groups, 76
Burton, 287
business analyst
    on the Adventure Works team, 262
    work streams, 188–189
Business Analyst role, 186, 200
business documents, uploading, 81
Business Intelligence Developer Studio, 223
business logic, testing, 139
business managers. *See* project managers
business sponsor, 262
BVT. *See* Build Verification Test (BVT)

C

CaliberRM product, 239
CANNOTLOSEVALUE field, 222
Capability Maturity Model. *See* CMM (Capability Maturity Model)
Capability Maturity Model Integration. *See* CMMI (Capability Maturity Model Integration)
Capability Maturity Model (CMM) Key Practice Areas, 179
Carnegie Mellon University, 194
Case tools, 93
change, adapting to, 180, 196
change requests, 82, 206
changesets
  adding to builds, 190
  compared to shelvesets, 31
  in TFVC, 28
Checkin Action, setting to Associate, 132
check-in notes. *See* notes, tracking at check-in
check-in policies, 32–34
  configuring, 38
  creating for source code control, 131
  custom, 80, 230–233
  including, 223
  overriding, 34
  sample code implementing, 230–233
  setting, 79–80
  version control, 134, 136
Checkin window, 64
check-ins
  associating with work items, 32, 131–133
  pending, 134
churn. *See* code churn
citizenship mindset, 199
Class Designer, 63–64, 125, 128–130
  allowing refactoring inside the graphical interface, 130
  creating a class diagram, 129
  features of, 129
  finding and launching, 63
  language support, 99
  opening a class in, 49
  providing a graphical interface, 128
  tightly coupled with source code, 63
Class Details window, 63
class diagram, viewing, 129
Class View window, 63
classes
  creating instances of, 129
  creating using graphical features, 129
  implementing in Application Designer, 112–115
  representing graphically in Class Designer, 63
classification service of Team Foundation Server, 227
Classification Structure System. *See* CSS (Classification Structure System)

classifications
  configuring, 38
  creating, 78
  hierarchy of, 78
Clean Build check-in policy, 80
Clean Build policy type, 33
client applications, 24, 37
  adding and managing work items, 83
  communicating with TFS, 23
client endpoints, 54
client object model, 22
client tier of Team Foundation Server, 23–24
clients, 225. *See also* Hosts
Closed state
  for a bug, 88
  for a quality of service requirement, 85
  for requirements, 206
  for a scenario, 84
  for a task, 87
  of a work item type, 223
Closed to Active state transition
  for a bug, 89
  for a quality of service requirement, 86
  for a risk, 90
  for a scenario, 85
  for a task, 87
closing bugs, 191
CMM (Capability Maturity Model), 193
  providing prescriptive guidance for process improvement, 194
  rating an organization's maturity based on tiers, 194
  specializing for various disciplines, 194
CMMI (Capability Maturity Model Integration), 9, 193
  agile approach to, 193
  combining several source models into a single improvement framework, 195
  Level 3 status, 193
  levels, 10
CMMI for Process Improvement, 10, 199
code. *See also* source code
  analyzing for known defects, 142
  changes to, 109
  checking in, 132
  confidence in, 137
  confidently refactoring, 137
  creating a unit test from, 139
  creating graphically, 128
  creating in Team System, 128
  generating with models, 93
  locks for checking out, 131
  profiling, 136, 144–145
  relating to a Quality of Service Requirement, 132
  reusing existing wrapped as a Web service, 99
  shelving, 31, 134
  traditionally represented as text, 128

treating as functionality, 128
   unshelving, 134
   writing as text, 128
code analysis, 150
code churn, 21, 253
code coverage, 141–142
   attained by tests, 252
   indicators, 142
   in Team Edition for Software Developers, 14
   in Team Edition for Testers, 14
   testing, 65, 136
   tool, 141
Code Coverage Results window, 66
Code Coverage window, 142
code development, 153–154
code libraries, reusing existing, 99
code profiler, 14
code profiling test, 65
code round-tripping, 110
code shelving, 131
code skeleton, 141
code structure, graphical representation of, 128
CodeChurn cube, 233
codenames, 287
coding conventions, 143
collaboration, 15, 82
collaborative advantages of WSS, 74
collaborative portal environment, 22
columns
   in Excel, 40
   in Microsoft Project, 43
command-line tools
   included with Team System, 37
   provided by the SDM SDK, 48
command-line utilities, 66–67
common cause variation, 195
common language, provided by SDM, 46
communication
   to a distributed team, 4
   fostering open, 180, 195
   gateways, 101
   global, 4
   pathways, 57, 105, 110
compatible endpoints, 120
Completed state transition, 86
components, defining initial, 214
Compuware QACenter, 242–243
Compuware TestPartner, 242
Conchango, 244
confidence as a benefit of TDD, 137
config round-tripping, 110
conflicts, resolving, 31, 135
connection pathways in Zones, 102
connections
   between applications, 99
   defining for an endpoint, 103

describing actual, 117
   lining up for two services, 106
   manually rerouting, 111
   tidying up with Redraw Connection, 111
consensus-oriented nature of role-playing, 200
Constant Load, 167
constituencies
   for each Advocacy Group in MSF 4.0, 179
   equally important to risk management, 197
   in the MSF 4.0 Team Model, 183–184
constraint metadata, 50
constraint violations, 120
constraints, 115–116
   for Application Designer, 56–57
   associating with fields, 221
   authoring, 116
   defining on endpoints, 103
   evaluating with the Deployment Designer, 116
   for Logical Datacenter Designer, 52
   providing individual diagram elements with, 120–121
   setting for Web application or service components, 127
   on system operations, 85
   types of, 116
   validating that a build reflects, 190
   validating with Distributed System Designers, 97
consultants, 72. *See* project managers
consumer dissatisfiers, 199
consumer endpoints, 53–54, 110
consumer expectations, 197
container, 158
continuous process improvement, 9
continuous tracks, 193
contractors. *See* defense contractors, evaluating software
     development capabilities
Contributor project group, 77
controller for Load Agent, 169
COPY element, 222
copy-modify-merge model, 35
core development team, 13
core ideas, 180
core services, extending, 225, 226–227
corporate naming conventions, 131, 143
Counter Sets, 168
Counters tree view, 168–169
coupling, 153
Create Instance menu item, 129
Create Tests option, 139
cross-tool reporting, 227
CSS (Classification Structure System), 208
CSS plug-in, 214, 216
cubes, 233
Currituck, 287
Currituck plug-in, 214, 217–218
custom application prototypes, 111–112

custom assemblies, 99
custom check-in policies, 80
custom constraints, validating, 97
custom Hosts, adding a tab for, 107
custom process templates, 177
custom prototypes, 110, 111
custom queries, 126
custom reports, 210
custom server type, 104
custom settings for logical servers and Zones, 53–55
custom templates, 113
custom test lists, 157
customer application prototypes, 109
customer extensibility, 239
customers, 197
    defining quality, 180, 197
    flow of value to, 195
    partnering with, 180, 195
customizing
    vs. extending, 211–212
    Team System, 210, 211, 212–224
Cut task, 87
Cycles and Iterations
    compared to tracks, 185
    in MSF 4.0, 184

D

DAD (Distributed Application Diagrams), 45. *See also*
    diagrams
daily builds, 35
data sources, binding request parameters to, 166
Data Sources node, 166
data tier of Team Foundation Server, 20–22
data warehouse, 233
Data Warehouse database of TFS, 20
database server constraints, 53
database tier, extending Team System on, 225
database type, 109
DatabaseClientEndpoint, 105
DatabaseEndpoint type, 110
databases
    defining connections to, 110
    installed in the data tier of TFS, 20
DatabaseServer logical server, 50
DatabaseServer prototype, 103
DatabaseServerEndpoint, 105
datacenter
    creating a logical representation of, 50
    designing using Zones, 102
    environment, 95
date field, validating, 222
.dd files, 47
debugging, time spent, 137
DEFAULT element, 222
default iterations, renaming, 78

default queries for viewing work items, 126
default unit test options, 140
default Word documents for new tests, 160
defects. *See also* bugs
    analyzing code for known, 142
    continuing to track, 248
defense contractors, evaluating software development
        capabilities, 193
Deferred bug, 88, 89
deferred scenario, 84
Deferred state transition, 86
Deferred task, 87
Define Deployment menu option, 58, 119
Defined tier (Level 3) of CMM, 194
deletion options for Zones, 102
delivery, frequent, 181, 198
dependencies in task group definitions, 217
dependencies section for each task, 218
deploy track in MSF 4.0, 193, 272–273
deployment
    of applications, 248
    of a configured use of applications, 117
    defining requirements during, 115
    errors or warnings list, 121
    increasing the predictability of, 44
    making a habit, 196
    validating, 119, 120–121
Deployment Designer, 58–60, 97, 116, 119–123
deployment diagrams, 45
    contained in a solution, 108
    creating, 119
    in a distributed system solution, 47
deployment environments, diagrams of, 50
deployment report
    generated after test-deployment, 248
    generating, 121–123
    reporting options available, 123
    saving the printed screen image of, 124
    sending to the IT operations team, 123
    in XML format compared to HTML, 122
deployment validation, 121
deployment verification step, 119
DeploymentReport.xsl file, 122
descriptions in the bug work item, 87–88
descriptive components of MSF 4.0, 181
descriptive framework, MSF 4.0 as, 177
descriptive SDLC model, 178
Design Application System, 118
Design for Deployment, 95
design surface
    dragging and dropping Web service applications
        onto, 99
    dragging application prototypes onto, 109
design tools, 96
designers, changes to reflected in code, 109

designing for operations, 45
details, 233
Details tab in Web Test Runner, 166
developer branch, 34
Developer Manager role, 202
Developer role, 16, 187, 202
developers. *See also* development manager; lead
        developer
    on the Adventure Works team, 263
    forcing to implement best practices, 136
    impact of restrictions on, 153
    implementing Web services, 112
    reports and, 152
    restricting, 153
    role of, 125
    synchronizing code changes with visual design, 96
    Team edition for, 14
    tools for, 62–65
    tracking for Sarbanes-Oxley, 34
    work streams, 190
Developer/Tester role, 16
development
    advocates for the technical solution, 265
    allocating resources based on the flow of value, 185
    fixing bugs during, 135
    model-driven approach to, 48
    with a process, 154
    solving problems, 6
    structure for, 125
    team-based, 24
Development advocacy group, 200
development constituency advocate, 183
development life cycle build, 125
development manager, 202
development organization, assessing the maturity of, 193
development tasks, 87, 188, 190, 207
    assigning work, 86
    implementing, 190
    in a scenario, 190
development team, 4, 5–7
Diagnostics. *See* Mercury Diagnostics
diagrams. *See also* Distributed Application Diagrams
        (DAD)
    creating in Application Designer, 108–110
    creating in Logical Datacenter Designer, 100–107
dimensions, 233
direct connection over HTTP, 54
disciplines, 179, 191
    defined by MSF for CMMI Process Improvement, 207
    in MSF 3.0, 179
    in MSF 4.0, 191
    multiple accommodated by CMMI, 195
    in process guidance, 179
    removed from the metamodel, 179
    specializing CMM for, 194

distributed application designers. *See* visual designers
Distributed Application Diagrams (DAD), 45. *See also*
        diagrams
Distributed System Designers, 50–61
Distributed Systems Designer prototype file, 48
Distributed Systems Designers, 44–45
    editor used by all, 116
    extending in Team Architect, 48
    security supported by, 97
    storing SDM information, 47
    in Team Edition for Software Architects, 95, 96–100
distributed system solution, 47
Distributed System Solutions projects, 56
DLL (dynamic-link library), 128
document libraries
    adding and managing, 38
    creating, 74
    quality of service requirements list, 85
documentation of bugs, 88
documents
    adding and managing, 38
    uploading, 81
dogfooding, 28
DREAD, tracking, 126
drop location, 149
DSI (Dynamic Systems Initiative), 14, 45–46, 96
DSL (Domain-Specific Language) tools, 48–61, 63
DSLs (Domain Specific Languages), 96
Duplicate bug, 88, 89
Dynamic Systems Initiative (DSI), 14, 45–46, 96
dynamic-link library. *See* DLL (dynamic-link library)

E

Eclipse Plugin, 240
Eclipse RCP application, 240
editing sessions, viewing changes made during, 65
editions of Team System, 71
ELead, 287
embedded diagrams in the HTML deployment report,
        121
embedded Hosts in Zones, 102
EMPTY field, 221
endgame, 247
Endpoint prototype, 112
endpoint specifications, propagating, 112
endpoint types, 105, 110
endpoints, 103, 110
    adding to a logical datacenter diagram, 101
    in the Application Designer toolbox, 109
    checking for compatible, 120
    connecting, 54, 105–106, 110–111
    contained in a logical server system, 48
    defining constraints on, 103
    lining up for two services, 106
    selecting in Deployment Designer, 59

enterprise architects. *See* infrastructure architects (IA)
Enterprise Library, 94
enterprise-scale software, 4
environment, modeling, 95
envision track in MSF 4.0, 192
envisioning track, 266–267
epochs, 78
error free code, 80
errors and warnings list for deployment, 121
Errors List window, 59
Errors window, 143
eventing service of Team Foundation Server, 226
Excel, 24, 37, 83
    connecting to a Team Foundation server, 40
    from inside Team Explorer, 39
    integration with Team System, 17, 39
    launching from within Team Explorer, 40
    as an offline client, 40
    as a project management tool, 39–43
execution order for tests, 169
execution status, 157, 170
explicit validation, 121
exploratory testing, suggesting, 86, 188, 207
express editions of Visual Studio 2005, 17
extended teams, disseminating information to, 73
extending
    vs. customizing, 211–212
    Team System, 211, 212
extensibility of Team System, 7–8, 73, 211
Extensibility Toolkit, 239
extension, supported by the architecture of Team
    System, 224
external resources, invoking for testing, 163
external Web service, connecting to, 99–100
ExternalDatabase application type, 56
ExternalWebService service type, 56
ExternalWebService settings, 57
Extract Interface, 130
eXtreme Programming. *See* XP (eXtreme Programming)

F
F1 codename, 287
F5 key, 35
facts at the center of star schemas, 233
fault management software, 243
Feature Driven Design, 177
feedback, facilitating continuous improvement, 198
field map, 43–44
fields, 27, 221–223
file types, 38, 223
files, selecting for check-in, 132
firewalls, 4, 51
Fixed bug, 88, 89
flow of value, 180, 195, 196

foundational principles, 178
framework, 196–197
    creating, 128
    interchangeable with metamodel, 178
frequent delivery, 198
FROZEN field, 221
functional goals, captured by scenarios, 189
functional requirements, 12
functional specification, 192
functionality
    deployable units of, 99
    testing all required of a solution, 142
    treating code as, 128
FxCop, 287
FxCop plug-in, 136, 142

G
GAC (global assembly cache), 52
gateways, 101
generic server constraints, 53
Generic Test Designer, 163
generic tests, 66, 159, 162–164, 172
    categories of tools, 162
    specifying behaviors of, 163
    test output from, 164
GenericApplication application type, 56
GenericApplication constraints, 57
GenericClientEndpoint, 105
GenericEndpoint type, 110
GenericServer logical server, 50
GenericServer prototype, 104
GenericServerEndpoint, 105
Get Work Items query, 42
glexport.exe, 220
glimport.exe, 220
global assembly cache (GAC), 52
global communication, 4
global groups, 76
global lists, 220
goals. *See* functional goals, captured by scenarios
governance, 185, 192, 201, 207–208
governance checkpoints, 207
    grouping the activities leading to, 192
    in MSF 4.0, 192
    tracks concluding with, 185
graphical bitmap image, specifying, 111
graphical interface for creating code, 128
graphical three-way merge tool, 31
Group of applications prototype, 111
Group of endpoints prototype, 112
Group of servers prototype, 106
Group of Zones prototype, 106
group security service, 226
Group Security Service (GSS) plug-in, 214

groups
    configuring, 38
    mapping to Team System, 76
    setting up, 209
GUI testing, 241
guidance, uploading to the project portal, 82
guiding
    iterations, 189
    projects, 189

H

hardened database Zone, 102
Hardware layer of SDM, 47
Hatteras, 287
hierarchy of classifications, 78
Host types, 103
hosting restrictions, 120
Hosts. *See also* clients; servers
    adding to Zones, 103
    binding applications to, 120
    connecting in a diagram, 105
    constraining endpoints in a Zone, 103
    deleting, 102
    forming a logical container of, 101
    reuse of, 106
    Zone as a logical collection of, 102
how-to guides. *See* guidance, uploading to the project portal
HTML report, generated for reference, 121
HTTP
    access through Web service interfaces, 35
    direct connection over, 54
    requests, 165, 166
HTTP-based Web content endpoint, 110
HTTPClientEndpoint, 105
hyperlinks, relating to work items, 42

I

IAs. *See* infrastructure architects (IAs)
IDE (integrated development environment), 5
Identify Software, 241–242
IIS Settings, importing, 104
IIS Web Server
    constraints, 53
    settings, 53
    Zone containing an, 106
IISWebServer Host, 104
IISWebServer logical server, 50
IISWebServer prototype, 103
IM (instant messaging), 4
images, adding file types for, 223
immutability of properties, 113
Implement All Applications feature, 112
implementation properties, setting, 114

implemented application, reusing, 112
implementing
    a class, 112
    classes in Application Designer, 112–115
implicit constraints, 116
improvement, suggestions for, 196
inbound endpoint for a Zone, 103
independent software vendors (ISVs), 47, 96
Infopath, editing process guidance documentation, 219
information system architects. *See* infrastructure architects (IAs)
Infrastructure Architect role, 16
infrastructure architects (IAs), 94–95
    communicating to developers, 44
    creating diagrams of deployment environments, 50
    creating logical abstractions and validating application design, 96
    defining datacenter policies, 51
    returning to Team System, 123
Initial tier (Level 1) of CMM, 194
install/uninstall scripts, automated testing of, 162
instance, naming a class, 130
instant messaging (IM), 4
instrumentation profiles, 145
instrumentation profiling method, 144
integrated development environment (IDE), 5
Integrated Program Management (IPM) Officer role, 204
integrated testing, 136–145
integration and system testing, 155, 160
integration points, 160
intelligent proxy layer, 239
intelligent whiteboard, 55
Intercept Studio of AVIcode, 243
interconnected application hosts, diagrams of, 96
interface
    consequences of changing, 153
    of Test Manager, 157
    of Test View, 158
Internet Explorer, 24, 37
    for all team members, 66
    extended with a utility recording HTTP requests, 165
    integration with Team System, 17
Internet Information Server (IIS) security, 97
interoperability, implementing, 97
intranet Web portal Zone, 102
inventory of all systems, 121
IPM officer, 204
IPolicyDefinition interface, 230
IPolicyEvaluation interface, 230
IRIS-on-Demand service, 245
IRIS Process Author, 244–245
ISO 9000/9001, 10
issues, 82, 206
ISVs (independent software vendors), 47, 96
IT environment, managing change in, 244

IT operations, communicating to developers, 44
IT Professional role, 16
items, copying from one project to another, 29
iteration names for development cycles, 209
iterations, 78
    for the Adventure Works scenario, 266–273
    closing down the current, 248
    creating, 78–79
    defining initial, 214
    guiding, 189
    planning, 189
    reducing the batch size for, 198
    renaming default, 78
    small, 184
IWarehouseAdapter interface, 233, 234

J-K

J2EE services, modeling, 100
Java applications, Allerton clients as, 240
KPAs (key project areas), 194

L

labels, hiding for endpoints, 110
languages
    selecting for test projects, 139
    specifying prior to implementation, 113
    supported by Visual Studio 2005, 99
    supported in Visual SourceSafe, 35
layers
    of architecture, 94, 189
    described by SDM, 47
.ldd files, 47, 101
.lddprototype file, 106, 107
lead developer
    on the Adventure Works team, 263
    implementing scenarios, 83
    role of, 202
learning, ongoing, 181
Levels of CMM
    Defined tier (Level 3), 194
    Initial tier (Level 1), 194
    Managed tier (Level 4), 194
    Optimizing tier (Level 5), 194
    Repeatable tier (Level 2), 194
linking service of Team Foundation Server, 226
links, 226
Links tab of a work item, 26
Linux, running Allerton from, 240
Load Agent, 169
load front end, 169
load profile for a load test scenario, 167
load test results, 168
Load Test Runner, 168
load test scenario, 167

load testing, 65, 142, 145
load tests, 160, 167–169
load Web testing, 14
local area network (LAN) performance booster, 35
local overwrite conflict, 135
locks, 131
logical datacenter
    designing, 101
    selecting to test a deployment against, 58
    understanding and modeling, 94–95
    validating an application against, 119
Logical Datacenter Designer, 50–55, 95, 96, 100–107
    probing for servers and configurations automatically, 104
    prototype file, 106
    toolbox, 104, 107
logical datacenter diagrams, 45, 50
    connecting endpoints in, 54
    contained in a solution, 108
    containing a Zone, 106
    creating, 97, 100–107
    defining element attributes, 116
    developing in tandem with application diagrams, 101
    in a distributed system solution, 47
    firewalls not directly supporting, 51
    logical servers contained in, 50
    renaming, 101
    steps for creating, 101
Logical Machines and Network Topology layer of SDM, 47
logical model, generating, 104
logical server constraints, 116
Logical server prototype, 106
logical server system, 48
logical servers
    contained in logical datacenter diagrams, 50
    no direct correlation with physical machines, 104
    placing in Zones, 51
Logical Servers section in the toolbox, 106
Longhorn, 47

M

Mac OS, running Allerton from, 240
main menu, accessing version control, 133
main process definition file, 214–215
Managed tier (Level 4) of CMM, 194
manual test runner, 162
manual tests, 65, 159, 160–162
    executing, 162
    as first-class project artifacts, 160
MATCH pattern field, 222
maturity of a software development organization, 193
measures, 233
memory leaks, finding, 241
Mercury Diagnostics, 243
Mercury Interactive Corporation, 243
Mercury Performance Center, 243

Mercury Quality Center, 243
merge history, updating for items, 31
Merge Wizard, 31
merging in TFVC, 30–31
merging technology, 80
metadata
  capturing about components, 46
  defining, 100
  saving in spreadsheets, 43
  tracking in DSI designs, 45
MetaData.xml file, 213, 216
metamodel
  built-in rules, 27
  for describing SDLCs, 175
  interchangeable with framework, 178
methodologies, 8
  configuring, 72
  customizing, 13
  defining for new projects, 208
  exporting existing, 73
  implementing different work item types, 126
  mid-course corrections to, 177
  multiple supported by Team System, 208
  need for, 8
  perceived as an impediment to productivity, 176
  popular, 8
  selecting, 72–73
  Team System supporting, 11–12
methodology process guidance, 179
methodology templates, managing, 39
MethodologyTemplate.xml file, 213, 214
  editing, 218
  metadata elements from, 216
methods
  implementing using Object Test Bench, 130
  strongly coupled, 137
metrics, recording in a central data warehouse, 209
.mht file, 124, 269
Microsoft, suite of tools used internally, 7
Microsoft BizTalk applications. *See* BizTalk applications
Microsoft Excel. *See* Excel
Microsoft Internet Explorer. *See* Internet Explorer
Microsoft Office Excel. *See* Excel
Microsoft Office Project, 24, 37, 83, 193
  creating and launching documents from inside Team
    Explorer, 39
  installation of, 44
  integrating with Team System, 17, 257
  limited set of columns, 43
  Professional Edition required, 43
  support for Team System, 43–44
Microsoft Operations Manager (MOM)
  leveraging SDM, 47
  management packs, 243
  possible deployment report future integration with, 123

Microsoft patterns & practices Web site, 94
Microsoft Solutions Framework. *See* MSF (Microsoft
  Solutions Framework)
Microsoft Source Code Control Interface (MSSCCI)
  plug-in, 18
Microsoft SQL Server. *See* SQL Server 2005
Microsoft SQL Server Reporting Services. *See* SQL
  Server Reporting Services
Microsoft Visual SourceSafe 6.0. *See* Visual SourceSafe
  (VSS)
Microsoft Windows SharePoint Portal Service. *See* WSS
  (Windows SharePoint Services)
Microsoft Windows SharePoint Products and
  Technologies 2003 (SDK), 236
milestones, 78
mindsets, 180–181, 196
minimum standards for code, 136
model-driven approach, 48
model-driven development, 94
modeling, value of, 93
models
  first-class development artifacts, 93
  generating code, 93
  as more than just documentation, 98
MOM. *See* Microsoft Operations Manager (MOM)
mouse pointer, no drop shape, 59, 120
MS Project. *See* Microsoft Office Project
MSBuild, 36, 146, 234
MSDN Enterprise, 15
MSDN Premium Subscription, 15
MSDN Universal, 15
MSF (Microsoft Solutions Framework), 8–9, 175
  evolution of, 175
  incremental improvement built into, 178
  management and development of, 175
  process templates for Team System, 176
  versions of, 176
MSF 3.0
  disciplines included in, 179
  foundational principles of, 178
  framework compared to the MSF 4.0 metamodel, 178
  Role Clusters in, 179
  team member roles, 179
MSF 4.0
  Advocacy Groups in, 179
  agile development techniques, 176
  core ideas, 180
  Cycles and Iterations, 184
  as a descriptive framework, 177
  disciplines included in, 191
  foundational principles of, 178
  governance, 185
  governance checkpoints, 192
  implementing with Team System, 208–210
  key concepts, 180–185

MSF 4.0, *continued*
  metamodel, 178, 181
  mindsets, 180–181
  principles, 180–181
  Process Model, 179
  structure of, 181
  Team Model, 183–184
  tracks, 192–193
MSF for Agile Software Development (MSF Agile), 9,
    72, 176, 186–193
  classification structure for, 208
  default queries, 126
  elements, 11
  methodology, 264
  process, 82
  process template for, 208, 213
  work items defined by, 25
  work items included in, 187–188
  work streams defined by, 188–191
MSF for CMMI Process Improvement, 9, 72, 176,
    193–208
  disciplines defined by, 207
  mindsets of, 196–199
  operational management separated from corporate
    governance, 208
  principles of, 195–196
  process template for, 208, 213
  qualities of service defined by, 207
  roles defined by, 203–205
  work items defined by, 82
  work items included in, 206–207
MSF Formal process, accessing guidance extensions, 240
MSF Governance Model, 207
MSF Team Model, 199, 264
MSI files, creation of stable, 248
MsProjProp.xml file, 44
MSSCCI plug-in, 18
multiple checkout, 31
multiple users
  checking out the same files, 80
  simulating for testing, 167
multitiered architecture
  of Team Foundation Server, 20
  of TFVC, 27
My Bugs report, 152
My Queries folder, 126

N

name, specifying prior to implementation, 113
Namespace Administrators global group, 76
Nant build framework, 146
nested systems, 60
.NET application, building to access the application
    tier, 239
.NET architects. *See* application architects (AAs)

.NET classes, 63
.NET code, analyzing, 142–143
.NET object model, 227
.NET Programmability Support feature, 44
network architects. *See* infrastructure architects (IAs)
network security architects. *See* infrastructure
    architects (IAs)
network types, defining, 168
New Load Test Wizard, 167
New state
  for bugs, 88
  for a quality of service requirement, 85
  for a task, 87
New Team Build Type Creation Wizard, 147
New Team Project Wizard
  data-entry screens for plug-ins, 216
  launching in Visual Studio, 214
  methodologies list displayed by, 208
New to Active state transition
  for a bug, 88
  for a quality of service requirement, 86
  for a risk, 90
  for a scenario, 84
  for a task, 87
New Work Item menu in Team Explorer, 90
no drop mouse pointer, 59, 120
No Test Run Configuration Available message, 172
North Carolina, Microsoft campus in, 28
notes, tracking at check-in, 33
Notes check-in policy, 80
notification
  alerts, 227
  mechanism, 226
  recipients, 226
NOTSAMEAS field, 222

O

Object Test Bench, 129, 130
objects, strongly coupled, 137
Obsolete bug, 89
Obsolete task, 87
Ocracoke, 287
OfficeApplication application type, 56
OfficeApplication constraints, 56
offline client, Excel as a, 40
OLAP, 233
open communications, 180, 195
operating systems settings, 52
operational management, 208
operational problems, 243
operations
  advocates for delivery and deployment, 265
  designing for, 45
  standard set for all Web services, 111
operations analysts. *See* infrastructure architects (IAs)

operations manager on the Adventure Works team, 264
Optimizing tier (Level 5) of CMM, 194
Orcas, 47, 287
Ordered Test Designer, 170
ordered tests, 160, 169, 170
organization units, defining initial, 214
organizational governance, 185
Osellus, 244–245
outbound endpoint for a Zone, 103

P
Page Viewer control, 235
pair programming of final fixes, 59
parameters, maintained by build types, 147
partner extensibility, 239
Partner Extensibility Kit, 220
partners, 239–245
paths
    branches as, 30
    highlighting un-followed in the code coverage tool, 142
    of user interaction through a system, 83
pattern matching, 222
Patterns and Practices team, 6
peak usage scenarios, 167
peers, team of, 181, 184, 197
pending check-ins, 134
Pending Check-ins window, 64, 133
performance
    aspects of, 192
    as a category of quality of service, 192
performance bottlenecks
    discovering, 167
    finding from inside Team System, 241
    identifying, 136
    revealing, 250
Performance Center. *See* Mercury Performance Center
performance counters, 168
performance metrics, 145
performance statistics, recording baseline, 167
performance trends, analyzing, 167
permissions
    assigning to a classification or iteration, 79
    assigning to groups of users, 77
    assigning to TFS artifacts and services, 226
    assigning to users and groups, 77
    required for build directory and drop location, 149
    setting for branches, 30
    setting up, 209
personas, 186, 197, 267
physical machines, no direct correlation with logical servers, 104
physical servers
    constraints inside a Zone, 103
    representing by logical servers, 50
plain text files, manual tests, 160

plan track, 192, 267–268
planning
    cycles in each iteration, 267
    iterations, 189
pluggable methodology, 27
plug-in section of the Methodology/Template.xml file, 216
plug-ins
    multiple within one task group, 216
    task groups not required for every, 216
    within Team System, 238
policies. *See* check-in policies
portal environment, creating a collaborative, 22
ports. *See* public ports
positive risk management environment, 89–90, 188, 207
pre-built constraints, 97
pre-built process templates, 177
pre-built reports, 21
predefined constraints, 116
PREfast, 287
Prescriptive Architecture and Guidance (PAG) team, 6
prescriptive components of MSF 4.0, 181
prescriptive methodologies, 177, 182
prescriptive SDLC model, 178
pride of workmanship, 181, 197
Primary Interop Assemblies, 44
probes, inserting, 144
problem resolution system in AppSight, 242
process definition files, 213, 214–215
process guidance
    customizing, 212
    defining, 214
    for a development team, 5
    documentation, 219–220
    documents, 81
process improvement
    framework, 193
    provided by CMM, 194
process metrics. *See* metrics, recording in a central data warehouse
process models
    comparison of, 179
    of MSF 4.0, 179
    short development cycles of, 184
process template items, tasks as, 188, 207
Process Template Manager, 210, 213
Process Template Plug-Ins, 213, 214
process templates, 208, 212
    adding, removing, and customizing, 208
    components of, 208–209
    configuring, 38
    creating custom, 177, 218
    customizing, 210, 212–219
    exporting and editing existing, 218
    importing into a test environment, 219
    importing into Team System, 213

process templates, *continued*
  included with Team System, 213
  making small incremental changes to, 218
  for MSF 4.0, 208
  for MSF for Agile Software Development, 214
  selecting, 177
  set of unique reports for each, 257
  third-party, 177
process types, 245
ProcessGuidance.xml file, 219
ProcessView Composer, 244
product management
  advocacy group, 200
  advocates for customer business, 265
  constituency advocate, 183, 200
Product Manager role, 200
product managers. *See* project managers
Product Studio. *See* Team System
productivity, increasing, 195
products
  building, 190
  creating shippable, 180
  incremental versions of, 185
  releasing, 191
  transitioning from development to production, 185
profiling code, 136, 144–145
program management
  advocacy group, 200
  advocates for solution delivery, 265
  constituency advocate, 183
program managers. *See* project managers
programmability with the .NET Framework, 44
PROHIBITEDVALUES field, 222
Project. *See* Microsoft Office Project
Project Administrators project group, 76
project areas, configuring, 72
project groups, 76
project infrastructure, 38
project leads. *See* project managers
project location, specifying, 113
project management
  as a discipline in MSF 4.0, 191
  software, 37
  techniques not included in MSF CMMI, 193
  tool, 39–43
Project Manager role, 16, 186, 191, 201
project managers
  on the Adventure Works team, 263
  other titles of, 71
  roles of, 71
  tools for, 38–44
  tracking the status of a project, 6
  work streams, 189
project portal, 66, 81
  configuring, 72, 73–74
  customizing, 212, 224

  defining, 214
  extending, 226, 235–237
  specified by a process template, 209
  viewing reports from, 152
Project Server, 258
project settings, 38
project structure of a process template, 208
project team, unification behind a common vision, 192, 266
project timelines, 266
project type, 158
project vision, capturing, 188
projects
  assigning work within, 86
  branching out from existing, 75
  classifying, 209
  as collections of value, 196
  configuring for multiple checkout, 31
  documenting, 209
  guiding, 189
  inherent risks of, 89
  managing ongoing, 75–90
  organization-level flow of, 205
  planning for, 192
  process templates configuring initial settings for, 208
  selecting a methodology for, 72–73
  starting new, 72–75
  system tests belonging to, 158
  technical or organizational risks of, 13
  traits essential for successful, 187
promotion levels, 34
properties
  associating with view fields, 221–223
  specifying before implementation, 113
  of work items, 25
Proposed state for requirements, 206
ProtoGen.exe, 48
prototypes. *See also* application prototypes; server prototypes
  creating custom, 106
  custom, 110, 111
  saving, 106, 107, 111, 112
prototyping, 190
provider endpoints, 53–54, 110
proxy endpoint, adding, 60, 118
public ports, 101
publication and subscription mechanism, 226
Publish Changes option, 41
publishing errors for work items, 41

Q

QACenter, 242–243
QoS requirements. *See* quality of service (QoS) requirements
qualities of service, 191–192, 207

quality, defined by customers, 180, 197
Quality Assurance (QA) group, 160
Quality Center. *See* Mercury Quality Center
quality first principle, 180, 196
Quality Indicators report, 152, 252–253
quality of service (QoS) mindset, 181, 199
quality of service (QoS) requirements, 82
    adding, 85–86
    addressing, 268
    closing, 85
    completing, 85
    creating, 189
    as an item type, 188
    in MSF Agile, 12
    resolving, 85
    state transitions, 86
    states of, 85
    testing, 190
Quality of Service Specialist role, 204
queries
    creating to view particular work items, 126
    defining initial, 214
    listing of definitions, 218
    returning an exact list of work items, 38
querying work items, 42

R
.rdl files, 223
reactivated scenario, 85
Reactivated state transition, 86
Reactivated task, 87
Reactivations Report, 254
Reader project group, 77
READONLY field, 221
read-only project portal, 66
red/green/refactor mantra, 138
Redraw Connection, 106, 111
Refactor, selecting in Class Designer, 130
refactoring, 137, 153
registration service, 227
regression test, 86, 89
regressions, signaling, 86, 188, 207
release iteration, 179
release management features, 241
release manager, work streams, 191
Release Manager role, 187, 204
release/operations advocacy, 184, 200
releases
    maintaining multiple, 29
    reducing the batch size for, 198
releasing products, 191
Remaining Work Report, 249–250
remote procedure calls (RPC), 35
Removed state transition, 86
Repeatable tier (Level 2) of CMM, 194

Report Builder, 21, 224
Report Definition Language files, 223
reporting services in TFS, 21–22
Reporting Services reports, 223
reports
    calling directly via a URL, 235
    creating, 223, 257
    customizing, 210, 212, 223–224
    defining initial, 214
    editing, 224
    enabled by Team System, 249–257
    extending, 225, 233–234
    generated at the completion of the build process, 248
    related specifically to testing, 171
    in Team Foundation Build, 147
    in Team Foundation Server, 151–153
    viewing, 152
Reports link of the Quick Launch bar, 152
repository for storing performance data, 167
request parameters, 166
REQUIRED field, 221
requirements, 82
    compared to QoS requirements, 85
    managing, 239
    types of, 206
    as a work item, 206
resistance to the implementation of TDD, 137
Resolve, setting a Checkin Action to, 132
Resolved state
    for a bug, 88
    for a quality of service requirement, 85
    for requirements, 206
    for a scenario, 84
Resolved to Active state transition
    for a bug, 89
    for a quality of service requirement, 86
    for a scenario, 85
Resolved to Closed state transition
    for a bug, 89
    for a quality of service requirement, 86
    for a scenario, 84–85
restrictions
    flexibility allowed by, 153
    placed on developers, 153
results, displaying for all test types, 170
reusable configurations, creating systems as, 118
reusable systems, designing, 61
reuse of Hosts on diagrams, 106
reviews, 82, 206
risk identification, 89, 188, 207
risk management
    creating a positive environment, 13, 89–90
    as a discipline in MSF 4.0, 191
    ongoing, 191
risk work items, 13, 89, 90

risks, 82, 83, 89
  adding, 89–90
  change requests, 82
  compared to issues, 206
  issues, 82
  as an item type, 188
  mitigating, 90
  reappearing, 90
  requirements, 82
  reviews, 82
  state transitions, 90
  states of, 90
  as a work item, 207
Role Clusters in MSF 3.0, 179
role-based security, 76
roles
  creating, 77
  in MSF Agile, 11
  in MSF for Agile Software Development, 186–187
  in MSF for CMMI Process Improvement, 203–205
  tools by, 67
rollout, managing, 187, 204
rollout plan, 191
Rosetta, 287
Rosetta plug-in, 214
round-trip developing with code, 109
RPC (remote procedure calls), 35
run configuration settings, 171
Run Settings, specifying, 168

S

sampling profiling method, 144
Sarbanes-Oxley requirements, 34–35
scaffolding, 244
scalability bottlenecks, 167
scalability scenarios, 167
SCC plug-in, 214
scenario work item, 12
scenarios, 82
  activating, 83
  adding, 83–85
  attaching quality of service requirements to, 190
  closing, 84
  completing, 84
  creating, 189
  creating and implementing, 83
  deferring, 84
  example, 261
  as an item type, 187
  reactivating, 85
  removing, 84
  resolving, 84
  splitting, 84
  state transitions of, 84–85

  states of, 84
  testing, 190
  writing, 187
schema, 46
Schwaber, Ken, 244
SCM (software configuration management), 24–36
scripted instructions for manual testing, 160
scripts, derived from browser sessions, 164
Scrum, 10–11, 177, 244
scrum master, 11
S-curve pattern, 250
.sd files in a distributed system solution, 47
SDK (software development kit)
  for building SDM Tools, 47
  command-line tools provided by, 48
  documenting the schema for an SDM document, 115
  extending Distributed System Designers, 48
  Visual Studio Integration Partner program, 239
SDLCs (software development life cycles), 8, 10, 175
SDM (System Definition Model), 46–48, 96
  application systems, 48
  benefits of, 46
  documents, 47, 114
  layers defined by, 47
  models, 48
  persisting the information in, 14
  SDK (software development kit), 48
  settings and constraints required to implement, 51
SDM Command Line Compiler, 48
.sdm file, 48
SDM Manager Generator, 48
SDM Prototype Generator, 48
search page, testing a Web site's, 164
security
  applying to classifications or iterations, 79
  as a category of quality of service, 192
  configuring, 30, 38, 76–77
  enabling role-based, 76
  requirements, 97
  supported by Distributed System Designers, 97
security groups, 214
security models, 97
security service of Team Foundation Server, 226
SEI (Software Engineering Institute), 193
  Capability Maturity Model Integration (CMMI) Level 3, 176
  of Carnegie Mellon University, 9
  Web site, 194
selection criteria for adding queries, 126
sequence diagrams of UML, 49
Serena Software, 244
server endpoints, 100
server prototypes, 103, 104
server settings in the HTML deployment report, 121
server types. *See* Host types

SERVERDEFAULT rule, 222
servers. *See also* Hosts
    application types constrained for, 116
    constraints inside a Zone, 103
    restricting in a logical datacenter diagram, 115
Service Accounts global group, 76
service notification mechanism, 226
service-oriented applications, 96
service-oriented architecture. *See* SOA (service-oriented
    architecture)
service-oriented architecture (SOA) designers. *See* visual
    designers
services
    combining into a system, 61
    types of, 109
settings, 115
    for Application Designer, 56–57
    importing from an IIS Web server, 105
    for Logical Datacenter Designer, 52
    for Web application or service components, 127
Settings and Constraints Editor, 116, 120
setup iteration, 179
shapes
    adding to a logical datacenter diagram, 101
    connecting in application diagrams, 57
    on a logical datacenter design, 54
shared services of Team Foundation Server, 226–227
shared vision, working toward, 180, 195
Shelve button, 134
Shelveset, selecting to unshelve, 134
Shelveset name, 134
shelvesets, 31, 32
shelving
    code, 134
    in TFVC, 31–32
    uses of, 135
shippable products, 180
skeletal structure. *See* stub code
skeleton code, generating, 127
SME. *See* subject matter expert (SME)
SMS. *See* Systems Management Server (SMS)
SOA (service-oriented architecture), 97
    applications, 108
    architectures, 98
SOA designers. *See* visual designers
SOAP-based Web service endpoint, 110
software
    change and, 10
    Microsoft's internal, 7
    quality, 191–192
    requirements, 85
software architects. *See* application architects (AAs)
Software Architects, Team Edition for, 94
software code. *See* code
software configuration management (SCM), 24–36

software developers. *See* developers
software development. *See* development
software development kit (SDK). *See* SDK (software
    development kit)
software development life cycles. *See* SDLCs (software
    development life cycles)
software development methodologies. *See*
    methodologies
software development organization. *See* development
    organization, assessing the maturity of
Software Engineering Institute. *See* SEI (Software
    Engineering Institute)
Software Factories initiative, 94
solution architects. *See* application architects (AAs)
Solution Explorer, 158
Solution Selection page, 147
solutions
    for build types, 147
    containing only one application diagram, 108
    in Visual Studio, 148
source code. *See also* code
    Class Designer tightly coupled with, 63
    conflict with target code, 31
    identifying performance-related issues, 144
    need for corrective work on, 190
Source Code Control (SCC) plug-in, 214
Source Control Explorer, 29, 30, 62–63, 65
source control integration, enabling, 18
Source Depot. *See* Team System
SourceGear, 240–241
SOX. *See* Sarbanes-Oxley requirements
spare capacity, 250
special cause variations, eliminating, 195
specifics, learning from, 181, 198
Split state transition, 86
Sponsor role, 201
spreadsheets, saving Excel, 43
sprints in Scrum, 11
SQL Server 2005
    data tier of TFS hosted on, 20
    integration with Team System, 17
SQL Server 2005 Web service access, 100
SQL Server Business Intelligence Developer Studio, 223
SQL Server Reporting Services, 210, 257
stabilizing track in MSF 4.0, 193, 272
stakeholder, 262. *See also* project managers
standard edition of Visual Studio 2005, 17
star schema databases, 233
start-up activities, 185
state transitions
    for bugs, 88–89
    for risks, 90
    for scenarios, 84–85
    for tasks, 87
    for work item types, 77

states
    of bugs, 88
    of risks, 90
    of scenarios, 84
    of tasks, 87
static analysis, 142–144
Static Analysis check-in policy, 80
Static Analysis policy type, 33
Static Analysis tab, 143
static analysis test, 65, 136
static analysis tool, 142–143
static analyzer, 14, 143
status field of a work item, 223
Stepped Load, 167
storage space efficiency of branching, 30
Stored Query Definitions task, 218
stressing, applications, 145
strong coupling, 137
structural elements, architecture defining, 189
stub code, 112, 113
subject matter expert (SME), 262
Subject Matter Expert role, 202
subscription mechanism, 226
SUGGESTEDVALUES field, 222
System Definition Model. *See* SDM (System Definition
    Model)
system design, TDD assisting in, 138
System Designer, 60–61, 97, 117–118
system diagrams, 45
    compared to application diagrams, 117
    contained in a solution, 108
    creating, 60
    defining deployment, 119
    defining element attributes, 116
    describing actual connections, 117
    in a distributed system solution, 47
system stability scenarios, 167
System View window
    in Deployment Designer, 58
    dragging an application from, 119
    dragging and dropping applications from, 120
SystemDefinitionModel Schema, 48
systems, 60, 117
    allowing nested sub-system architectures, 118
    application reuse and, 112
    creating as reusable configurations, 118
    designing reusable, 61
    documenting required characteristics of, 188
    nested, 60
    selectively exposing the behavior of applications, 118
systems architects. *See* infrastructure architects (IAs)
Systems Management Server (SMS), 47, 123

T

target code, 31
Task class, 234
task groups, 216, 217
task list files, 217–218
task work items, 86
    adding, 86–87
    in MSF Agile, 12
tasks, 82, 83, 126
    coding custom, 234–235
    as an item type, 188
    state transitions for, 87
    states of, 87
    types of, 87
    as a work item, 207
taskXml section
    of a plug-in, 218
    for the Stored Query Definitions task, 218
    for the Work Item Definitions task, 218
TDD (Test-Driven Development), 137–138
    ability to refactor confidently, 137
    benefits of, 137–138
    best practices, 138, 141
    reduction in time spent debugging, 137
    revealing flaws in the architecture of a system, 138
Team Architect edition, installing, 112
Team Build, 36, 247–248. *See also* Team Foundation
    Build
    API for, 22
    creating custom tasks, 234
    data, 20
    extending, 226, 234–235
    node, 147
Team Builds
    creating and executing, 38
    screen, 150, 151
Team Edition for Architects, 45, 47, 127
Team Edition for Developers
    installing, 112
    load testing not accessible in, 145
Team Edition for Software Architects, 14, 94
    implement feature available only in, 112
    saving printed screen images from, 124
Team Edition for Software Developers, 14, 127
Team Edition for Software Testers Load Agent, 169
Team Edition for Testers, 14
    built-in validation rules, 166
    load testing available in, 145
    tools provided by, 156
    types of tests supported by, 159
Team Explorer, 15, 24
    Active Bugs list, 88
    creating a new work item query from, 127
    installing, 39
    launching Excel from within, 40

making tools visible as nodes on, 239
New Work Item menu, 87, 90
tasks performed by, 38–39
Team Build node, 147
Team Foundation Build, 145–151. *See also* Team Build
extending MSBuild into a full build automation system, 146
forming a tight integration with Team System tools, 146
outlining the general health of a build, 147
Team Foundation Build Service, 148
Team Foundation Client
API, 210
object model, 22
Team Foundation Notification Service, 226
Team Foundation server, connecting to from Excel, 40
Team Foundation Server (TFS), 15, 19, 151
architecture of, 20–24
components of, 19–20
configuring settings, 38
connecting to a specific, 38
creating source code control check-in policies, 131
extensibility of, 224
features of, 19–20
handling complex development tasks, 131
infrastructure and workflow of, 27
installing, configuring, and troubleshooting, 19
more reliable than VSS, 131
projects under source control on, 62
reporting capabilities of, 21
shared services, 226–227
team members authenticating to, 74
version-control capability of, 74
Web services port number, 22
Team Foundation Source Control, 64
Team Foundation Version Control. *See* TFVC (Team Foundation Version Control)
team leads. *See* project managers
team members
authenticating to Team Foundation Server, 74
classifying, 77
information needed about each, 72
roles of, 71, 186–187
Team menu, 213
Team Models, 178, 183–184
team of peers, 181, 184, 197
team portal, 22
Team Project Creation Wizard, 239
team projects, 38
Team Suite editions, 15, 127, 145
Team System
with Active Directory, 20
add-ins introduced by third parties, 7
architecture support features in, 94
areas of integration possible with, 239

back-end infrastructure of, 19
build management, 35
client applications, 24, 37
code coverage tool built into, 141
configuring, 175
configuring security, 76–77
customizing, 210, 212–224
customizing templates, 113
default methodology in, 9
DSL tools in, 50–61
editions of, 13–15, 71
extending, 224–239
extensibility of, 7, 73
generating stub code, 112
goals of, 6–7
Implement All Applications feature, 112
implementing MSF 4.0 with, 208–210
integration with Active Directory, 76
integration with Excel, 39
integration with Microsoft Project, 257
integration with other Microsoft products, 17–18
interacting directly with, 22
intrinsic rules, 27
life without, 3–4, 5
MSF process templates, 176
no Web-based work item support in the initial version, 72
overview of, 3–18
plug-ins within, 238
as a powerful engine for managing SDLC, 175
prebuilt process templates, 177
prebuilt reports for, 21
prescriptive methodologies implemented in, 177
Process Template Plug-Ins provided with, 214
process templates included with, 213
processing of task groups, 217
project manager role in, 71
suite of testing tools, 155
suite of tools for developers, 125
support for Microsoft Project, 43–44
support for unit testing in, 139
supporting methodologies, 11–13, 208
synchronizing aspects of a project, 258
testing support pieces provided, 136
tests belonging to projects, 158
tools for managing the entire software development life cycle, 176
Web-based interface not provided for, 66
windows relating to testing, 66
Team System Application Designer. *See* Application Designer
Team System toolbar, 26
Team System Web site, 19
Team Test. *See* Team Edition for Testers

Team Test Load Agent, 169
Team Test Load Controller, 169
TeamBuild.proj file, 235
teams
   disseminating information to extended, 73
   geographically-separated, 4
   organizing, 71–72
technical architects. *See* infrastructure architects (IAs)
technical documents, uploading, 82
technical risk, 89, 188, 207
Template drop-down control, 113
templates
   creating for manual tests, 160
   customizing in Team System, 113
   specifying prior to implementation, 113
Test advocacy group, 200
test advocates, 265
test cases
   designing a series of, 139
   encapsulating the requirements of code, 138
   managing, 66
test constituency advocate, 183
test deployment, 58
Test Failed state transition, 86
test failed status for a scenario, 85
test lists, defining custom, 157
Test Manager, 157, 162
Test Manager role, 203
Test Manager window, 66, 141
test metadata files, 150
test mix for a load test scenario, 167
Test Project, 157
test projects, 158
Test Results, 157
Test Results Details report, 152
Test Results window, 66, 141, 157, 170
test run configurations, 171–172
test scripts, migrating, 160
test tasks, 87, 188, 207
   assigning test cases, 86
   closing, 87
   in a scenario, 190
test types, 159
Test View, 157, 158
Test View window, 66, 141
test-case management tools, 14
TestComplete from AutomatedQA, 241
Test-Driven Development. *See* TDD (Test-Driven Development)
Tester role, 16, 187, 203
Tester/IT Professional role, 16
testers, 65
   on the Adventure Works team, 264
   creating and managing tests, 156–158
   Team edition for, 14

tools for, 65–66
types of, 155
work streams, 190–191
testing
   popularity of, 136
   purpose of, 203
   quality of service (QoS) requirements, 190
   scenarios, 190
   technologies, 162
   tools, 65, 155
   in Visual Studio 2005, 159–170
Testing Policy check-in policy, 80
Testing Policy policy type, 33
TestPartner. *See* Compuware TestPartner
.testrunconfig extension, 171
tests
   access to a focused subset of, 158
   authoring, 159–160
   managing, 157–158
   retrieving previous versions of, 158
   status of currently executing, 157
   types of, 155
text, representing software code as, 128
text view, opening, 142
text-based manual test, 161–162
tf.exe command line utility, 29, 66
TFS. *See* Team Foundation Server (TFS)
TFS Everyone global group, 76
TFS WorkItemTrackingAttachments database, 20
TFSActivityLogging database, 20
TFSBuild database, 20
TFsBuild.exe command-line utility, 67
TFSDeleteProject.exe command-line utility, 67
TFSIntegration database, 20
TFSVersionControl database, 20
TFSWarehouse database, 20
TFSWorkItemTracking database, 20
TFVC (Team Foundation Version Control), 27–35
   audit trail support, 35
   branching, 34
   capabilities for branching, merging, and shelving, 29–32
   interacting with, 66
   minimizing required storage, 30
   Sarbanes-Oxley requirements and, 34–35
   switching to Visual SourceSafe, 28
threat modeling, 192
threshold rules, applying to counters, 168
threshold violations, 168
tiers
   of Team System, 225
   used by CMM, 194
tight coupling, 138
time zones, developers in multiple, 35

toolbox
    adding a server, service, or application to, 61
    in Application Designer, 109
    in Logical Datacenter Designer, 104, 107
tools
    for architects, 44–61
    for developers, 62–65
    establishing links between data elements, 226
    integrating into Team System, 238–239
    for project managers, 38–44
    raising events to the eventing service, 226
    by roles, 67
    suite provided for developers, 125
    Team Build integration with other Team System,
        247–248
    for testers, 65–66
    using multiple for development, 5–6
tooltips, provided by Deployment Designer, 119
tracks
    defined by MSF 4.0, 185
    leading to checkpoints in the governance model, 192
    in MSF 4.0, 192–193
traffic, specifying for a Zone, 103
transferred risk, methods of, 90
triage, assessing, 255
triaging bugs, 193, 272
trial deployment
    defining, 119
    performing, 119
    report documents generated from, 123
trivial code, unit tests not necessary for, 138

U

UI. *See* user interface (UI), integrating into the Visual
    Studio 2005; user interface testing
UML (Unified Modeling Language)
    diagram tool, 130
    diagrams as a compile program source, 98
    limitations of, 48
    as a significant step forward in using models in
        software development, 98
    tools, 98
    toolset with Visual Studio 2005, 98
    usage by Microsoft developers, 98
Unapproved state of a work item type, 223
UNC share, 149
uncertainty, dealing with, 191
Unicode support in Visual SourceSafe, 35
Unified Modeling Language. *See* UML (Unified
    Modeling Language)
unit testing, 14, 65, 138–141, 155
unit tests, 159
    automating methods of testing, 138
    building, 139
    capabilities integrated into Team System, 136

    copying and pasting, 139
    creating groupings of, 141
    determining the location of a failure, 138
    developed in TDD, 137
    executing, 141
    generating for class members, 140
    not necessary for trivial code, 138
    revealing flaws in the architecture of a system, 138
    running before check-in, 33
    verifying the overall quality of a build, 150
Universal Naming Convention (UNC) share, 149
Unplanned Work Report, 251–252
unshelving code, 134
use case in UML, 12
use-case diagrams of UML, 49
user defined constraints, 97, 116
User Education Specialist role, 205
user experience
    advocates for the most effective solution, 265
    as a category of quality of service, 192
    constituency advocate, 183
User Experience advocacy group, 200
User Experience Architect role, 205
user interface (UI), integrating into the Visual Studio
    2005, 239
user interface testing, 162
User Profile for Web tests, 168
users
    adding to groups, 209
    assigning permissions to groups of, 77
    built-in TFS rules involving, 27
    checking out the same files, 80
    mapping to Team System, 76
    simulating multiple for testing, 167

V

V model, 155
Validate Diagram option, 59, 121
ValidateRuleRequiredTag, 166
validation errors, 59
validation rules
    attaching to HTTP requests, 166
    configuring, 166
validation tests for a build, 190
ValidationRuleFindText, 166
ValidationRuleRequestTime, 166
ValidationRuleRequiredAttributeValue, 166
VALIDDATE field, 222
VALIDUSER field, 222
value, increasing, 180
velocity
    of the development effort, 36
    planned, 256
Velocity Report, 250–251

version control, 27–35, 130–136
  accessing from the main menu, 133
  check-in policies, 136
  configuring, 72
  creating an empty folder, 75
  creating a new branch, 29
  customizing, 212, 223–224
  extending, 225, 229–233
  integration with Visual Studio, 29
  plug-in, 28
  in a process template, 209
  sample code automating, 229–230
  settings, 74–75
  supported by Allerton, 240
  tests getting the benefits of, 158
version control database of TFS, 20
version control event log database of TFS, 20
Version Control Explorer, 133
version-code-control check-in policies, 134
version-control capability of TFS, 74
version-control functions of Source Control Explorer,
  62–63
View Class Diagram, 63, 129
Visio, 49
Visio 2002 Network Tools edition, 104
vision
  capturing for a project, 188
  unification of the project team behind, 192, 266
  working toward, 180, 195
vision statement, 267
Vista, 47
Visual Basic, 99
Visual C#, 99
visual designers, 14
visual engineering, 48
visual feedback, 119
Visual SourceSafe (VSS)
  compared to TFVC, 27
  development of, 35
  limitations of, 35, 130
  migration utilities for, 18
  switching to TFVC, 28
  working through firewalls, 4
Visual Studio, 24, 37, 83
  accessing source control inside, 133
  Add Web Reference dialog window, 57
  browser integrated into the start page of, 81
  communication tightly integrated inside, 19
  editions of, 16–17
  executing generic tests, 162
  express edition, 17
  features by edition, 67
  integrated development environment (IDE), 152
  integration with Team System, 17
  languages supported by, 99

Merge Wizard, 31
professional edition, 17
profiling engines built into, 144
result data interface, 162
return control interface, 162
SDM integration of, 47
shelving code from, 32
solutions, 148
standard edition, 17
testing in, 159–170
tool integration, 238–239
transformed by Team System, 7
UML toolset with, 98
viewing work items, 126
Visual Studio 2005 Team Edition for Architects. *See*
  Team Edition for Architects
Visual Studio 2005 Team Edition for Software Testers
  Load Agent. *See* Load Agent
Visual Studio 2005 Team Explorer. *See* Team Explorer
Visual Studio 2005 Team System. *See* Team System
Visual Studio Integration Partner program SDK, 239
Visual Studio Integrator Program (VSIP), 7
Visual Studio Source Control Explorer. *See* Source
  Control Explorer
Visual Studio Team System Web site, 47
VSS. *See* Visual SourceSafe (VSS)

W
warehouse dynamic schema modification facilities, 239
Warehouse Web service, 22
Web application, generating code for, 127
Web archive (.mht) file, 124, 269
Web Browser tab, 166
Web content endpoint, 110
Web farm, 169
Web Part Library project, 236
Web parts
  adding or building for the project portal, 235
  as ASP.NET server controls, 237
  creating custom, 235
  sample code implementing, 236–237
Web portal, creating, 209
Web service applications, dragging and dropping, 99
Web service endpoint, SOAP-based, 110
Web services. *See* ASP.NET Web services
Web services architects. *See* application architects (AAs)
Web Services Description Language. *See* WSDL (Web
  Services Description Language)
Web site, testing the search page of, 164
Web Test Designer, 165
Web Test Recorder, 165
Web Test Runner, 166
Web tests, 65, 160, 164–167
WebApplicationX, 57

Web-based interfaces
    automating the testing of, 164
    not provided for Team System, 66
web.config file, 110
WebContentEndpoint type, 110
Weblog (blog), deploying, 261
WebServiceEndpoint type, 110
WebSiteEndpoint, 105
WebSphere Software, 240
Whidbey, 287
whiteboard, intelligent, 55
Whitehorse, 287
willingness to learn mindset, 181, 198
Windows authentication, 97
Windows client constraints, 52
Windows Client logical server, 50
Windows client settings, 52
Windows Forms testing, 162
Windows Server 2003, hosting a project portal, 224
Windows SharePoint Portal Service, 17
Windows SharePoint Services. *See* WSS (Windows
    SharePoint Services)
Windows Vista, 47
WindowsApplication application type, 55
WindowsClient constraints, 56
WindowsClient prototype, 103
WIT. *See* Work Item Tracking (WIT)
witexport.exe, 220
witimport.exe, 220
Word documents, manual tests implemented as, 160
work, measuring as scenarios, 249
work item definitions, 218
Work Item fact, 233
work item tracking
    database, 20
    extending, 225, 227–228
    process template plug-in for, 217–218
Work Item Tracking (WIT), 22, 25–27
work item types
    customizing, 212, 220–223
    defining initial, 214
    Excel and Project reflecting customizations, 40
    exporting existing, 220
    importing definitions, 220
    in MSF for Agile Software Development, 187–188
    in MSF for CMMI Process Improvement, 206–207
    securing the state transitions of, 77
    status states, 223
work items, 25, 82, 187
    adding and managing, 38, 82–90
    adding or retrieving, 43
    associating changesets with, 28
    associating check-ins with, 131–133
    associating linked artifacts and other attachments to, 43

associating multiple with a particular check-in, 133
associating with check-in, 32
automating the creation of, 228
as the base tracking mechanism, 126
configuring, 209
creating and managing, 15
creating or editing a list of, 40
customizing the tracking of, 26–27
defined by MSF Agile, 25
extensibility of, 126
initiating action in a development life cycle build, 125
keeping partitioned for project phases, 78
linking to other artifacts, 26
in MSF Agile, 11–12
publishing changes, 41
publishing or refreshing from a Microsoft Project file, 43
querying, 42
as records in a SQL Server 2005 database, 26
spawning, 227
types and names given to, 126
types of, 126
uploading to Team Foundation Server, 41
viewing, 125–127, 156
Web service tracking, 23
Work Items check-in policy, 80
Work Items Definitions task, 218
Work Items icon, 132
Work Items policy type, 33
Work Items Project Queries, 126
Work Items task, 218
work products, configuring, 209
work streams
    configuring, 209
    defined by MSF for Agile Software Development,
        188–191
    in MSF Agile, 12
workflow, setting for work items, 223
work-item client application, choosing, 83
workmanship, pride of, 181, 197
work-stream approach, 11
WSDL (Web Services Description Language), 57, 100
WSS (Windows SharePoint Services), 22, 66
    altering the look and feel of the portal project, 224
    collaborative advantages of, 74
    creating a Web portal, 209
    disseminating information to an extended team, 73
    plug-in, 214, 216
    port number for, 22
    portals, 22, 81
    Project Portal site, 38
    sites, 74

X

XML
  deployment report as, 121
  process definition file, 219
  schema for an SDM document, 115
XML-based script for MSBuild, 146
XML-formatted documents, storing SDM information
    in, 47
XP (eXtreme Programming), 10, 59
XSL template, converting the XML deployment report
    into HTML, 122

Y-Z

Yukon, 287
Zone constraints, 52
Zone endpoints, 100, 103
Zone prototype, saving, 106
ZoneEndpoint, 105
Zones, 51, 101–102
  adding Hosts to, 103
  adding to a logical datacenter diagram, 101
  containing other Zones, 102
  custom settings for, 53
  defining, 100
  deleting, 102
  designing a datacenter, 102
  naming, 102
  placing logical servers in, 51
  removing, 102
  representing boundaries, 101
  specifying the traffic supported by, 103
  steps for creating, 102

Richard Hundhausen

Recently awarded the title of Visual Studio Team System MVP, Richard Hundausen (a Solid Quality Learning mentor) is a software architect, author, trainer, and Microsoft Regional Director. He specializes in constructing useful Microsoft® Windows®–based and Web-based applications using Microsoft products and technologies, and he has led development efforts in the agricultural, engineering, medical, telecommunications, and military sectors. Richard has coauthored other books on ADO.NET, Web services, and Microsoft Visual Basic®.

What do you think of this book?
We want to hear from you!

Do you have a few minutes to participate in a brief online survey? Microsoft is interested in hearing your feedback about this publication so that we can continually improve our books and learning resources for you.

To participate in our survey, please visit:

www.microsoft.com/learning/booksurvey

And enter this book's ISBN, 0-7356-2185-3. As a thank-you to survey participants in the United States and Canada, each month we'll randomly select five respondents to win one of five $100 gift certificates from a leading online merchant.* At the conclusion of the survey, you can enter the drawing by providing your e-mail address, which will be used for prize notification *only*.

Thanks in advance for your input. Your opinion counts!

Sincerely,

Microsoft Learning

Microsoft | Learning

Learn More. Go Further.